THE FALLING ANGELS

THE
FALLING
ANGELS

JOHN WALSH

HarperCollins*Publishers*

HarperCollins*Publishers*
77–85 Fulham Palace Road,
Hammersmith, London W6 8JB

Published by HarperCollins*Publishers* 1999
3 5 7 9 8 6 4

To Madelyn, the best of sisters,
whose memories of all this
will, I fear, be very different

ACKNOWLEDGMENTS

Warm thanks to all who contributed memories, corroborated half-memories, contradicted family myths, lent books and photographs and gave me their time and understanding in bringing this very personal saga to a conclusion. I'm indebted to my aunt Peggy Moran, my cousins Caroline, Cecily and Marjorie, to Michelle Hargreaves and Catherine Barker; to my sister Madelyn Brody and my cousin Louise for reading the manuscript and offering dozens of useful and, shall we say, stimulating, suggestions; to George Bull, my first editor and mentor, for his unrivalled knowledge of Dante; to my agent David Godwin and commissioning editor Michael Fishwick for their vigorous and enthusiastic support of this project, from soup to nuts; to Kate Johnson for her awesomely meticulous editing and tactful shaving-off of a thousand textual excrescences; to my boss and friend Simon Kelner for generously allowing me a three-month compassionate sabbatical to get the book under way; to Carolyn Hart for putting up with my Tolstoyan flights of egomania over the last year; to Sophie and Max for enduring their father's wild-eyed and unshaven refusal to come out and play badminton in the garden, as successive deadlines loomed; to Clementine, my stroppy angel, for sitting on my knee in mid-composition and homing in, unerringly, on the Delete key. And I owe a special debt of thanks to Ruth Padel, poet, Hibernophile, muse and friend, without whose constant encouragement, wise counsel and passionate criticism this book would never have got anywhere.

CONTENTS

PROLOGUE

Two men are walking through a wood. They are brothers. They carry guns.

The morning is fine. Early rain has yielded to a passionate August sunlight; hardly a cloud disturbs the kingfisher blue. But their view of the sky is restricted by the linking branches of elder and sycamore above them. In the expansive woodlands around Ballybacka it's easy for a stranger to get lost. Every turning looks the same, every clearing resembles the last. But they know the territory. This is, after all, their home turf, their backyard.

John, the elder, tall and muscular, bound for the priesthood, could never lose his way here. He knows the woods inside out. He knows everything. Martin, six years his junior, is less sure of the tracks. He is soon to begin his long induction as a medical student. He doesn't share his brother's insistence on knowing the name of every tree and bird and every plant in the outlying fields. He studies enough biology to get by. He stays home in the evenings and dreams of the girls he has seen passing by in the town of Tuam, where he is still at school.

The brothers' serge trousers taper down inside black rubber gumboots, a sensible precaution, for the night rain has muddied the pathways. Their jackets, initially buttoned against the woody chill, have become uncomfortably warm. They are on the lookout for pheasant and woodcock, whose plump corpses they hope to bear home for a family supper some days hence, a luxury break from the standard diet of mutton-with-dumplings, bacon-and-cabbage and big floury potatoes. John has, in his magisterial way, instructed his little brother about the safety catch, the trigger guard, the snug fit of the shotgun stock into the shoulder, neither too arm-dislocatingly high, nor too low to strain the twanging tendons around the armpit.

They have walked perhaps a mile into the woods when the older brother calls, 'There!' He has seen what Martin has not – a cock pheasant breaking into a slouchy, Groucho-Marx run that means it's about to fly. You can't shoot a pheasant until it's in the air. Only a starving or desperate man would think of blasting away at a bird that was just walking around. Ignorant of this protocol, the pheasant takes off on a low, graceful trajectory. John brings up the gun, sights along the barrel, following the line of the foresight until it's slightly beyond the beak of the iridescent bird, and squeezes the trigger. Just one barrel does the trick. The pheasant collapses, mid-air, into a confused wreckage, its soft plumage aghast at its own destruction. It lands somewhere out of sight, beyond a rough defile of bushes. John lets out a whoop of exultation. 'Good man!' shouts Martin. John plunges into the undergrowth to find his trophy. Martin, a little discomfited by his brother's easy success, turns down a lonely track, ducks in between two pillar-like trees, and walks into the darkest part of the wood.

He has never been here before. He has never penetrated the woodland around his home so deeply. This is alien country, so shaded, so dank and crepuscular that prickles of gooseflesh course like cold electricity along his arms. There is no sun here. The blue sky is now only a memory. Toadstools grow in gross outcrops around the trunks of thousand-year-old trees. It should be the perfect place to find a colony of rabbits, or perhaps spring a woodcock.

Martin flips the safety-catch of his gun, ready to shoot at anything. He moves through the trees into a greater darkness. Instinctively, he shivers. Though he is out in the open air, he feels claustrophobic. The trunks are closer together than he's ever known trees to be before.

Suddenly out of nowhere, as surely as if he'd been hauled up in the air in some booby-trap net, he is poleaxed by a blow to the stomach. It isn't a physical assault. Nothing living has struck him. It comes from inside, draining him of energy. Empty except for pain, torn with pangs, clawed at by a yearning for sustenance, he can feel his ribs tear against his skin, as if they may soon burst through. What seems at first a dull, far-distant ache resolves itself into a terrible, nitric heartburn. He is doubled over by the strange attack; it feels as though his stomach is trying to eat itself.

The shotgun falls from Martin's hand, dangerously, since the safety catch is off, but miraculously it does not fire. He stands hunched over the ground like a question mark and collapses to his knees, head bowed to breast as if awaiting execution. He is as weak as a drowning kitten. He feels his bowels give way, as much from fright as from the invading virus. Tiny don't-blink scenes from his young life switch on and off in his mind. He could be dying, but he doesn't know why, which only makes it more distressing.

'John,' he calls out. 'John . . .' but he hears himself making only a pathetic, mewing sound, his face pressed, as he kneels there, against the earth of this cheerless wood. A choking smell of open graves fills his nose and mouth. He feels the stock of the shotgun by his side. Putting all his weight on his forehead, as it rests on the soil, he walks a limp hand up the wooden sleeve of the gun until it finds the cool metal circle of the trigger-guard. He painfully inserts two fingers and squeezes.

The explosion is loud but seems to come from far away. For Martin has entered a new place with soundproofed walls and tinted glass over everything. He is leaving behind the world of pheasants and blowing grasses and the ordinary sounds and sights of Galway. It is useless. He will die here, actually die on his knees, without even knowing the name of the condition that did for him, this sudden tearing of the guts, this out-of-nowhere, chilly, dark, unexplained evisceration.

It takes an age for John to come. How could he have known anything was wrong? 'Morcheen,' he shouts at his brother, as he rolls him over on the ground and prepares to pick him up. 'Didn't I tell you never to go into that wood? Will you never listen? Didn't I warn you?'

John, who knows everything, has heard about the woods where the great hunger resides and its way of striking down the unwary. He knows that all you can do if you find a victim, and are not stricken yourself, is to sling him over your shoulder and run out of the wood as fast as possible. This he does. He throws his brother across his back like a sack of meal and lumbers off. He doesn't stop until he reaches the doors of Ballybacka. Martin is put to bed. He stays there for three days, with delirium and awful dreams.

Thirty years later, Martin Walsh broods on this experience in his London surgery. Blue smoke from his cigarette spirals up a wall covered in elaborate timetables and drug information. He nibbles a thumbnail – his fingernails are chronically bitten but the thumbnails are mostly spared – as he considers what happened to him in 1934. It was the only unexplained illness this professional man of science ever suffered. Was it hysteria? An acute burst of hyperventilation in a dank wood? Some viral attack on the central nervous system, made worse by auto-suggestion? He stubs out his cigarette in a novelty ashtray, a plaster skull inscribed with the legend: 'It's Better To Smoke Here Than Hereafter.'

Martin is not a man generally susceptible to ghostly visitations. The surgery where he sits is full of the paraphernalia of diagnosis and treatment – the little sink, the examination couch, the weighing scales, the elaborate rubber tubing of the sphygmomanometer. Behind him, ranged against the side wall, is the medical chest of drawers he inherited from his partner, each drawer fronted by a tiny square of carved mahogany, each one containing a little trove of pills in blister packs, rolls of lint, metallic circlets of Elastoplast, round tin boxes of Durex finger-cots for *per rectum* examinations.

'It was called the Fér Gurtha,' he says to the small boy in pyjamas in front of him. 'It means "the hungry grass". The whole wood was supposed to be haunted, you see, because back in the 1840s, the potato crop was blighted for three years, and lots of people starved to death. And up in Galway, your ancestors were driven mad with the hunger. They'd try eating grass and the bark off the trees because they had nothing else. They became like animals. And there was no help from anyone. Some people say that the spirits of people buried in that wood can come down and affect the living, though of course that's just a lot of cod.'

Tonight is a Saturday night. Martin came down to the surgery to hunt for a packet of cigarettes. Guards are his brand. Despite the foolish connotations of the brand name ('guards' are policemen in Ireland) he sticks to them. He collects the Green Shield Stamps which come with each packet, and is now rummaging through a drawer full

4

of half-empty packets in search of a couple of full ones, to slip into the pockets of his formal black, satin-seamed dinner suit.

'But Daddy,' I say. 'It happened to you, didn't it?'

I have not yet been shooed off to bed by Corrie, the Dutch au pair, because my sister and I have been allowed to stay up late and see our parents in their finery. I'm prowling in the surgery because I love it here: the mysterious apparatus of doctoring, the patella hammer which bangs the funny bone in your knee, the 'guessing tubes' of his stethoscope, the auroscope with its gross circle of hardened wax trapped inside the tiny 'O'.

Tonight my father's habitual smell of worsted and nicotine is overlaid by Brilliantine which plasters his black hair to his scalp. In his tuxedo and bow tie, his waistcoat with its silver lighter in a fob and a tiny diamond of handkerchief sticking out from his pocket, he is amazingly handsome.

'Ah,' says the man of science dismissively. 'Something happened to me all right. But what it was, I couldn't really say.' He will never mention it again for the rest of his life.

Why has he chosen tonight to tell me about the Fér Gurtha, which struck him down at eighteen, nearly a century after it scythed down a million other Irishmen and sent a further million falling off the edge of Europe bound for America? Is it because of the great Irish feast that lies before them?

My parents are going to a dinner-dance, to mark the feast day of St Patrick a couple of days before. There will be a ceilidh band at the Irish Club in Eaton Square, and lots of dancing after dinner, and spot prizes, and probably a guest appearance by some high-profile Irishman, like Eamonn Andrews.

Upstairs in their bedroom, I find my mother seated at her triptych vanity mirror, her opulent torso strapped inside a white liberty bodice, the size and texture of a medieval cuirass. She is patting her neck and the underside of her chin with a curious object, a double moisturising pad on the end of a handle. Slap, slap, slap, slap, slap. Pause. Slap, slap, slap, slap slap, the other way. The soft flagellation continues for several minutes. I never think to ask her why she needs to do this to herself, why all the tinkling trays of slimy lotions, the cut-glass perfume bottles with their trailing, tasselled rubber bulbs, the tins of freesia-scented talcum powder that leave a soft, perimeter snow on the glass-topped table when she lifts them up. To me, they're just part of the infinite paraphernalia of motherliness, like my father's surgical equipment downstairs; as mysterious as the ancient, threadbare fur coat she lost interest in long ago, that hung on the back of the nursery door when I was small, and was finally used as a blanket to cover the toy rabbits and teddy bears at the end of my bed, so they wouldn't be cold at night.

Mother's chin is tilted dictatorially upwards, as she concludes her flesh-percussing ritual and squeezes, in three rubber puffs, a soft rain of Balenciaga Le Dix across her front from ear to ear, as though sketching an invisible necklace. But it does not preclude her talking.

'Oh, Giles and Hetty will be there, and Maureen O'Sullivan, and lots of friends. You remember Father Bill Sheridan, with the loud voice, he's on our table too. All the tables will have little lights on them. It'll be great fun. And we'll probably have prawn cocktail and some delicious beef and roast potatoes, and some fruit, and then everyone will dance. Your father is a great dancer. He wasn't when I met him though. Now Giles, *he's* a great dancer. But then he's a Durkin, like me. Now you'll be a good boy and go to bed when Corrie tells you. And have you done your homework? I haven't time to hear it out to you. What was it, Nature Study? What's the smallest bird in the British Isles? A wren. Good boy. Pass me that blouse on the hanger . . .'

The doorbell rings below. It is the taxi. Madelyn and I will sit on the stairs, waiting for the big departure. Dad straightens his bow tie in the bathroom mirror, peers more closely, turns his face this way and that, inspecting his five o'clock shadow. Rather than remove tuxedo, waistcoat and shirt all over again, he pulls an electric razor from a shelf, goes into the living room, hoicks a sixty-watt bulb out of the side-lamp on the mantelpiece, plugs in the razor and sails it urgently over his face, twisting it and preening before the long, gilt-framed mirror, as vain as a canary. I have followed him into the room to watch this dashing, masculine performance.

The taxi driver is getting impatient. Madelyn and I meet on the stairs, as the bell peals again. Mad is a year older than me, and has been in with her mother, to scrutinise the dress, tie up the huge bow at the back, do up my mother's emerald necklace with the fiddly catch and watch the ritual with the shoes. Corrie answers the door, calms the driver with her curly-haired Dutch charm and shouts, 'Time to go!' from the hallway.

One by one they appear. The bulb in the landing light has gone, but they're both backlit by the strip-light in the bathroom. My father is resplendently monochrome, feeling his chin, checking his wallet inside his unaccustomed jacket. My mother's petticoat makes a noise like swept leaves. The seemingly-endless gold ballgown cascades in a moiré waterfall over her bosom, pulls in at the waist and then flows down all over the carpet. The hallway is not wide enough to accommodate it all. She pulls long satin gloves up to her elbows, and asks, 'The keys, Martino, have you got the keys? I can't find mine.'

My father looks her up and down with a kind of appalled pride.

'Do you not know, Anne,' he says as she moves towards him, 'a hundred years ago you could be put in prison for rustling?'

He winks at me as they go down the stairs. Mad and I stand by Corrie in the hall and watch them leave.

With the apparitions departed, the house seems suddenly full of night. My sister returns to her homework. I am sent to brush my teeth.

Whatever else happens, I decide, as the Colgate foams around my innocent gums, when I'm older, I'm going to go to parties all the time, and dance and eat prawn cocktails in a black-and-white suit. Whatever this Irish club might be, I'm going to join it.

I

THE WANDERERS

The Devil is selling margarine on the road from Galway Cathedral to Galway Regional Hospital. By the bus-stop, an advertisement for some low-cholesterol designer grease called 'Low-Low' features a mincing figure dressed in Satanic crimson silk, with the words 'So tempting . . .' emblazoned across his spindly chest.

The hospital lies on the outskirts of town, low and squat and hopeless, like an extruded-plastics factory that has fallen on hard times. You enter through a prefabricated waiting room where people sit reading the papers, puffing Carrolls tipped and cuffing their whining children. New arrivals come in and out of the rain through the automatic sliding doors, survey the personnel in this curious bunker, and are eyed in turn by the sitters and smokers. Inside, the tea room is always full: patients well enough to walk, chatty visiting women in solid winter coats, priests doing their rounds, staring-eyed caffeine addicts, children with bags of Hula Hoops who have seen too many gothic sights in pyjamas and nighties in the last hour, young interns in their whites and their air of newly-minted importance, carpenters and plasterers (for the hospital is being re-decorated), mill about constantly. A great wandering of stern-faced, peripatetic Irish souls, coming and going with ponderously slow deliberation, from health into sickness and out again.

On the third floor, none of the clocks is working. They have all stopped but with their hands in different places, as though from an earthquake whose precise timing nobody could agree on. The corridors are painted a municipal yellow, the exact shade of the skin that forms on custard after a day or two. The overhead lights are dim, foggy, fortywattish, and they cast a Bosnian gloom over your footsteps.

The smell of hospitals at lunchtime is probably uniform from Gdansk to Galway, a noisome melange of drowned greens, monosodium glutamate, puddingy starch and strangers' bottoms. But in St Anne's ward, it is head-swooningly joined by the fume of lilies. Lilies carry images of funeral parlours and nun's robes about them, but there's no denying their spectacular, go-for-it efflorescence, their surging, sexy incense and the festering drainage smell with which they sulkily close their act for good.

In the nurses' room, a flash of blue announces the presence of Sister Mary O'Keefe. She is a pretty woman in her mid-forties, a bustler and a talker. She is always doing one or the other, or both. She treats her elderly charges like large babies, who need to have their backs rubbed to bring up the wind, who need reassurance and treats, who have to be groomed and primped and rendered beautiful every day for fear that they will fall into slovenly habits. She is famously good with her nurses. She doesn't bark at them. She is sensible and practical and knows what is to be done. Her hair is blonde and her skin shines with a faint moisturiser glow. It wouldn't be all that difficult to fall in love with Sister O'Keefe.

At the end of St Anne's ward, in a fenced-off area by the windows, four beds are occupied. Rosamund, from Strokestown, Co. Roscommon, is cross-looking, vulpine and broken-veined, and sleeps with her mouth open. There's a frightened look in her eyes most days, as if she's sure they will come and take her away soon. She sometimes sits on the side of the bed clutching the castored trolley with one hand and goes to sleep in this position, the living image of a refugee.

Mary the Yank is a tiny, bird-like woman whose crinkly, marmalade hair sweeps back from her forehead into a startling beehive. From certain angles she looks like Elsa Lanchester in *The Bride of Frankenstein*. She lived for many years in Connecticut but (by a strange coincidence) comes originally from Tubbercurry, my mother's village in County Sligo. Also like Mama, she was a star of her local drama group and her husband died of leukaemia, as my father did. It's by no means certain that she always tells the truth.

The third woman is another Mary, impossibly sweet-faced, snow-haired and kindly-looking; she has a vast extended family who visit her mob-handedly and sit stolidly around her, reading the Irish *Sun* and eating bananas.

The fourth patient is my mother. Her name is Anne. She is an Irishwoman in her late eighties who has spent the bulk of her life in England, working, nursing, raising a family and being a doctor's wife. Thirteen years ago, she and my father retired to Oranmore, a town on the outskirts of Galway city; she has lived there ever since. Now, at the end of her life, she lies here sleeping a blissfully shagged-out sleep. Her mouth is turned down as if from some terrible disappointment. A small scale cancer scare eight years ago – nothing special, just an imploded facial mole that turned malignant – led to an operation that left her with a twisted lip. All the muscles between nose and chin have loosened and her skin is pouched and puckered and lined like the crosshatching on a Piranesi drawing. Everything about her handsome face now tends towards the mouth, as if it were a drawstring purse pulled firmly shut by a miserly hand.

My mother's left hand rests Napoleonically inside the pink stripey pyjama top. It is covered in liver spots, so many and so profuse that, together, they look like a blotchy suntan. Her right hand, where they have stuck three different needles when attaching a drip, is even worse. There seems to be a horrible, dark, subcutaneous something-or-other dwelling beneath her browned and blackened flesh, a nasty suspicion of decay. Even asleep she looks faintly aghast with worry about what is going to happen to her. The skin, at eighty-seven, is full of secret folds that one never saw or suspected before, the pleats and pouches of a fat woman who has suddenly shed a load of flesh – though Mother was never fat. It's a whole new territory of orangey crêpe, a landscape of whorls and striations and overlapping lines, of crevices and bluffs, a new Monument Valley for the eye to ride around as we sit by her side every day. The tendons in her neck are stretched and taut as lianas round a baobab tree. The cavernous depression created by her skeletally bony clavicle is as deep as a rock pool. She is slowly and sneakily turning into someone – or something – else.

Yesterday, out of nowhere, as one of our conversations dwindled to nothing, she suddenly clutched my hand and said: 'All my beauty is gone.' It was as stark as that. She had looked at no mirror, responded to no question, been prompted by no flattery. It just came to her that her looks had disappeared, like the sun going in for the afternoon and never emerging again.

She had never been exactly beautiful. Her face was a little too long and equine and her jaw too firmly set, to be a dreamboat. The nurses with whom she trained in the thirties used to call her 'Sister Ingrid', because of her fancied resemblance to Ingrid Bergman, but I, the child who inherited her looks, could never see it. She was handsome, though. Her face was full of resolve and determination. She always won arguments with difficult neighbours, patients and policemen. With tradesmen, butchers, customs officials and priests she was chatty and flirtatious. She was good at giving people she liked the impression that they were funny, or incorrigible or mildly shocking. 'You don't improve,' she would say, shaking her head with mock disapproval. She had a sweet, artless smile and laughed like she really meant it. You wish she would laugh like that now, or even feel like laughing, or have anything to laugh at, or have something to think about except the only thing that she is stuck with thinking about.

All the other ladies in this medical barracks are thinking about eternity, and they are faced with the most potent physical evidence that there's something wrong with you – amputation. Rosamund, Mary the Yank and Mary Snow-White are waiting to have bits chopped off their legs. Their conditions are all diabetes or smoking-related, and the grisly prospect of losing limbs, because of a habit whose attractions I understand very well, must be hard to bear. Snow-White Mary and Rosamund have both lost a foot already, and it remains to be seen whether the surgeon will determine that the next cut will be just above the ankle or right up to the knee, and if that doesn't do the trick, if the gangrene continues its corrupting course like a seducer's hand, stealing unstoppably over its victim's knee, then it will be the whole leg as far as the mid-thigh. And if that doesn't work . . .

Do the old ladies lie here marvelling at this unlooked-for penetration of their frail bodies, this invasion by an invisible intruder? Or do they, as my mother's generation were trained to, offer it up for the souls in Purgatory? Here they are at the end of their lives, these tough Irish Catholic ladies, grown old and de-sexed and attitude-free, full of kindliness, as inoffensive as balls of wool, offering everything up in a modest fit of transcendence – after the example of Our Lord on the Cross. They have stopped fighting for their families or their rights. They have turned into the very image of the sweet, wonderful, charitable little Irishwoman that seems mandatory at their age – whatever class of tomboy or vamp or bitchy termagant they were in their prime.

And this, apparently, is where I am too. This is my space now. I am an English journalist, five hundred miles from home in the capital of Ireland's mystic west, caught in a ceaseless daily orbit between this hospital and my sister's house in Athenry where I am staying while awaiting the prognosis.

I had rushed over from London to Galway when she was sent into hospital, and sat by her bed for days. My sister's children, Annabel, Giles, Justin and Simon, had come to see her too, and found her with a hideous death's-head apparatus called a nebuliser clamped over her nose and mouth on a length of elastic. Through holes in the plastic mask, clouds of breathy steam furled and billowed. The children trepidatiously advanced towards the apparition. For Simon, aged two, it was like creeping up on a seething dragon with its chin resting on its breast. His eyes were as wide as oysters. Why was his tough, kindly grandmother turning on him like this?

After a week, she seemed much better. Her appetite had returned. 'There's no point in you hanging round here,' she told me. 'You have your family to think of. Go on home. I mean, I'm not going to die just yet, am I?'

She said the last words with such crushing, oh-please sarcasm.

I went back to London, where I was due to broadcast a programme for Radio Four. Mid-transmission the call came from my sister to say Mother had been put on oxygen and they didn't know whether she would last the night. A flurry of telephone calls secured a 'compassionate' emergency Aer Lingus flight, ones they keep on constant standby for just such get-me-to-Ireland-quick-my-mother's-dying eventualities. I changed planes in Dublin, glumly drank pints of Guinness in the transfer lounge, and tried to read Don DeLillo's *Underworld* as we sped to Galway at 600 mph, racing my mother's dwindling heartbeat. Frank, my brother-in-law, met me at the airport. I came through the tiny arrivals hall with the words 'Is she alive?' on my lips. 'Oh, she's fine,' he said shortly. He picked up my overnight bag, packed with a minimal wardrobe of toothbrush, three shirts, a change of underwear and a funeral suit. I followed him to the car, suddenly realising I was in for the long haul.

Now I sit, as though chained to my mother's bedside, a slave to fondness and filial duty, imprisoned by the uncertainty of death. I could be here another twenty-four hours, or twenty-four days or several months, in this Irish hinterland that's at once so familiar and so foreign. Galway has been my second home for over forty years, but it has never been a real home. It's an accent I can do as easily as my real voice. It's a special-occasion set of clothes, rather than one I actually wear. It's a holiday destination, not an everyday one. It's a place to be inspected for its alien qualities, not ignored for its over-familiarity. And I've suddenly found myself living here, with no immediate prospect of going home.

'Well John,' said one of the visiting nuns, who used to call on my mother in Oranmore, 'back again? Sure why wouldn't you? Isn't this your home now?'

'No, Sister. I live in London. Didn't you know?'

'Well of course you have your work in London, and your little ones and all. But it's here that your father is buried, and your mother will be beside him, and your grandfather and uncles and all Martin's people in the one place up in the Athenry graveyard, and your sister living just down the road with her lovely family. Sure of course it's your true home. And you'll be coming back here eventually, won't you?'

My true home? Well of course I know the place. I'm fond of Athenry. Some of the townspeople have become friends. I've been coming here so often, I'm used to Irish ways and behaviour, the drift of conversation and friendship, of getting rounds in pubs, and avoiding giving offence; it's second nature to me now. Yet every time the visitors pass through here, in that incessant, wandering Irish way, every time I open my mouth, I'm reminded how much I don't fit in with this Hibernian gang, how little I share their mind-set, their sympathies, their prejudices, their devotion to strange gods and crackpot myth-ologies. With my mother I'm the same as I've always been, only perhaps more English these days. With my sister, I've become more Londonish than usual, perhaps to underline the fact that she started out as English too. Maybe I'm trying to save her from this little rectangle of mourning that is St Anne's ward, to take her away from this room, this bed, these sheets, these screens, these walls, away from the hospital and all the sympathetic voices and from this dismal end of the city, and from Galway itself, and away from Ireland altogether, where these awful things are happening. But you can't shake off Ireland quite so easily.

Wednesday morning was the beginning of Lent, the Catholic forty-day period of fasting and abstinence in the run-up to Easter. Pat, the male nurse, a very precise and faux-prim class of orderly, appeared by my side bearing a little bowl full of black ashes. He could have been a sales representative from the offices of Mr Boffin, the dust millionaire in Dickens's *Our Mutual Friend*. From the bowl he flourished a metal plunger, the kind you might once have seen stamping library books.

'Would she like some?' he asked, indicating the stricken figure in the bed, lying on a dozen pillows with her mouth cavernously open. 'Some ash for Ash Wednesday?'

I regarded him coldly.

'My mother is dying,' I said. 'She has no immediate need of a *memento mori*, thanks very much. In fact I think it's pretty tactless . . .'

Without taking the slightest notice, he dunked the plunger into the ashes and stabbed a black cross onto my mother's innocent forehead. An Arizona cowpoke branding a heifer would have been more subtle. My jaw dropped.

'Now,' said Pat, with an eager nod. 'Would you like some yourself?'

He made it sound like a treat. It was a tricky decision. Would I like to have my face anointed with the debris of some unknown graveyard, to remind me of the imminence of death while seated beside my disintegrating mother?

'Not today, thanks,' I said coldly.

Pat turned away with a flounce and went to minister to the others. By lunchtime he had done the rounds of the ward, both male and female. Everybody had been branded with ash. The elderly women, the snow-haired amputees, the creaking grumpy farmers, the battered itinerants, the comatose post-operatives from Sligo and Roscommon, they all lay marked with a reminder that they were going to die sooner or later, and probably the former. I went for a walk along the corridor.

A couple of sweet young nurses barely out of their teens appeared, their foreheads streaked with grime. A young mother shuffling to the lavatory bore the mark of Cain like nasty make-up in need of renewal. I hurried on. The porters heading for the lifts, the visiting relatives lurking in the recesses, the girls preparing lunch in the kitchen, the tiny children bringing a posy of March violets to their aunt Bridget – all were walking advertisements for the certainty of extinction. Even the divine Sister O'Keefe, stopping for a chat about my mother's progress, had a perfect dusty cross on her brow like the crosshairs of a huge gun. More of the Ash Wednesday gang appeared. They seemed to be milling together and heading my way. It was like *Night of the Living Dead* when the zombies start closing in.

Down at floor level, I sought solace in the tea room, among the muffins and Danish pastries and Lucozade bottles, where people read the papers and munched fruit, there were ordinary non-ill people who, like me, couldn't get out of a hospital fast enough. They all looked up from their steaming polystyrene cups, crumbs of pastry flaked their cheeks – and the rubble of Ash Wednesday stared from their foreheads, like stigmata. They'd all been done, every one of them, young and old, from the cool Galway babe in combat trousers and a stud in her nose, to a tired-looking mother holding a grimy, yowling urchin on her knee. It made me think of the plague years of the Middle Ages, when the quick and the dead, the lucky and the doomed were separated by a cross daubed with pitch on the doors of houses where victims lived. The difference here was that none of the Irish victims, none of those earmarked by mortality, seemed the least bit concerned about their condition. 'Remember, man, that thou art dust and to dust thou shalt return', is what the priest says when anointing you with the black ash; then, the idea is, you go away and forget about it.

I stood there feeling like a marked man, the only person (apart from the yowling urchin) who hadn't been favoured with a thumbful of grit. I hadn't 'received' (as they used to say about Communion). I hadn't 'communicated'. I hadn't joined in. I swear that one or two of the believers in the tea room looked my way, saw my pristine, un-ashed forehead and thought: 'You? What makes *you* so different?'

The smell of vanilla is getting to me. It's the only flavour of Ensure that Mother likes. The nearest thing to solid nourishment she can keep down is a thick, viscous glue called Ensure. She sips it once an hour from a polystyrene cup. You can get blackcurrant and orange flavours too, but Mother sticks to vanilla for fear of becoming sick. The stuff is available in cardboard cartons or in little tins with pull-back tongues like small 7-Up cans. A discussion has broken out between my mother, my sister and a nurse about the relative strength, taste and efficacy of the two forms of packaging:

'No, Mum, the one in the tin is *Ensure Plus*, and is more concentrated than Ensure, so you obviously need a smaller dose. And it'll be better for you, because it won't fill you up with fluid.'

'I don't want it,' says Mother grumpily. 'I can't drink that stuff. It's too thick. And it's not better for you just because it's thicker.'

'You can't beat the Ensure, Anne,' put in the nurse.

'My point,' says Madelyn, 'is simply – this one, you take less of it, there's not so much peeing. That one, takes lots more peeing. Think of it logically.'

'They do an apple flavour now,' says the nurse irrelevantly. ''Tis lovely.'

'Madelyn,' says Mother, making a suddenly terrible face. 'Will you not just give me the one I want?'

My sister Madelyn has lived in Athenry, my father's village, for fifteen years. Though born and bred in south London like me, she bolted from the trendy metropolis in the late 1970s, left her friends and aspirant lovers and went to work in Ireland for a hotel company. She used to pay visits to her relations in Galway most weekends and it was there that she met and later married Frank Brody, the local vet, whose father and grandfather would have known our father and grandfather.

Although my father is buried in the cemetery at the end of the road out of town, Madelyn is still an outsider around here – a 'blow-in', an Englishwoman, someone who is not part of the tribe. This despite her status as founding member of the Athenry Women's Group, committee sitter on the Athenry Heritage Trust and leading light of the Athenry Arts festival each summer. She has, as far as is humanly possible, discovered and penetrated the social nexus of this modest town, but her essence remains unchanged: she's an Englishwoman living 'over here'. She is more easily acceptable as Frank Brody's wife (it is not uncommon to find that local men around here have acquired wives from America or Australia or France by some baffling process) and as the nice woman who answers the telephone and greets callers to the house with their stricken animals in a back-trailer, like the one pulling up the driveway as we sit together in the kitchen.

Madelyn and I are a compassionate double-act. We take it in turns to sit with Mother. Sometimes we sit together, one on either side of the bed, holding her two hands in ours, but there is something off-putting about this arrangement, as if we were in competition with each other for her attention, or else keeping her imprisoned and immobilised between us. So we have an hour each, one of us sitting and reading, topping up her drinks, talking to the nurses and welcoming visitors like a social secretary, while the other prowls the corridor, talks to other patients, visits the tea room, goes across the road for a cigarette, or into Galway on the constitutional walk that takes in the Salmon Weir bridge, the green bulk of Galway Cathedral, the tight academic pile of University College Galway and the image of the dancing low-fat Satan.

The mornings are spent killing time. We know Mother will wake early, be washed and spruced and hair-combed and fed her tiny, sparrow's diet of cereal and Lilliputian slices of toast and meagre sips of tea and vanilla slugs of Ensure, before sleeping again for most of the morning. Madelyn and I will get to the hospital at noon and set up our eight-hour vigil, but for the moment we prolong the sense of furlough, of time off. We procrastinate. We compare notes about our children's education. Then we look out the window and see an unusual sight.

Athenry in late February is not an exciting town, but this morning a record has been broken: for the first time in Frank's history, a patient has driven to the veterinary surgery with a pregnant cow in the trailer. Lamb deliveries, yes. Pregnant dogs and cats, fine. Cows, no. The vet visits the cow, not the other way around. Cows are too bulky and unmanoeuvrable. But this cow's owner is worried about her progress and has rushed her to Frank's attention. He and a young farm hand explain the most recent symptoms: the cow is past her full term, but has not gone into labour. She cannot stand up. She is terminally gravid. They don't want to lose her, as well as whatever calf is lurking inside her.

Frank puts on his professional dungarees and encases his right arm in a kind of detachable mackintosh sleeve, in order to reach up the cow's vagina to find the womb. But the cow cannot be shifted from her trailer, where she sits on the metal floor in an attitude of the utmost comfort. She is as immobile as a vast brown statue, a Rodin Minotaur, haunches spread like a bulky tarpaulin. The men shout and yell at her, hurl imprecations, but without result. Frank undoes a rope from the trailer, knots it, doubles it over and thrashes the cow's smug, deliquescent flanks – once, twice – trying to sting her into action. No dice. Simon, Madelyn's youngest child, toddles onto the trailer and aims a ferocious toddler kick at the bovine *horizontale*. The men wave their arms and yell some more.

The morning is going by and nothing is happening. Nothing is being born, and nothing is dying. We are waiting for some eternal verity to arrive. Instead, rain comes on; little stinging drops through the trees, borne on the wind that soon resolve themselves into rain. The men, frustrated by the turn of the weather, attach some implement of persuasion to the cow's nose and, with much shouting, pull hard. Finally she rises with magnificent reluctance, awkward and bandy-legged, a frail old lady looking for her stick. The cow totters off her trailer onto the soft earth outside Frank's surgery – and collapses there, exhausted by her efforts.

The men groan. Watching from the surgery window, I groan with them. The rain lashes the trees, the door, the skylight. It is Irish purgatorial rain, thin and mean and whipping. When I next look at the scene outside, the three men are sheltering inside the metal trailer while, outside, the cow sits on the grass verge, as comfortable as Ferdinand the Bull under the cork tree. The men roll cigarettes and smoke thoughtfully, looking at the cow like spectators in a livestock museum. The cow looks back at them with unbothered calm.

An hour later it is all over. The calf is born dead, pulled from its mother's womb on heavy ropes. It is long and floppy and dismissively flung away like a Belsen corpse. It seems to have no insides.

Inside the hospital, a crisis has broken out concerning an amaryllis. Despite, or perhaps due to, its egregiously phallic appearance when in full flower, amaryllises are very popular among elderly Irish ladies. Their vivid red-green solidity affects Catholic matrons like the pillars of a cathedral, in which the natural and the metaphysical are happily enshrined. Some kind soul brought Mother an amaryllis the other day and she admired it as it grew and opened out. She asked us to put it across the gangway from her bed, beside Mary the Yank's flowers, so that she could have a proper view of it.

Days went by and it became more engorged and spectacular. Then, one day it disappeared. Mother woke from a deep sleep and was upset to find the great floral trumpet suddenly gone. ''Tis a terrible thing now,' said staff nurse Adrienne, 'when you cant even protect the flowers that visitors bring from thieving hands.'

Sister O'Keefe was informed. She was shocked. Nobody was going to pinch flowers from St Anne's ward as long as she was around. Last week, some thieving bastard pinched the old ladies' television – just rolled it on its castors out the door and down the corridor. That was, at least, understandable. But to walk off with Anne Walsh's amaryllis, right from under her very nose, was an act of un-Christian selfishness and cruelty. Investigations began. Who could possibly? Then I heard one of Mary's Sligo friends confiding to her that the big plant was thriving just fine, and she was keeping it watered and making sure it wasn't left standing in a puddle because those flowers didn't like that, did they?

Had *they* taken the amaryllis?

'We thought, since Mary was going to another hospital in a few days, there'd be no one to mind her lovely flower,' came the reply. 'So we said we'd take it home and mind it for her.'

All was suddenly explained. After a couple of dozen visitors had remarked on the amaryllis's great thrusting stem and its His Master's Voice fiery bowl, and had asked Mary the Yank who had given her such a lovely thing, she had finally supposed that it must be hers, and named some plausible donor. From that moment, the ownership of the thing had been transferred from Mother to Mary, and it had been borne away in triumph by her busybody friends. There was no chance on earth of getting it back.

I went out at lunchtime and bought Mother three more amaryllises and arranged them in a great jug. 'They won't be out yet awhile,' said the man in the shop. 'Your mother won't see a flower for ten days or so.'

But will she be around to see one? And will I?

★

Religious visitors arrive in packs. Mother was very friendly with the local nuns from the convent up the road in Oranmore, and they took to her. They used to send Victoria sponges and milk puddings round to her house. They used to call by in relays. Recognising her as a nun in the making, from the way she combined the most prostrate devotion to the Pope and the Catholic religion with the most unslakeable love of scandal, they would bring her news and leave with shocking stories about affairs in Oranmore and south London ringing in their ears.

Sister Teresa and Sister Nuala used to visit her in Oranmore every Sunday for two hours of gossip, reminiscence and digestive biscuits. They were expected at 2 p.m. sharp every week. If they were five minutes late, Mother would ring the convent, demanding to know what had become of them. And then the nuns came a-calling at the hospital. They were her most welcome visitors.

Sister Catherine, the head nun, is a large and worldly woman with a broad, intelligent face capable of registering several emotions you don't generally associate with nuns, from the satirical to the sultry. For reasons I never understand, she doesn't wear a nun's habit, just an ordinary jumper and skirt. Sister Paul, her face tightly framed by her black headdress, is more a nun from Central Casting. She is a talker of Olympian stamina and relentless invention. In hospice or hospital, schoolroom or funeral parlour, she is never at a loss. No matter how terminal the patient or how hopeless their condition, she knows how to amuse them. She is the convent's secret weapon.

'Now Anne,' she says to Mother, 'you're looking marvellous.'

'Indeed I'm not marvellous, Sister,' says Mother, 'I'm dying.'

'And what harm if you are?' Sister Paul breezes on, 'Won't you be seeing Martin again, after all these years? Won't he be waiting there to welcome you?'

'If he's been behaving himself, Sister,' says Mother. 'And I'll find out that soon enough.'

This trope of reassurance – of death being like an invitation through the post to a big party with your deceased loved ones – becomes familiar over the next couple of weeks. Visitors tend to say either that Mother is about to make a complete recovery and will be back on her feet probably playing squash by the weekend; or they talk about Heaven and the afterlife. She is getting a little tired of the latter tendency. People assume an easy familiarity with Heaven and

Hell that grates on her nerves – she is, after all, a lot closer than they are to finding out about one or other of those places.

It is twelve years since Martin, my father, died. Mother nursed him through his last three months, nursed him for all she was worth, brought all her ward–sister expertise to bear on his sleep patterns, his diet, his regimen of medicine, even his prayers. She approached his bout of leukaemia and his imminent death as if they were themselves difficult patients, troubling and malevolent presences in the ward, to be given appropriate treatment and sent packing as soon as possible. She intoned special prayers, made novenas, said rosaries, struck deals with the Almighty and all the saints under his control. Martin could not possibly die, she decided, not with her rooting for him, not with her hotline to the top.

When he died, she almost lost her faith. If God was capable of doing that to her, she said, then she wanted nothing more to do with him. What would be the point of going on believing in someone who could let you down so badly; he who was so ineffectual when it came to the wire? The priests worked on her night and day. 'Think of it, Anne,' they would say. 'Did he have any pain and suffering at the end? Did he not have you by his side through it all? We cannot know why God called him away but . . .' It had worked. Now, I was afraid she was beginning to lose it again.

In the doorway, I am introduced to Sister Catherine, the convent's boss: 'So you're John,' she says guardedly. 'Well we certainly heard all about *you*.' I run a quick mental check list of what they will know about me over the years, from my mother and from the town gossips: that I'm a lapsed Catholic living in sin in Dulwich with an English woman and three children out of wedlock; that I wrote a book about religion that poured scorn on the Pope, the Virgin Mary and the Blessed Sacrament, that I'd appeared on *The Late Late Show* and that I refused to go to Mass despite my mother's dying wishes.

'There's no doubt,' Sister Catherine continued 'you were the apple of your mother's eye.'

'That's er, very nice to know,' I said. 'Though I can't imagine why.'

'No,' said Sister Catherine shortly, 'nor can we.'

★

Back at the bed, Mother and Sister Teresa are discussing diarrhoea. Sister Teresa recommends drinking flat 7-Up. I have heard the same bland palliative recommended in Galway for a score of ailments, from gastroenteritis to infant croup. It is thought to have some mystery ingredient that is a powerful cure-all, just as tonic water is supposedly crammed with enough quinine to save you from snake bites in the jungle and Coca-Cola allegedly used to contain amphetamines. It is about as likely to cure Mother's bowel complaint as to cure the common cold.

My mother has gradually become engulfed in panaceas, in miraculous medals, lucky charms and amulets and Mass cards. Her bedside table is crammed with cards promising that a Mass will be said especially for her, a powerful weapon in the artillery against sickness and the Devil. Within reach of her hands are little prayer cards in polythene sheaths: there's a Prayer to Our Lady of Knock, complete with a picture of the Apparition of the Virgin in that small town of Mayo that has been enshrined like Lourdes, complete with its own airport. There's a novena to St Martha (she at whose house Christ lodged in the New Testament) which is more than usually direct about its terms: 'One Our Father and three Hail Marys, and light a candle every Tuesday for nine Tuesdays, and the above prayer be made known . . . This miraculous Saint grants everything before the Tuesdays are ended. No matter how difficult.' There's also a curiously didactic little poem called 'Don't Say A Word', enjoining the classic Catholic response to adversity which is to *offer it up*. It starts:

Are you nervous and blue?
In doubt what to do?
Misunderstood too?
Don't say a word.

And ends:

Climb bravely life's hill,
Seek only God's Will,
Trust Him and be still –
Sh! Don't say a word.

It is odd to find such a sentiment recommending quiescent passivity as the best way of conducting your life anywhere near my mother, whose natural disposition was to knock others into shape until they did what she told them. It must have held some curiosity value for her.

After the nuns have left, Eilis, the young curly-haired catering girl, sidles up to me:

'Was that not Sister Teresa?' she asked.

'Yes,' I said, 'do you know her?'

'I do not know her,' said Eilis, 'but,' her eyes widened, 'isn't she the one that's got Padre Pio's glove?'

Padre Pio is now an Italian saint, the Friar of San Giovanni. His hands used to regularly, and inexplicably, bleed as he was saying Mass in apparent emulation of the wounds of Christ on the cross.

'Goodness,' I said. 'A souvenir of the True Stigmata?'

'They say she's the only woman in Ireland that's got one,' breathed Eilis.

'Where's the other glove?' I asked. 'Assuming there must be two.'

Eilis gave me an old-fashioned look. Some things, it said, are too important to have smart feckers making fun of them.

It is the turn of the priests to arrive. One, moving with awful majesty, is Father O'Connor, the parish priest of Oranmore. A tall, bald and impressive pastor in his seventies, he has a look of unshakeable melancholy on his weary face, and speaks in the grudging drone of one who always expects to hear bad news. He is fantastically grand, an elder statesman of the tribe, deserving of, and expecting, the respect of all, due to his advanced years, his wisdom and his doctrinaire vigour.

'How is she?'

'She's not eating much. They persuaded her to have some toast for breakfast but she's waved away lunch and I think . . .'

He ignored me. 'Anne,' he called, in a low insistent rumble. Mother had dozed on, cast off on a temporarily untroubled sea.

'She's sleeping,' concluded the priest. 'But she's looking better anyway. Will they operate, do you think?'

'I've no idea, but I doubt it'll do her any good. An operation would probably finish her off,' I said.

'Maybe I'll just give her some of this,' said Father O'Connor, extracting a bottle of holy water from his jacket. At the end of the bed, he said prayers, then uncorked the bottle, hooked one finger over the spout and flung half a dozen gouts of water all over my mother's sleeping body. The attendant visitors all blessed themselves, just in case any of the divine liquid might have landed on them.

Shortly after Father O'Connor departed, Mother began to come round from her all-consuming sleep in time for the arrival of Father O'Dwyer, a foxy-faced man in his late forties who looked like he knew how to handle people.

'Good day to you, good day to you,' he said generally, to left and right; then he addressed the drowsing figure in the bed.

'Hello Anne. This is Father O'Dwyer. It's Tuesday, it's February the twenty-fourth, and it's about half past three in the afternoon.'

We looked at him.

'I always like to start by telling them the day and the time of it. Some of these elderly ones like to be told. It gives them something to hold on to.'

'Why stop there?' I asked. 'You could also give them a weather update. You could tell them what's on television tonight. You could tell them the winner of the 2.30 at Leopardstown.' But he was oblivious.

'Anyway Anne,' he said. 'You're looking much better. We'll have you out of here in *no time*.'

Madelyn and I were summoned to see the cancer specialist, Mr Courtenay, to get the big news. You have to go to the other end of the hospital for this, the business end: park your car by the mortuary and its great tactless chimney stack, go through Casualty, with its bewildered-looking young men with plough-boy forearms sitting in wheelchairs and bleeding from head wounds, forge past the hospital chapel and form a queue before a kind of ticket office, where patients suffer the indignity of having to voice their complaints out loud in front of everyone.

Upstairs, past a crowd of prospective patients sitting gloomily on chairs, comes Mr Courtenay. He is a large, well-built man in a suit and, seemingly, a state of permanent affront. He has a very solid-looking moustache, the sort you'd seen worn by a cruel circus boss with designs on Paulette Goddard in a Chaplin movie. Mr Courtenay is not happy to see us. So soon after lunch he has some bad news to convey and, frankly, he can think of better ways to spend his afternoon. He motions us to sit down.

'We've run some more tests,' he says, 'and it looks like your mother has got cetes in the stomach fluid.'

'Cetes?'

'Cancer cells.'

'You mean she has cancer of the stomach?'

'It's hard to tell if the primary site is the stomach or the bowel or the colon,' says Courtenay, 'short of opening her up and taking a look, and I'm reluctant to do that in view of her great age.'

'So, what you're saying is?'

'I'm saying I do not propose to operate on your mother.'

There was a silence.

'Will you send her home?'

'She's too ill to be moved.'

'Can she stay here, even though you're not going to operate?'

'I see no alternative.'

'So the treatment is?'

'To make her as comfortable as possible.'

There was another silence, a different quality of silence, something altogether heavier.

'How long has she got?' asked Madelyn.

'Could be three months, could be three weeks,' said Courtenay shortly. 'I'm not going to speculate.'

Madelyn and I looked at the floor. So it was a death sentence after all. I was trying to find something to hang on to.

'Look,' I said. 'Do you think she might have secondaries on her lungs; you see she has this awful cough and I thought it might be because of all the pressure on . . .'

'It's completely *academic* where she has the cancer,' Courtenay virtually shouted at me. 'The woman has cancer and that's all there is to it.'

Madelyn had tears in her eyes. We had both known for a while that whatever Mother had, it was inoperable. But to discover there was nothing that could be done, no chemotherapy, no radiotherapy, no pills, no medication except painkillers and a large, bottomless hypodermic on a spring-release mechanism – it turned my mother's amazingly long life into not so much a fight against disease as a long, slow capitulation to it, a marathon of waiting for an end that would surely come, but knowing that the act of waiting would turn, as these things do, into an act of wanting it to happen.

I had no wish to lose my mother, whom I loved. But I dreaded what was going to happen to her and wished her out of it, and wished us all out of there. I wanted to be a non-combatant in this grisly war. I wanted to get back to the life I knew in England, of London friends and my children's conversation, of sun-dried tomatoes and bottles of expensive Burgundy in Dulwich wine bars. I wanted to escape from everything, to lock myself into a library, to find a cinema and watch some closely textured movie, *The Double Life of Veronique*, for instance, with the sultry-and-mystified Irene Jacob dying in Poland and being simultaneously reborn in Paris. Anything but sitting in this draughty room listening to this large Irishman telling me what's what about life and death.

Back by my mother's bed, watching her drink from a puny poly-styrene cup, the smell of vanilla flavoured Ensure starts getting to me. I will never again, ever, wash with vanilla soap, go into branches of The Body Shop, eat ice cream or drink Coca-Cola for fear of inhaling that sweet essence which is now the scent of death. I can't imagine why it's called Ensure, except to make bloody certain that you never want to get ill. Or old.

I look at her frail body as it twists about on its mountain of pillows, trying to get comfortable. Mother is definitely shrinking. I noticed when I hugged her last Christmas that her shoulders had become a little cage of bones; but now her arms are fat and as solid as a prize-fighter's, and her legs are becoming equally enormous. Once or twice a day she asks me to reach under the covers and lift her legs from under her knees, up and down as though she were pedalling a bicycle. Her feet are the size of Minnie Mouse's and need to be dusted daily with antiseptic powder.

I remember one of our many religious chats – her absolute belief on one side, my absolute scepticism on the other. This one was about corporeality and the afterlife. Mother believed that we would get our bodies back after we were dead and would be able, when reunited, to hug each other again.

'Oh yeah,' I said. 'And what would we look like?'

'Like we did on earth, of course.'

'But when? When we were children? When we died? Imagine all those decrepit octogenarian faces, all those palsied limbs, all those hospitalised deadbeats and crones, the cancer victims, people with Aids, the accident corpses who died in a road smash or a fire . . .'

'No John,' she said patiently. 'It won't be like that at all. We'll all come back looking like we did at our best. In our prime.'

'Hang on,' I said, 'you mean we'll all be looking well fed, middle-aged, buffed by success, and about forty-fifty? So you and I and my son and your great granny who died in the famine, and your sisters in America, we'll all be walking around looking handsome and fortyish, with no distinction of rank or seniority, of time or era or Englishness or Irishness?'

'That's exactly how it'll be,' said Mother triumphantly.

'But Ma,' I complained, 'your parents' (who died before I was born) 'could walk past and I'd never know them.'

'John,' she snorted, 'don't be so stupid. Wouldn't I introduce you?'

There's less to smile at now, as her body daily betrays her, as her sense of who and what she is is beginning to come apart.

In 'The Old Fools', Larkin wrote: 'At death, you break up; the bits that were you/ Start speeding away from each other forever/ With no one to see.' But with Mother, even the run-up to death is full of fleeing bits, that one can see all too clearly. Of limbs that have escaped the jurisdiction of her will and gone AWOL. Of organs that don't know or recognise their owner any more. Of skin that is disguised with liver pigmentations, like battle camouflage. Of bruises in their fancy, Francis Bacon palette of atrocious purple and black, the colour of hospital grapes. Her chest has developed a fierce malignancy of its own – a terrible racking cough that sends her feeble body into a spasm, a tusseration at whose first agonised whisper I have to bound forward from my chair and pull Mother upright in the bed, and pat her back until it is over and her wheezing subsides and her bleary eyes come back to normal.

'John,' she says, painfully.

'Poor Ma.'

Her lips opened to speak, but she thought better of it. A minute went by.

'John . . .'

'What is it Ma?'

She gave a pathetic, sidelong half-smile.

''Tis very hard to die.'

'To leave everyone?'

She shook her head.

'To go down there.'

'But Mum,' I said. 'You can't think for a minute that you're going anywhere but Heaven. After your endless loyalty to the Lord.'

'Down in the grave,' she said, and turned her head away.

The prancing Devil beside the bus-stop suddenly came back to me, in all his idiocy. And the graves of my ancestors and of my father, ten miles away in Athenry cemetery, and his brother Walter, his father Henry, his mother Margaret, his rich uncle Martin. I thought of the choice of fates that used to confront the Irish fishermen in years gone by, the green grave of the sea and the black grave of the turf on dry land, and how much one is lost to the tribe when the green grave has claimed another of its sons. And an image from Synge came into my head. It's from his book *The Aran Islands*, a record of the four trips he made between 1898 and 1902 to the three great plates of limestone that sit out on the Atlantic, shadowing the coasts of Clare and Connemara. On Inishmore, the largest of the islands, he met Mairtin Conneely, an old, blind but strikingly earthy islander who explains to Synge about the exiled angels of the upper air:

> When Lucifer saw himself in the glass, he thought himself equal to God. Then the Lord threw him out of Heaven, and all the angels that belonged to him. While he was 'chucking them out' an archangel asked him to spare some of them, and those that were falling are in the air still, and have power to wreck ships and to work evil in the world.

In Synge's book it's all over in a moment. But as the scene unfolds in your head you can imagine the great would-be dictator, the failed usurper of Heaven, folding his wings around him with a kind of bad-tempered dignity and taking a step out of the door to nothingness, stepping off the edges of Paradise like a paratrooper under the exit sign and plunging through the spectacular sky to the dark regions of Pandemonium. And you can see all his black-winged hosts following him, teetering for a second on the brink, like lemmings trying to change their minds, but eventually falling beyond the doorway through which there is nothing except exclusion and darkness.

The islander's story is full of the pathos of angels. You can imagine a soft-hearted archangel like Gabriel taking pity on the multitude of bad guys being bulldozed out of the crystal wall of Heaven, saying: 'Don't do this. Don't send us to Hell. We were only obeying orders. You can't consign us to perdition for all eternity just because we were loyal.'

Gabriel, a decent policy adviser, would have taken their petition to the triumphant Son of God saying, 'Do they all have to go to Hell? Maybe just a few might be allowed.' And God in turn, confronted with this appeal for clemency, would have said after a moment's thought, 'Oh very well then. You don't have to go to Hell. But you can't stay here. *You'll always be falling.*'

And that's how come they're always around, the falling angels, drifting through the upper air, a constant danger to the tall masts of ships, to fisherman, to low aircraft, to lighthouses, fishing smacks, lifeboats. They don't mean any harm. They're just frustrated by the endless hanging in the air, constantly, eternally in transit between one place and another, deprived of a sanctuary, denied a final refuge, never finding a real home. No wonder they turn into trouble-makers.

And that's what we are, the new English-Irish, caught between two cultures, between the Anglo-Saxon and the Celtic, between scrupulous, God-fearing, Apollonian decencies and the careless, pagan, Dionysiac strain, never able to integrate the two since they are antithetical, pulling our human sympathies in two different directions.

And so I sit here, between Battersea and Galway, two poles I know with two levels of intimacy, one of them my resting place, the other my 'true home', though it feels as awkwardly foreign as it's always done. Before me is my mother, herself hovering between life and death, an object of interest to friends, neighbours, family and busybodies alike, to all of whom I must act as the master of ceremonies, cheerleader and reclaimed prodigal son.

I, who am not Irish, feel I'm being sucked into a new Gaelic identity. And yet I've spent forty-odd years growing up with this Irish strain, this Celtic gene that had invaded my English soul at a million turns. While the figure who did most to turn me into this curious hybrid lies dying beside me. I begin to remember the years I'd spent being both English and Irish, the constant switchback of my relationship with both countries, the condition of being between the two cultures my mother straddled like the consummate actress she was; her's, my father's, my sister's and my own endless falling between sense and sensibility, between south London and the west of Ireland.

II

INGRID BERGMAN AND
GEORGE RAFT

My eyes are squeezed shut to keep out the stinging suds and the cascade of water, and her thumbs on the back of my head feel monstrously large, as if I am being worked over by a giant. I am four years old, and I'm standing on a chair, bending over the bathroom basin. All I can see is darkness, all I can smell is perfumed sudsy water; all I can feel is the manipulation of her strong fingers. There is a controlled violence about the way she is washing her only son's hair, as there is a yielding, brutalised passivity in the roll of my head as I am kneaded this way and that. Perhaps sensing that some form of comfort is required during this ritual, my mother decides to recite a little poem to me. Which shall it be? Ah yes. Her voice trembling, with a fake-wistful note she learned thirty years earlier in Sligo, she begins 'My Dog Tray':

> On the green banks of Shannon, when Sheelah was nigh,
> No blithe Irish lad was so happy as I,
> No harp like my own could so cheerily play,
> And wherever I went was my poor dog Tray.

Even a four-year-old could tell that something terrible was in the offing. It was given away in the clues about 'my poor dog', and the figure of the wandering harpist, and the assurance that he was once happy in the past. You just knew the man in the poem was bound to meet a sticky end. If you'd had any doubts, my mother's delivery would have ended them. Nobody could make an otherwise neutral phrase throb with pathos the way she could. Even the first line, recited in her mournful contralto, sounded like the prelude to some very bad news — although I couldn't tell whether Sheelah was a place or an adjacent lady friend. By halfway through her recital I was crying, my hot tears creeping through my squeezed eyelids, pushed out by more little gushes of scalding rain. Above my head there was no respite:

Oh the day it was dark and the night had got cold,
And Pat and his dog had grown weary and old.
How fondly he slept in my old coat of grey,
And he licked me for kindness, my poor dog Tray.

And if you thought the state of this poor man was a temporary glitch, a bad night spent *al fresco* by the roadside on the way to somewhere more welcoming and hospitable, you could think again:

Where now shall I go, poor, forsaken and blind?
Shall I find one to guide me — so faithful and kind —
To my own native village, so far far away?
I had ever a friend in my poor dog, Tray.★

To this day I can not remember what went wrong with 'Pat', between the announcement of his former happiness and the revelation of his present misery. The connecting narrative passed me by, or upset me so much that I stopped listening. But the image of the old musician, cold and tired and *blind* to boot, sleeping rough with his doomed dog inside his ancient grey overcoat, had a powerful effect. It was the first impression I had of what being Irish was like. It meant being happy, then sad; being companionable, then lonely; being young, then old; being surrounded by greenery, then enfolded in grey melancholy. Everything tended towards an inevitable decay. Everything was going to get worse. A whole cluster of impressions went with the poem and with my mother's declamatory voice.

★ It's called 'The Harper' by Thomas Campbell, the Glasgow poet who wrote 'Hohenlinden', but it is hellish difficult to find in any anthology.

Her fondness for depressing verse did not end there. Wherever she picked them up, whatever Victorian *Treasury of Melancholy Parlour Poetry* they'd been collected in, she knew a dozen little poems of tragedy among the rustic poor. Another began:

> The cottage door was open,
> The collier's steps were heard.
> The father and the mother met,
> But neither spoke a word . . .

and featured a dying child and his distraught mother's demand that the good Lord take her away instead. I must have had a triple-strength dose of these cheerful items one evening, because my father came home from the surgery to find me weeping into my pillow.

'My poor man,' he said. 'What's wrong with you?'

'It's Mummy,' I said, lachrymose little sneak that I was. 'She was saying about the child who was dead and his mother was so sad and . . .' Minutes later, I heard my father downstairs in the kitchen berating his mystified wife.

'Will you *not* be saying them sad poems to the children!' he shouted.

'But they're nice,' retorted my mother, 'I used to say them when I was young.' To demonstrate the harmlessness of her taste in verse, she began to recite another one at my father, probably concerning another hapless collier.

'That's awful depressing stuff,' said my father. 'It upsets the children. You mustn't do it.'

I stole back to my cold bed, impressed to think that my mother could use misery as a weapon, could just open her mouth and make people cry with a few words in a certain tone of voice – but could, evidently, be stopped if you spoke sharply to her.

Years later, my eyes still prickle when I remember these glutinous little rhymes. Thinking they were my property and nobody else's, I was amazed to discover an echo of 'The Harper' in Paul Muldoon's 'Sleeve Notes' – a poem in which he uses a U2 concert in California to dramatise his own condition as an Irish exile in America:

the night we drove all night from Palm
Springs to Blythe. No Irish lad and his lass
were so happy as we who roared
and soared
through yucca-scented air.

And as with Pat the harpist, Muldoon's initial happiness that evening is followed by 'a sense of loss . . . that would deepen and expand', following as inevitably as night follows day. The expectation of things going wrong was the first Irish lesson I learned. The second was that some grown-ups thought it was a perfectly normal and natural thing to upset children.

I started life in Balham, south London, in a house near the fast thoroughfare of Nightingale Lane, SW12. My father, Martin, was the junior doctor in a London GP partnership. His partner was, confusingly, named John Walsh, though apparently unrelated to our family.* In due course, the boss doctor mutated to 'Jack' and became my godfather. His wife, Cora, was a pitilessly sophisticated woman who played bridge and wasn't overly keen on other people's children. They, like my parents, had made a life in London after the war, to escape from an Ireland that was rigid with religion, economically stagnant, politically backward-looking and culturally moribund; a place that seemed to offer little to the landless, non-inheriting sons and daughters of rural communities. London had jobs and money and free health care, or at least had enough of all three to balance the less appealing metropolitan texture of rationing, austerity and bombed-out streets.

My parents were as Irish as Connemara marble. They were both from the west coast, from areas later known to tourist maps as, respectively, 'The Joyce Country' and 'The Yeats Country'. Their fathers were both farmers, their mothers both thinly-remembered figures, the point of whose lives had become lost after, or during, the years of child-rearing. My parents, Martin and Anne, were both educated with little reference to intellectual enquiry or independent thought. Martin

* Walsh is the fourth most popular name in Ireland, after Murphy, Kelly and O'Brien, and simply means 'Welshman, Celt or stranger.' In the Middle Ages, it was the name given to just about anyone who wandered into town from the east.

was taught by the priests at St Jarleth's College, Tuam in north Galway. He went on to study medicine at Galway University and became a doctor. Anne went to state school in Tubbercurry, Co. Sligo, and always resented her lack of a university degree. It was, she said, the result of her having to remain at home in Sligo and care for her ailing mother. For her, becoming a nurse was a means of escape from home, the farm backyard and Sligo drizzle, and she seized it with both hands. Once you'd learned the dread regimen of bedpans, hospital corners, pills, medication and ward management, she reasoned, you could go anywhere.

So, in 1937, she went to London, aged twenty-six. She lived in London during the Blitz, but the only evidence of this is a rent book discovered after her death, charting her life in a Paddington flat, paying her rent of 10/6 a week, apparently oblivious to the bombs, the firestorms and the collapsed terraces around Euston and Bayswater. Early photographs show an Irish girl of shining-eyed optimism and naiveté: my mother looks out beyond the camera with the dazzling smile of a teenager given her first screen test. Her hair is a rich chestnut, shingled into brutal waves in the twenties style and worn like a helmet. It is approximately a million miles from the hairstyle of a Sligo farm girl.

She would never have been happy on a farm. Her home town of Tubbercurry, with its ploughboys and farm labourers, was never going to be her sort of thing. She didn't wish (you could tell from her expression in photographs) to be fondled or mauled by gauche young country lads, and nor would she bother making up her face for them at country dances. She was destined for better things.

Mother always had ideas above her station. To the end of her life she gave herself airs, like a queen in exile. Her favourite diversion when young was amateur dramatics. She starred among the local thespians in a variety of parish-pump dramas with titles like *The Young Man from Rathmines* and *Spreading the News*. She had a walk-on-and-expire role in a patriotic drama, playing a genteel insurgent, executed by the perfidious British. In her seventies, she could still enact the play's climactic scene, in which she faced down the nasty soldiery with a martyr's scorn. Called on to inform on her rebellious colleagues, she dramatically tossed her Cathleen ni Houlihan locks and said: 'This is my answer – Death before Dishonour,' to which her sneery British tormentor replied: 'Then, you rebel dog–', and bade his soldiers shoot her. My mother was mown down in a fusillade of bullets and her noble corpse carried off the stage, night after night, in a stark, muffled-drum semi-silence – except when the company Lothario, Gerard Ryan, tickled her feet and made her (posthumously) squirm.

The truth was that, like many young girls of her generation, she couldn't wait to get out of Ireland. Home was a place of ignorance, want and illness. Her favourite sibling was her brother John, who gave her rides on his shoulders when she was little. At four or five, she was awakened one night by the sound of an ambulance, and watched, with the candlelight leaping on the banisters, as John and one of her sisters were carried out of the house. They were taken away to the hospital in Mayo. The house was silent all day as the family waited for news. Next morning, they brought the daughter back, but John had died. It was tuberculosis. He was sixteen. The disease was to claim another brother, five years later.

You could say the whole family was destined for export. My mother's elder sisters, Catherine, Bridie, Margaret and the eldest, a nun called Sister Xavier Maria (known as Auntie Sister) sailed for America when the war started. Catherine married a quiet Irishman, Tom Whyte, and they set up home in Brighton, Massachusetts. They had two children, Marion and Jack. Bridie became a social secretary to the Kennedy clan, but never married. Margaret came home to County Mayo and had six children who emigrated back to Phila-delphia.

Mother, however, wanted to be a nurse and there were nursing jobs a-plenty to be had in England. She had taken care of her mother for years, she could tell patients what to do, she understood drugs. She had a country girl's respect for medicine as the practical underside of prayer. Unlike prayer, it mostly made good things happen. Without being obviously connected to virtue (treatment never seemed to involve the mortification of the flesh or acts of contrition or the absolving of sin) it made the good better, though it often seemed equally well-disposed towards the wicked and the indigent.

So my mother made the trip to London in the mid-1930s. She trained as a nurse at St Thomas's Hospital near Waterloo Station and at St Mary's, Paddington, and rose to become a ward sister. I can imagine her being a severely efficient nurse – but I howl to think how naïve she was, how innocent in the Big Smoke before the war. She once told me, in a shocked whisper, how she was befriended, in the Lyons Corner House in the Strand, by a chatty London woman called Christine, who suggested they hang out together. 'It's more fun hunting in packs,' Christine had said, mystifyingly. Mother liked her new chum, and agreed to meet her in Piccadilly for a drink. As they sipped their cocktails – a horse's neck for Christine, a sweet sherry for my mother – she was quizzed about men and boyfriends and where in London she went 'to meet people'.

'I meet a lot of people at the hospital,' said Mother, reasonably. 'We go out with the doctors and have great fun.'

'Yes I dare say, dear,' said her new friend, 'but where do you go when you want to meet, you know, men?'

Mother was puzzled. Didn't she meet plenty of nice men at St Thomas's – young doctors who'd be always teasing you, and male nurses, and even the odd gentleman patient who'd try his luck asking you out, sometimes just as a way of getting his own back on you for having seen him half-naked and sick and horizontal? Where else did a girl meet men?

'Oh, Quaglino's,' said Christine, 'or the Café Royal, or there's a little club in Shaftesbury Avenue. They're very nice to the girls there.'

'But how on earth can you afford it?' asked my mother. 'The drinks at them places would cost half my wages.'

'You don't buy drinks, silly,' said Christine. 'The gentleman you're with pays for them.'

'But why should he spend all that money on someone he hardly knows?' asked my mother, mystified.

'Anne,' said Christine, '*How* old did you say you were again?'

Christine tried to take my mother to the Westbury Hotel and other plush joints around St James's and Berkeley Square, where good-looking girls with the right amount of conversation and lipstick drank Martinis and laughed at their gentleman friends' worldly stories, places where they were bought drinks on the loose but gradual understanding that they would accompany them to a convenient hotel, once they were sufficiently oiled. Christine was, it seems, more a wartime good-time girl than a prostitute. She must have realised that co-opting a coltish, chatty, Sligo virgin as her Plain Friend wasn't necessarily going to raise her game and the friendship soon lapsed. But, my mother recalled it at the end of her life as an odd introduction to the social round of the West End during the war. That was, to her, what London sophistication supposedly meant if you were a single girl in your twenties.

'What do you think would have happened, Mum,' I asked her once, 'if you'd gone off with one of Christine's gentlemen, and he'd put his hand on your thigh and said, "How about it, eh?"'

Mother pursed her lips. 'He wouldn't have had the chance, or the breath, to do it twice,' she said darkly.

It must have been a relief when she discovered the more elegant side of English manners among the aristocrats of the Home Counties. She became a private nurse to a series of families with addresses in Burke's Peerage, and spent her thirties in surroundings she could previously only have dreamed about. She looked after the dowager Lady Hambledon, who was the Wodehousian dragon-aunt of Lord David Cecil, Oxford don, literary critic and author of *The Victorian Novelists* – a charming but unworldly chap, more an appreciator of literature than a critic in the true sense. He was immortalised in Kingsley Amis's caustic *Memoirs* as a neighing silly-ass lecturer – and Cecil sometimes lived up to the caricature in my mother's recollections.

Once, as she prepared a bath for the dowager, his lordship was reading a volume of poetry in his bedroom nearby. As Mother poured bath salts and oily unguents into the cascading steam and manoeuvred the old lady down the hallway towards her aromatic lavabo, it entered Lord David's head that the running water must be meant for him. So he undressed, and put on slippers and a dressing gown, never relinquishing his hold on the poetry book in his hand. Whispering a particularly fine passage sotto voce to himself, he elbowed open the bathroom door. From her seated position in the bath, Lady Hambledon regarded her nephew crossly but said nothing. It was only when he slipped off his dressing-gown and, still holding his slim volume aloft, raised one elegant leg over the side of the bath on top of his naked aunt, that she thought to remonstrate:

'David *really*,' she squawked, 'Can you *please* wait your turn?'

Mother would tell us this story, punctuated with embellishments and girlish shrieks, as she had once been invited to tell it at a dozen amusing *soirées* among the English. How she must have amused them, this easily-shocked Irish nurse with her startled blue eyes and her fondness for indiscretion. I grew up listening to her tales of life among the gentry: other families, other manor houses and stately homes where, as

Nurse Durkin, she was a semi-professional part of the household without ever actually being treated as a servant. She was private nurse to Lady Honor This and Lady Violet That. She took care of General Sir Aylmer Haldane, the war hero and brother of the surgeon G. D. S. Haldane, who wrote a poem about bowel cancer that memorably begins, 'I wish I had the voice of Homer/ To sing of rectal carcinoma'.

Mother was allowed to eat lunch with the families (perhaps as a form of insurance against anyone choking on a fishbone) and went for drives and picnics with the younger members of the family. Wholesome as a barm-brack, toothy and giggling, she was a perfectly acceptable addition to the household – the kind of girl the young Betjeman might have sought solace with, had he failed to get his hands on Joan Hunter Dunn – on the understanding that she was owed nothing but her monthly wage packet and could be dispensed with at a moment's notice. She always spoke of this period as the happiest time of her life, before marriage, domesticity, children and the London streets all ground her down. It's not hard to see it as living in an English idyll: the houses, the walks, the badminton court, the arboretum, the honeysuckle trellis, the regular meals announced by gongs and bells, the nursery, the monogrammed bedlinen, the vast headlamps of the Bentley she was occasionally allowed to drive, the soup tureens, the endless discretion and murmurous noblesse oblige of her employers. She would proudly show us photographs of her various beaux from these years: a moustachioed RAF-type called Derek, various doomed-looking youths in dinner jackets, snapped with their arms around the available girls, and a bespectacled intellectual beanpole called Bobby in tweeds and a Fairisle V-neck jumper who romanced her for several months. Their photo taken in June 1939 looks like an engagement portrait – he frighteningly innocent and earnest, she, at twenty-seven, fashionably marcell-waved and decidedly in charge. She never married any of them though. Bobby, she said, was a near miss: he had to go off to the war, and she never knew what became of him. Their conversations, as she relayed them to me, sounded like communication breakdowns: he, tongue-tied about emotional commitment, she, chattering on about patients, chronic diseases and the power of prayer, all the time wondering why he was being so cold and unresponsive. Look at them, gazing at the camera – Anne and Bobby, two people separated by a common language and two hemispherically different religio-cultural poles.

It's not surprising that she didn't marry until she was forty. Members of the English aristocracy, however much they may sometimes admit commoner genes into the chromosomal family soup, do not go around marrying Irish nurses whose fathers are poor farmers from Sligo. They let them work for them, they allow them to be amusing, and they let them be grateful for small indulgences. And that – unless the Irish female in question is exceptionally beautiful (as with Grace Kelly) or amazingly scheming (as with King Charles's mistress, Kitty O'Shea) – is pretty well that.

So Mother gave up any hope of marrying an English milord, worked her way through the war years, and resigned herself to a spinsterish existence, like her Irish girlfriends back at the hospital. In its place she developed a carapace of skittish, Celtic-English flirtation, and it was that which endeared her to my father.

They met in Rome in 1950. They were both pilgrims on their way to see Pope Pius XII and the Vatican for the first time, as enjoined by the Catholic Church in recognition of it being a Holy Year (there's one every twenty-five years). Martin Walsh and Anne Durkin sat together at the back to the coach and chatted about Ireland and their families, and about medical matters. He was thirty-four, shy and short on small-talk, but impressed by her worldly air. She was forty and forthright, a colleen who'd made good in England, impressed by the fact that he was a doctor. She had a Thermos flask in her travel bag, full of cold vermouth, which she measured out for them in the flask's capacious plastic lid. This struck my father as the last word in sophistication. She was clearly his kind of girl. They drank a toast to Ireland. My father gazed on her spectacular bosom, her infectious laugh, her air of wiry and capable determination, and was lost. He courted her around the Eternal City, took her for drives in a rented Fiat, miles away from the other coach-stranded pilgrims, photographed her in toothy poses against the Trevi fountain and romanced her thoroughly. 'Arrivaderci Roma' became their song, and remained so until the end of their lives. She took to calling him 'Martino' as if he were a Latin lover – or indeed a cocktail that might go to your head, a Dry Martino – instead of the sharp American gangster he tried to resemble at the time. (My father always thought, with some justice, that he looked like the villainous actor, George Raft; my mother, flying in the face of both evidence and tact, always said she had wanted to marry 'a nice ugly man'. She who was, or so she thought, a dead ringer for Ingrid Bergman).

They married a year later in Brompton Oratory, the enormous Catholic church on London's Brompton Road. His best man was Martin Hession from his home town of Athenry. Her bridesmaid was Maureen O'Sullivan, a handsome, chuckling fellow nurse from Cork. It was a wholly Irish affair. The English aristocracy were not invited. Martin and Anne were exiles who had found a haven in each other, amid the lonesome wastes of post-war London. It was going to be all right after all.

My parents suffered from an identity crisis. My father didn't dislike the English, he just lived in the constant suspicion that they undervalued or disrespected him. My mother didn't dislike the Irish, she just wanted to distance herself from their rude familiarity. He was too Irish to be happy in England; she had become too English to be happy anywhere else.

My mother used to answer the phone with a hilarious dual voice: an opening, exploratory 'Hell-ay-ow', as English as Celia Johnson, and, once she'd recognised one of her Irish nursing friends on the line, a secondary, gratified slippage into pure Sligo, 'Arrah Biddy, is it you?' With the local Battersea butcher, whom she treated as an educated man, a subtle technician, like a surgeon though on a more basic level, she was coquettish; she liked to imply that he alone knew her exact requirements in the leg of lamb/rib of beef/pork-chop-with-kidney department. With the greengrocer, whom she treated as a lesser being, brawny but a bit of a yob, like the chap who brought the coal, she was gracious but distant, implying no familiarity at all. With the car mechanic, Gerry, a pipe-smoking, rakish Englishman who said things like, 'She'll be humming along nicely in no time, mark m'words,' she reverted to being a sassy flapper in slacks, her hands stuck in her pockets, her conversation full of wartime badinage. With English policemen and customs officers, she was a saucy colleen.

Once, as we returned from a holiday in Italy, I watched as an exciseman in a peaked cap wearily directed her to open a shoulder bag full of brown paper parcels. 'What's in here?' he asked. 'Italian peaches,' said my mother, 'would you like one?' I was shocked, as you are when your parents go into unexpected flirtation-mode. She had a lot of what she'd have called 'cheek', but reserved it mostly for English officials and Irish priests.

My father tended to mutter when faced with the English. He was a shy and secretive fellow, wary of strangers and condescension, diffident about 'being too open', constantly on the look-out for those who would con you or patronise you or fleece you or take the mick out of you. But he was no Mick. He was an intelligent, respectable doctor with a degree from University College, Galway. He was not going to be considered slow or stupid by English people because of his accent.

On arriving in England in the late 1940s, his first locum job was at a cottage hospital in Kent, where he was required to perform minor operations, cyst removals, that kind of thing. On his second day, he was bent over a nasty gashed leg, trying to remove some tiny black pebbles from the burst flesh. Beside him stood a young nurse from the Home Counties.

'Forceps,' he said. She handed him one.

'Swab.'

She handed him one.

'Kidney dish.'

She picked it up and held it near the wound.

'Dammit,' said my father, 'I'm gointa need a retracther.'

'I'm sorry?' said the nurse.

'A retracther,' said my father crossly.

'I'm really sorry, doctor,' said the girl, 'but I can't quite make out . . .'

'I said a RETRACTOR,' my father shouted, 'for pullin' back the SKIN. Are you DEAF or somethin'?'

The nurse bit her lip. She was not used to being shouted at by anyone, and certainly not by visiting junior doctors just off the Dublin ferry. She might have cried or run out of the theatre but instead she just stared at him (which was worse) and slapped the instrument into his hand. Afterwards he felt bad. It wasn't just that he had been made to feel like a thick fellow with an accent to match, it was the way the word 'tractor', with all its agricultural connotations, had somehow become involved as well. My father never forgot the incident and resolved in the future to keep his temper; but some damage had been done.

He had an inferiority complex about the English. My mother had a superiority complex about the Irish. Heaven knows how they got on in London, surrounded by Irish friends, listening to Irish singers, watching TV shows specifically because the entertainers had Irish connections. But while my mother was keen to put a lot of distance, real and class-wise, between Ireland and herself, my father was a Galwayman through and through, and he never lost a strong affinity with west-coast ways.

He found most English sports boring, effete, or excessively jingoistic. 'My God,' he would groan at the sight of footballers (even during the World Cup final of 1966) embracing in the aftermath of a goal, 'Will you look at that? All the kissing and cuddling? What kind of men are these at all?' The memory of one boxing match stayed in his head for years afterwards, because of the commentary, which shifted from the merely partisan to the flagrantly one-sided in a matter of seconds. He would recall it with relish: 'And the British boy is in there and he's fairly belting him now. One! Two! One! Two! A left to the head, a right to the body. He's got him on the ropes. It's nearly over. He's . . . Oh! The British boy is down! And he's out! The referee's counted him out!' He would end this recital with great laughter, both from joy at seeing the old oppressor given a hammering, but also for the reversal of the smug British assertion that they were morally bound to win sporting contests.

My father had been captain of the Minors hurling team at Galway University, a fact of which he was hugely proud. They'd given him a medal for some championship game, an award he treasured, and somewhere along the line he'd picked up a livid scar above his right lip, the result of being lashed in the face, apparently by a member of his own team. I used to regard it with interest, this Irish version of the Habsburg Lip. Hurling seemed to me to be an impossible game, so fast, so barbaric, so hard to follow. Instead of nice English hockey sticks, rounded and inoffensive like candy canes, hurleys were flat and bladed, like machetes. Instead of 'bullying off' (that uniquely English sporting term), you had to scoop up the ball – a sullen, non-bouncing, stitched and rigid leather bomb – using your ash machete as a kind of shovel to whack the thing a hundred yards up the pitch, apparently without any sense of where it might land.

From the age of ten or so, on Sunday mornings before lunch, I would go for walks with Dad and my sister across Clapham Common, leaving Mother to cook a leg of lamb for lunch. We would take a scooter, a bicycle, a football, a tennis ball, a cricket bat and stumps. Arrayed with an arsenal of non-Irish sporting implements, we would make our way through the small mini-common, cross the Avenue ('Don't *hop* the ball where there are cars,' he'd always say on the pedestrian crossing) and trek through the main common with the grand early-nineteenth century houses on the left and the mild sub-urban forest of spiky bushes and long grass on the right. There were rumours that horrible people lurked in there by night, and you could occasionally find fragments of noisome evidence: brown paper bags with murder victim's shoes inside (though you didn't actually look), fluttering leaves of lavatory paper . . . My father tended to bustle us past the wooded bits, and out onto the sunlit uplands, where we'd plunge the stumps into the soft ground and play cricket for an hour.

I played cricket at school so I knew how leg breaks and off-spinners worked, though I couldn't make the tennis ball turn in the air no matter how hard I tried. I knew where third man was supposed to stand, and first slip and extra cover. My father knew nothing of these matters. They were English terms and damned stupid ones. Silly mid-off? The man in the gully? Long leg? 'What kind of an eejit,' he'd say, 'would come up with daft names like that?' He never learned to bowl overarm, so all the spin strategies in the world were lost on him. He never learned to bat at any angles except cover and mid-wicket. To my father, the whole elaborate science of batsmanship could be reduced to a single technique with two variants – a great ploughboy wallop or a haymaker swing, sending the ball miles off to the left or right.

Cricket wasn't his game. His was back in Galway where seasoned hurlers wound yards of dirty bandage around the splintering heel of their sticks and ran themselves ragged after a ball that passed up and down the pitch at 200 mph, a speeding bullet. Dad pined for it.

One day on the Common, as he prepared to hit the tennis ball over the trees once more, he saw a wondrous sight: a group of Irish sporting bravos had set up a hurling game beside us, using real hurley sticks, gracefully pocking the ball through the air to each other. Dad was entranced. He gazed at them and couldn't go on batting. I bowled him out, middle stump, but he refused to move. His eyes were on the Irishmen, the way they ran like hares with the ball balanced on the hurley, as though in a peculiar Irish egg-and-spoon race. I couldn't help but look at them too, at the delicate way they scooped the ball off the green floor and swiped it away, while turning in a muscular, circling motion, like dancers, like the most agile of dervishes.

'John,' said my father over his shoulder. 'Throw me the ball.'

'But you're out, Daddy' I protested. 'It's Mad's turn.'

'John, throw me the feckin' ball,' he said, irritation shading his voice. 'And I don't mean bowl it.' I think I realised what he was up to. I threw him a long slow arc. He swung the cricket bat and whacked the ball straight up in the air, in what was called a Garryowen shot. With my child's cricket bat (the 'Colin Cowdrey Junior Sports' bat – slick with linseed oil and inscribed with my name), he tried his best ever hurling stroke, getting right underneath it, like a golfer trying to explode out of the rough with a 9-iron. It went up like a rocket, almost out of sight, at which point, of course, the captain of the hurling team should have approached, hand outstretched and said: 'That was a rare old belt you gave the ball – you wouldn't be Irish, I suppose? And you wouldn't by any chance ever have tried your hand at hurling, would you? Because, if so, we could do with a man of your calibre. We play every weekend and afterwards we always go for a few jars and talk about the old country. So if you'd care to . . .' But he didn't. The hurlers didn't even notice my father's application for membership. They were too busy playing the game to spot any overtures signalled at them by exiles with hurling scars on their faces. Dad tried one or two more wallops with my cricket bat but finally gave up in disgust and we went home.

He was quiet. The encounter had clearly bothered him. I knew how much he'd wanted to hang out with the players, and to be asked where in God's name he'd learned to puck the ball like that. I could hear his frustration at not being able to say, 'I played a bit for the county in my time. Only for the Minors, o'course, but . . .' I knew how he wanted to find out where they were from, when they'd arrived, how they were doing. But it wasn't possible, any of it. He suddenly seemed to me rather solitary, a man stuck on the edge of the life he grew up with, with a kid's cricket bat in his hands.

Two days later, he went out to a sports shop in Balham and ordered three hurley sticks from a Dublin supplier: one for him, one for me and a camogie stick for Madelyn. (Camogie means a female hurley player, and therefore the stick would be – what? Softer?

46

Gentler? Less violent? When the sticks arrived, there seemed to be no difference between them).

Armed with our new hurleys, we prowled the Common for weeks, the cricket now abandoned, looking, though we'd never admit it, for Dad's team. If we ran into them now, it would be so much easier, surely, to establish his credentials as the sporting Irishman, to make a connection with this tribe of exiles. It didn't happen.

We never saw them again. I was a great disappointment to my father when it came to hurling prowess. It seemed an impossible task to hit the bloody ball with the wide sweeping arc of the wooden machete, and tears of frustration would spring from my eyes. Madelyn soon lost interest in the camogie (its gentle qualities notwithstanding) and Dad had to concede defeat when, one day, as we ineffectually swatted the tight leather bladder at each other by the Clapham band-stand, he was approached by a very English class of person. 'Those sticks are jolly interesting,' he declared. 'What are they for – men's lacrosse?'

On Sunday afternoons during my teens, my father would disappear upstairs, like an anchorite off to say his prayers. It was the dead time of the weekend, when the only available beguilements were *The Golden Shot* on television or an hour spent trying to make a Schubert sonata emerge, with painful slowness, under my fingers, as I peered at the staves on the sheet music. I would seek out my father's company from pure boredom. I always knew where to find him. He'd be at the top of the house, in a lonesome boxroom, once the demesne of the au pair, where he had shifted the big wireless from the kitchen. He was convinced that the reception would be better if he were nearer to the roof.

From the wireless, a cacophonous high-pitched baying noise could be heard, which meant Dad was tuning in to Ireland, listening to a football or hurling match on the Athlone frequency. It was incredibly indistinct, like trying to hear someone shouting in a foreign language through a rainstorm. For some reason it was always the same man doing the shouting, no matter what the game. He was called Michael O'Hehir and, if you could make out the words through the blizzard of static, he possessed two fine qualities. He had the same capacity as Peter O'Sullevan, the English racing commentator, for making late gallops and sudden sprints sound incredibly exciting, and he had a gift for the colourful, if faintly ludicrous, phrase: 'I wonder if we shall see the blond head of Patsy Fagan on the pitch today,' he would cry as the teams were coming out, leaving me with an indelible image of a decapitated hurler and a cruel Berber tribesmen game being played with a severed bonce.

Whatever I said to him, Dad would go 'Shush,' as if expecting a momentous climax to the game, just at that second. I'd ask who was playing, expecting an enthusiastic run-down of the Gaelic Athletics Association premier league, or perhaps some bit of gruff, fatherly sporting lore; but all he'd say was 'Offaly and Kilkenny, shush'. I'd leave him to it, canted over the muffled wireless, passionately plugged into a game whose warring territories he hardly knew. Galway was his home, his land and sacred turf, his old team. Why should he care about Offaly or Kilkenny, or any other team? Did he get worked up about it just because it was his game? What was it that kept him closeted away on a Sunday afternoon, two floors above *The Golden Shot* and the awfulness of England?

He had an eccentric streak, of an imaginative kind. Whenever he heard the front gate click out of surgery hours, meaning that an unwelcome patient was heading for the front door, he would rush to the metal bell in the hallway, seize a piece of muslin cloth that lived between two banisters in expectation of just such an eventuality, and jam the cloth between the clapper and the bell, pre-emptively stifling its nagging summons.

'*There*,' he'd announce with satisfaction, 'that'll fix him.'

'But Dad,' we would say, 'just because you can't hear the bell, it doesn't mean the man's *not there*. Look – you can see his shadow through the glass beside the front door. Who do you think you're fooling?' He would give a little smile, like a mad scientist whose logical sense is light years above the common herd's, and would wander off, saying: 'He'll think twice before trying that again.'

I used to wonder what the man on the doorstep made of it, as this family squabble was conducted, in hushed whispers, in the hall of a supposedly empty house.

My father was the local Battersea GP, with a panel of patients that extended all the way from Clapham Common to Chelsea Bridge. For a man who had done his medical training in Ireland, doctoring in England seemed a terrible disappointment to him. He used to advise me against ever thinking of going into medicine, at least on the English model. Working as a GP over here was, he said, like being either a lowly civil servant or a failed grocer. His Hippocratic fervour was sapped by repeat orders for Haliborange tablets and Mogadon sleeping pills, and for non–urgent prescription items – in those days you could get a whole supermarket trolley of things free on the National Health, including hot water bottles and blackcurrant pastilles. It was no life for a real doctor.

But these mundane objections concealed a different reason why my father was disillusioned with English medicine. It was a matter of excitement. The unusual, the odd, the gothic and the bizarre were commonplace in treating the infirm and unwell of Galway in the years he had left behind. He always remembered one night when, as a newly qualified doctor, he was on duty at Galway Regional Hospital and was wakened by a porter at 3 a.m. with the news that there was a tinker in Casualty waiting to see him.

The man had fierce red hair and was in a state of agitation. No, he was fine himself, he said, but his Da' was dying and the doctor had better come quick. He had come on horseback, four or five miles. My father rang for an ambulance but none was to be found, the crews all asleep in their beds. So my father, in his long coat and surgical bag, mounted the horse along with the tinker and they rode for an hour through the rainy night until they reached an itinerant encampment along the main road beside Oranmore. Four old-fashioned caravans stood together, their front shafts resting on the mulchy ground. Their horses, unsaddled and unbridled, cropped the short grass at the roadside. In one of the caravans, in the spooked and spicy gloom of the interior, hung with a single lamp, a monumental figure lay groaning on a raised divan couch, clearly an important figure of the travelling community. Around the divan, kneeling on the thick blankets that spilled off it, were perhaps a dozen others, mostly women, watching the figure in the bed with hawkish scrutiny, as if each wanting to be the first to tell of his passing away. My father established that the pain was coming from the patient's lower back. The man reluctantly removed his thick, dusty corduroys, to reveal a pair of grey long–johns and grudgingly eased them off over his elderly buttocks. My father shone a lamp towards the white mass before him and discovered a vast and bolted abscess, in an advanced state of putrefaction. He would have to operate. He asked for boiling water and, fifteen minutes later, lowered his instruments into a bucket of seething water. He swabbed the hinterland around the tinker's abscess with surgical spirit and, with the scalpel, sliced off the top of the volcanic spot. The tinker chief let out a yell and wriggled convulsively. My father's response was immediate but potentially life-threatening. He smacked the man on the bottom and said, 'Stop that!' It was second nature to a doctor who had lanced a thousand boils and knew that wriggling patients only made things worse.

In this company, however, it was the wrong thing to do. The attendant family, seeing their chief assaulted by an outsider, leapt to his defence. As my father used to tell it, 'a dozen thin blades gleamed in the darkness.' A dozen gypsy shivs (most of which had done more in their careers than whittle wooden flutes), were held against his face, ready to slice through his cheek or his eyeball if he made any further hostile move. He looked around the caravan. It was, he later said, the most dangerous moment of his life. 'I mean no harm,' he told them, 'nor disrespect, but if he writhes about it will only make it worse, because he'll be losing blood. The poison is out of him and I must finish dressing the wound. Will you let me finish what I came here to do?'

It was a good speech, and it worked. They withdrew the knives from his face and backed off. The episode, which I must have heard him tell six or seven times, has a painterly quality about it – something from Caravaggio or George Wright of Derby – with the lined and wary faces of the travellers etched with shadows, staring at my twenty-six-year-old father in his rolled-up sleeves and boyish slick of Bryl-creemed hair; the necessary intruder, the young townie with his bag of tricks whom they relied on but never trusted.

I never heard how exactly he got back to the hospital that night, nor if he ever saw the patient with the abscess again. It was the picture of the encounter, in all its vivid 4 a.m. chiaroscuro, that summed up for him the charm of Irish country medicine. It might have been more perilous and unpredictable than doctoring in London, but it wasn't boring. And it gave you better stories to tell.

III

AN IRISH STEW

It was a big house, but hardly a Big House. It stood at the crest of a hill and it resembled the prow of a ship. Where Battersea Rise and Lavender Sweep met at a sharply acute angle, our back garden formed a thin V-shape, with a black wrought-iron lamp at its apex, the figure-head of the SS *Walsh*. Seen from the road, the house had a certain naval quality, with its big forecastle of rooms sticking out at odd angles, and its dramatic air of forging ahead, as if it were surging through the waves of Battersea and pulling the neighbouring shops along with it.

When we first moved there in 1963, I was ecstatic to find an air-raid shelter at the end of the garden, even though it was dank and evil-smelling and the steps down to its murky interior were spongy with mildew and home to a thousand weevils. From the garden you could see the edge of Clapham Common. The war had left its scars there in the form of two great ugly blisters of concrete, where anti-aircraft batteries had once stood during the Blitz, and had been sub-sequently turfed over.

It was a very English sort of place. It had been a haven of middle-class luxury in the nineteenth century, home to well-heeled merchants and City gents who rode up to town each morning in gigs and stove-pipe hats. E. M. Forster's paternal cousins lived in a mansion called 'Battersea Rise' on the west side of the Common. His fond great-aunt Monie (Marianne Thornton), whose legacy of £8,000 got his career as both writer and traveller under way, moved after a family row to the east side of the Common, where still, she told her diary, 'I can hear the sound of the Battersea Rise dinner bell.' Forster himself wrote, in a 1934 review of a book about the Thorntons, 'Battersea Rise! What a thrill the name gives me. Can it really be the house that once belonged to my family? And did I ever go to the house in the early eighties, led by some cousin in my peacock-blue velvet suit?' He regrets that the name of the house will mean 'nothing to the post-war generation' and deplores the way the loveliness of the place, its historical glow, its connection with tradition and the Clapham sect of evangelicals – its *Howards-End*iness – inevitably vanished under the creeping spread of London. 'Clapham,' he sniffily concludes, 'once infested by highwaymen, turned first into a pleasant and then into an unpleasant suburb.'

He would have done more than wrinkle his nose had he seen what became of the place by the time we got there. The Battersea end of Clapham Common was a dump, a service area for Clapham Junction: the busiest, noisiest and dirtiest railway junction in the country. It was a stridently working-class and immigrant neighbourhood then; a tough, coarse-grained part of inner suburbia. The skinhead phenomenon of the late sixties started around the Junction, where gangs of forty or fifty bald adolescents with braces and Doc Marten boots would congregate, before marauding across the Common in search of homosexuals, hippies and (later on) Asians youths to bash up. The pedestrian walkway that led to the station featured in the movie *Up the Junction*, giving my backyard a sudden, dodgy gleam of trendy squalor. In the film, a smart Chelsea girl (played by Suzy Kendall) leaves her parents' posh SW3 residence every morning to cross Battersea Bridge and go to work in a horrible factory in Clapham. Her intentions in doing so are inscrutable – something to do with working-class life and conveyor-belt banter being more 'real' than hanging out among the well-bred but bloodless rich folk – as are her reasons for going out with a local biker and van-driver's assistant (played by Dennis Waterman). But it put Clapham Junction on the map as the essence of 'Sarf Lunnen' – a place of gormless, listless, violent, Philistine, charmless non-endeavour – occasionally enlivened by shrieks of laughter from big girls with ragged stockings and white lipstick, who all looked like Adrienne Posta.

That, at any rate, was one perspective of Battersea – my home town. But, between the ages of ten and seventeen, I had a different view. I knew it as a tripartite ghetto, shared among the blacks, the Irish and the Poles.

The Polish community in London SW11 kept themselves to themselves, were invariably bilingual and modest, and were mostly refugees from the war. You only knew of their existence because of the special Polish Mass they attended at the Catholic church in Clapham Common on Sundays. They all wore discreet dark-grey coats and black hats, and moved in a kind of monochrome filter, as though still dazed by what had happened to their families just twenty years earlier. I struck up a friendship round at our local church with a handsome Polish father of two called Danny, with whom I used to alternate the reading of Bidding Prayers on the altar, but we fell out over some absurd misunderstanding about whose turn it was. He simply melted away and I never saw him in the church again.

The blacks and the Irish, by contrast, were noisily competitive about whose place it was. I remember a day when my mother and I (aged twelve) were returning home from church, when she stopped dead in the middle of the pavement.

'Will you look at the cheek o'that,' she said. I looked and saw a man parking his beaten-up Austin 1100 outside the back door of our house, precisely in the spot overlooked by a printed sign that announced: 'DOCTOR'S HOUSE. NO PARKING HERE PLEASE.'

'Leave it, Mum,' I said. 'He isn't doing any harm.'

'Isn't he indeed?' she said, her mouth setting in a grimace like a mantrap. She strode over to the Austin, where the driver was yanking on the brake, and rapped sharply on the window. A black face looked out. 'Would you mind offaly,' said Mother in her most piercingly polite voice, 'not parkin' here? Because you see, the doctor needs to park his car here, where he can get to it easily if he has to go out on an urgent call. Otherwise, he might have to park half a mile away and by the time he'd found his car the patient'd be dead, d'you see?' Having sketched this tragic scenario, she subsided. We both waited for a reply.

'Lady,' said the man in the car, equably. 'Why don't you go back where ya came from?'

She flinched as if she'd been hit in the face. 'Lookit,' she said. 'I was livin' in London a long time before *you* fellers came near the place.'

'That so?' said the man, unimpressed. 'Time ya went back.'

'Mum . . .' I said, worried that we might have an interracial war on our doorstep if this went much further.

'Park this thing somewhere else,' she said, rapping a finger on the roof of his invasive vehicle, 'and don't be so disrespectful. There'll come a time when you'll be needin' a doctor and God help you then.'

'God save us *ahllll*,' said the man, 'from people like you.' But he drove off anyway, to park in some less contentious territory. A small victory, but Mother marched home in triumph.

There were black families living in Lavender Sweep who seemed to run what passed for nightlife in sixties Battersea. They had fantastic parties that lasted until dawn. At Number 45, they'd moved in a life-size fifties jukebox, on which they played reggae at teeth-rattling volume through the night, punctuated by women's screams and raucous male cries of 'You, man – yaw a disgrace to de human race.'

Every Saturday, the Northcote Road market would move in and transform the bottom of our road into a multi-coloured souk of vegetables, meat, fish, groceries, American comics, old-style weighing scales, sheets of the *Daily Sketch* and the *People* to wrap your carrots in, and brawny men calling out, like so many Stanley Holloways playing Eliza Doolittle's dad, 'Gitcha lovely spuds 'ere, ahnly two bob a pahnd'; the Irish matrons would gaze suspiciously at the yams and sweet potatoes and plantains on display, and my mother would look away disgustedly from the sight of a woman emptying her nose into the gutter.

At the Northcote pub, where the market road met Battersea Rise, the jukebox in the lounge bar had four rows of song selections printed in green to signify they were for the delight of the Irish – Big Tom and the Mainliners, Brendan Grace, the Dubliners, 'Lovely Derry on the Banks of the Foyle', 'Among the Wicklow Hills' – and a form of apartheid prevailed. The Irish exiles hung out in the lounge bar, while the blacks congregated in the public bar and drank only there, in their glazed hats. The two deracinated races just didn't like each other's company. They never hit it off.

Some of them seemed to like my father though. Every Christmas he would get seasonal cards from his black patients, specially personalised with the message, 'Happy Xmas to a Great Doc.' He was pleased but puzzled by these items of mail, because he swore he had never seen, in any gift shop, any newsagents or card emporium, a greeting card on sale with such a message on it. Nor had I. Was it a specifically Afro-Caribbean salutation? Were the cards available only in shops patronised by the black community? Whatever it was, my father was a popular doctor.

Everywhere from Clapham Common to the river was his manor. He had two surgeries and thousands of patients on his panel, and therefore, in the community of Battersea he counted as an elder – on a par with the local magistrate, the JP, the headmaster, the parish priest, the vet, the senior accountant, the businessman, the local council chairman, the president of the golf club and so on.

But we didn't know the local community. My sister and I went to school miles away, in Wimbledon, where Mother would drive us every morning and return us therefrom every evening, so we didn't know any local teachers. My father's accountant lived in Surrey. There wasn't a vet in Battersea, or at least the afflictions that beset our tortoises and Nicky the mynah bird weren't deemed sufficiently important to warrant ever calling one out. My parents didn't get involved in local politics, so they knew nobody on the council. Battersea wasn't the kind of place that encouraged you to linger when you visited, or made you feel like getting to know it when you lived there. It was a boring, dusty, Junction-serving corridor between the smart end of Clapham and the newly proliferating suburban sprawl of Wandsworth. And our road, Battersea Rise, a name that had once caused E. M. Forster such a thrill of excitement, had become subsumed under a later name: the South Circular Road.

It would have been pleasant to grow up in a town, or to feel oneself becoming part of a town; but we weren't a town. We weren't a village. We were barely a district. We were just an artery, a migratory conduit, just as England had mutated into 'Airstrip One' in Orwell's *Nineteen Eighty-Four*. Huge, coughing trucks, immense Italian jugger- nauts, transporters carrying cages of new and reconstituted cars from Dagenham and Cowley to London dealers came wheezing and crash- ing up the Rise each night, their headlights sending long bars of light marching across my bedroom ceiling, making my whole bed shake. For years, on holidays and school trips, I couldn't get to sleep if things were too quiet outside. Silence unnerved me. I was used to the sound of machines going places, grindingly, relentlessly, effortfully. I could only sleep to the rhythm of things in transit.

We didn't know our neighbours. Our house was at the end of a row of shops. There was nobody on one side, and a nondescript terraced house, in three flats, on the other. The inhabitants of Number 10 changed from time to time, but nobody ever dreamed of coming round to say hello when they moved in. For years the ground floor was occupied by a hard-faced thirtysomething tough guy, a typical sixties figure with his Jeff Beck haircut, his tinted shades, his nasty green Ford Capri and his amazing blonde girlfriend. She had once been beautiful, but her looks had hardened into a permanent, heat-sealed sulk. Her hair, though, was cut like Julie Christie's and, at thirteen, I thought she was a goddess. I schemed about rescuing her from the clutches of her nasty beau, as I watched them leaving the house together, he steering her with a claw-like grip on her elbow, as if half-expecting her to run away.

I did a lot of watching from windows. I became a shocking voyeur, a real curtain-peeper, even going so far as to acquire a telescope mounted on a tripod through which I'd observe the comings and goings on Rise and Common. I told myself I was doing interesting field work in applied anthropology, watching the herd of metropolitans congregate and part. I was a little too young to be looking for girls standing innocently in their underthings at upstairs windows. My motivation was obscure, but I suspect I liked the way the telescope lens's foreshortening effect made it look as if everyone was bunched up together, walking together in a solid phalanx, meeting each other in a soft crash of converging humanity. I was anxious to make a form of community from this random slice of life that had fortuitously and coincidentally come to live in the same region. It was a fruitless enterprise.

Because we went to school in Wimbledon, I saw Battersea only at weekends. I didn't have friends in the street. Walking around the streets, en route to the shops, I would occasionally encounter two of the local bad boys – one Bunteresquely fat, the other skinny, rat-faced and argumentative – who went about together in glum camaraderie. They would listlessly suggest we have a fight. One of us would punch the other on the shoulder or try a tentative tap on the jaw, the other would retaliate by affecting to be furious, and we would switch to calling each other names. We knew, on both sides, that we preferred the preamble of tough-guy threats ('You startin' somethin'? Cos if you are, I'm gonna finish it . . .'), to actually being hit in the face.

Realising that this wasn't much in the way of local socialising, I enlisted, aged twelve, as an altar boy at the local Catholic church, St Vincent de Paul's in Altenburg Gardens. Was this where I could Meet Friends and Influence People? Not exactly. Most of the other altar servers seemed to me brutally crude and thick; they made jokes about farting that outraged my polite, sensitive little soul. One of us, Brian, surreptitiously took (technically sinful) swigs of Communion wine from the bottle when the priest had gone home. He liked discussing the way people snogged in television plays and movies – the way they did it, where the noses went, the tongues, the teeth, the breathing requirements, how slimy it must feel, how disgusting to have someone else's spit in your . . . It was evident that puberty was hitting him with sharply conflicting impulses. Then there was Rob, who was slow and dependable and rarely said anything apart from 'Pack it in!' to the young servers noisily disrobing in the cassocks-and-cottas cupboard.

Gregory was, by some way, the most intelligent and sophisticated of all the altar boys, a flaxen haired, sharp-nosed teenager who modelled himself on Ray Davis of The Kinks – whom I watched singing 'Sunny Afternoon' and 'Waterloo Sunset' on *Top of the Pops* and took to be the epitome of English lordliness. Unfortunately Gregory fell in love with an older woman, a Greek pianist who lived off Lavender Hill, whom he would visit at her marital home every week, drawn not so much by her Aegean loveliness as by the blind homing instinct of his fourteen-year-old cock. She liked playing exhibitionistic games. Once, her alarmingly hairy husband was at home when Gregory arrived; she pretended Gregory had come to borrow some sheet music. The husband made some manly small-talk about football, and the wife went to telephone a friend. In the hallway, as Gregory walked past her on the way to the bathroom, she unzipped the fly of his jeans and began to massage his penis. He stood rooted to the spot with embarrassment, while her husband shouted questions from the kitchen: 'Grigori ees stayin' for tea?' 'Wan lump o' two, Grigori?' The woman just smiled at her plaything and went on moving her hand up and down, talking in Greek all the while to her unseen confidant. Or that's how he told it.

Their affair went on for a year and left a psychic scar. After it, Gregory could never again stay at home in the evenings, but took to wandering the roads of SW11, calling on people to tell them what new indignity had befallen him. I thought he was uncomfortably weird, and when he called, I pretended to be buried in homework.

And that was London – my London – in the sixties. Whatever the music industry said about it, however much the Beatles-loving American magazines like *Time* and *Newsweek* stuck its swinging credentials on the cover, whatever inanities Simon Dee, the television chat-show host, spouted about 'dolly birds' and E-type Jags, not all London was swinging. Battersea certainly wasn't, despite *Up The Junction*. Now and again, I'd take the Number 19 bus to the King's Road, Chelsea, and marvel at the shops, be dazzled by the Bacofoil sheen of the Chelsea Drugstore, look in puzzled rapture at the frontage of Granny Takes a Trip and Kleptomania and the rest of the shops with wacky names, and feel a tremor of good times in the offing. I knew that Chelsea was where it was all happening. On the houseboats in Chelsea Reach, in the flats on Beaufort Street and Prince of Wales Drive, in the galleries of Robert Fraser and the ateliers of World's End. The sixties were taking place there and then, right under my nose. You could practically hear the daily procession of groovy events hardening into mythology: orgiastic parties and people in trumpet sleeves and Afghan waistcoats taking posh drugs, of Paul and Jane and Mick and Marianne and Terence and Julie going from recording and film studio to some fancy mansion in the Oxfordshire countryside for languid cocktails and brittle chat beside a pool and an Afghan hound.

I read all about it in the London *Evening Standard*, where Maureen Cleave and Ray Connolly interviewed the stars. I sometimes felt they were almost neighbours. Of all the people in my school, I was nearest to the crucible of the action. I may have lived in the heart of Battersea yobdom but it was barely a mile away from the Beautiful People in Chelsea. There was only a bridge between us. Surely I could cross it? In the meantime, Battersea grew more alien, hard, unwelcoming and unhomely than ever.

But then, I had Ireland and the Irish. They were everywhere. Irish things, Irish people, Irish faces, Irish songs, Irish voices, Irish names, Irish drink, Irish newspapers, Irish gossip, Irish tales, Irish woe, Irish exile – it permeated the life I lived in Battersea, it hung around like a great green fug. In a part of London where I didn't know the neighbours' names and local people remained strangers, the Irish ghetto-dwellers hung out together as they might have hung out in a three-street district of Brooklyn. Irishness got in your hair and under your fingernails.

Even the smell. Every Saturday morning, my mother would make Irish stew for lunch. She made it the traditional way, with mutton neck chops rather than lamb, with carrots and onions and potatoes layered on top of each other and gently simmered in boiling water for two hours. All you had to do in the meantime was occasionally skim off the fat, add more black pepper, and savour the heady pong.

Upstairs, in the study, I would be doing my homework when the smell first hit: frying onions, then hot stock and lastly the slightly gross, earthy tang of mutton coming to the boil. As I wrestled with Artesian Wells, Algebra, the Rise of Stalin and the Descending Fifth, the aroma stole up the stairs and wrapped itself around me like a cloak. There was a distinctly orange tang about it, synaesthetically speaking, a slight hint of decay and offal outraging the nostrils, but you didn't mind that. You could almost hear the elderly meat falling off the bones in the saucepan. You could practically see the faint little curlicues of iridescence in the seething water that announced a potato had begun to disintegrate in its whirlpoolly depths. You could not sit still. Details of *pi* and *pizzicato* and Purges became indistinct in the face of this smelly onslaught. It was hard to care what had become of the Australian drainage system when the stew was in such roaring form. By 12.45, when my mother called us downstairs, I was gagging for it.

One Saturday, when we had not been in Battersea for long, I left the table after lunch and ventured out for a walk in the street. I was doing whatever meagre window-shopping was available on Battersea Rise – Edwardes Furnishing, Ingo Finke Picture Framers, Midwinters the Greengrocers, Kalsi's the Dispensing Chemist – and absently sniffed the air. The air smelt funny. Whatever was causing it, it was both horribly familiar and rather off-putting – a combination of overdone carrots, well-hung meat and essence of dishwater. I smelt it all along the Rise, past the bus-stop and the traffic lights, right up to St John's Road. It was everywhere. What on earth could it be? It was the smell of my mother's stew, but a nasty debased version – underseasoned, neglected, utterly stewed. How could it be permeating the whole neighbourhood like this? Months went by before I discovered it was in fact the smell from the Ram Brewery in Wandsworth, four miles away, whose filtration facilities occasionally packed up at weekends, sending the smell of hops, barley, sugar and roasted yeast across the southern metropolis. But I didn't know that. I hadn't previously met the real smell of the borough, head-on. And so I stood there, glowing with delight and the warmth of camaraderie, convinced that everyone in my new home of Battersea, everyone that lunchtime, in every kitchen in every house, was making Irish stew. My heart swelled with a sense of involvement. So this was how it felt when a people shared a culture – they all have the same thing for lunch. Battersea had turned into a vast, Hibernian soup-kitchen, dishing out gallons of boiled mutton and carrots to a grateful giant family.

It wouldn't have seemed very strange to me if it had been true, since so much of Battersea grown-up life was, or seemed to be, Irish. All my parents' friends were from Galway and Sligo and Mayo. All the professional types they dealt with, all the artisans they hired, all the people who entered the house for any reason, were Irish. Our cleaning lady was Mrs Geogehan from Cork. The man who tiled the roof was Pat Hines from Dublin. My mother's assiduous gardener was Joe Fergus from Galway. My father's Surrey-dwelling accountant, who came on regular visits with his plump, pretty, perfumed wife, was Tony Freeman from Donegal. My father's dentist was Eddie Cashen from Waterford. In my pram I'd been wheeled around Clapham Common by a sweet granny-spectacled old friend of my mother's called Molly O'Connor. When I was older I traipsed up the murky, mouse-scented stairs of Grove Mansions on the north side of the Common, to take piano lessons from her equally spinsterish but less sweet Eily O'Connor, both of them naturalised London-Irish *vielliardes* with fond memories of the war, when half a dozen American GIs were briefly billeted on them.

If my mother wanted a watch mended, she would ignore the half-dozen jewellers' shops on nearby Lavender Hill, and make a detour to Mrs Laucher's scruffy little shop on the wrong side of Chelsea Bridge. Mrs Laucher was a lean, dark Irishwoman, long exiled from Sligo, with one of those strangled, rhotic vocal deliveries you associate with *Mitteleuropean* ladies on the Orient Express. Hearing her tell my mother that a watch was 'verrry dearrrr' was like listening to a cat purr.

It was quite a gang this freemasonry of London Irish who were casually keeping each other busy, offering each other employment, implicitly refusing to trust the perfidious Brits to do any job with honesty. The tribe may have been far from home, but they brought their numbers together by way of network and introduction, until everybody was sharing the same Cavan osteopath, the same Wicklow plumber, the same Connemara bookie. My mother always had 'a little man around the corner' who could be got to do something for her – as if the corner in question was a promontory of the Irish Sea. Workmen and family friends tended to shade into each other. The charladies and gardeners might not get invited to supper, but they were expected, after the day's work, to sit and have tea and cake and spill the beans about what had become of their families.

The kitchen at Battersea Rise was where I first heard grown-up secrets: people talking in sudden *pas devant les enfants* whispers, insultingly implying that my hearing, rather than my maturity, might not be up to scratch. It was there that I first heard the expression 'she slipped her elbow', meaning some unfortunate girl had had a baby out of wedlock. It was there I marvelled at the casual racism which marked Irish conversation. 'Arrah why would she even think of marryin' him?' one of my mother's friends would say. 'He's just an oul' Jewboy.' I wasn't generally invited, or expected, to join in the conversations in the kitchen, partly because I was a kid and didn't know anything, and certainly wasn't worth telling about the fate of Breege or Concepta in the wicked city of Leeds or Stroud or wherever they'd fetched up; but also because I had, by the age of eleven, turned into a little Englishman. I'd sit doing my homework, still in my school uniform, and would answer questions politely, but anything I said out loud amidst these rough, murmurous voices sounded impossibly stiff, like someone preparing to deliver a lecture. If I asked a question of Joe or Pat or Bridie or Margaret-from-the-church ('So, er, Joe, what do you think might win the Grand National on Saturday?'), a silence would fall, as though I had committed a frightful social gaffe. I felt as formal as Little Lord Fauntleroy and no more appealing.

At home there seemed to be a strict demarcation of rooms. The kitchen was Mother's domain, a warm fug of complicity. She would leave the chattering company around the kitchen table and disappear into the tiny closet-like roomlet where the ancient cooker and the sink resided. She'd stand there, adjusting the heat, rinsing dishes, stirring soup, straining vegetables through a green colander, prising pan-lids without handles from their seething iron cauldrons by jabbing a two-pronged black fork into one of the steaming eye-holes, turning monstrous beef sausages with forensic precision – half an inch nor'-nor'-east or west – until they became a uniform glistening ochre, prodding them, provokingly, over and over, until at last they burst from their smooth, sun-tanned skins, spilling their guts into mad efflorescent shapes, as if unable to stand her motherly nagging any longer. She could never leave things alone, to just cook or blend into a harmonious dish by themselves. She overcooked every green vegetable that came her way. And she'd come out of that tiny hothouse, minutes later, her arms and face reddened by these scullionly endeavours, anxious for a précis of the conversation she'd missed. 'What was that, Margaret, about poor Maura O'Shaughnessy? Did she marry the airman with the wooden leg?'

My father, meanwhile, presided over the dining room. He sat at the end of a long rosewood table around which he would gather a dozen London-Irish professional mates: Tim, the locum who turned out to be an illicit raider of the drugs cupboard, Mary Lynch a handsome Donegal doctor and Joseph her schoolteacher husband, Father Luke O'Reilly (a noisy cleric once interned in wartime China), Nuala and Eddie, respectively a sweet-faced, chuckling doctor in Balham and her enragingly polymathic English librarian husband; Giles and Hetty, two more London medics, Eddie the dentist from Wicklow and Jack and Cora, my retired godparents. Their dinners would go on for hours, sometimes half the night. After puddings and brandies would come Irish coffees, the cream poured out with ostentatious delicacy over the back of a dessert spoon above the reeking mix of Nescafé, Jameson's and sugar; then boxes of half-moon candied oranges and lemons; then everyone would light up. Given the high incidence of medical people around the table, this may seem odd, but everyone, bar my mother, smoked away like laboratory beagles at the end of these dinners, turning the dining room into a fuggy Irish speakeasy, and then the singing would start. Conversation which had veered in its *ad hominem* way from world affairs (Kennedy, before and after his assassination, Castro, Kruschev) to Irish and English politics (Harold Wilson, Enoch Powell, De Valera), came down to sport (Cassius Clay, Christy O'Connor) and music and shows, and by natural extension, someone, usually my father, would call for a song: 'I'm as Corny as Kansas in August' from *South Pacific* or 'On the Street Where You Live' from *My Fair Lady*, and the company would be away. Nobody seemed to mind that all chance of a proper conversational exchange was scuppered for the night as one song begat another. It was the Irish way.

Turn and turn about, they would sing for each other. My mother would quaver a faux-religious romantic thing called 'My Prayer', which began, unreligiously, 'My prayer is to linger with you/ At the end of the day/ In a dream that's divine.' Joseph Lynch would sing 'The Whistling Gypsy' with its artless chorus of 'Audi-doo, audi-doo-dah-day'. Everyone did their stuff, buoyed up by final (always the very-last-ever) slugs of Jameson's and Bushmills and, for the incorrigibly sophisticated, Courvoisier. It went on and on. You could have found them all still at it at 6 a.m. Nobody seemed to worry about working in the morning. Once or twice, my father recalled actually rising from the dinner table at 7.30 a.m., when there were only three guests still alive and game for more, in order to get my sister and me up for school. 'I swear if the police had ever stopped me on the way to Wimbledon and set a match to my breath,' he once told me. 'We'd all have been jet-propelled.'

Every Sunday, we'd drive off to visit my parents' single Irish friends. It was a duty visit, a kind of ritual expression of support for the lonesome and the exiled, though the parents did it enthusiastically enough. The Irish Singles lived all over London. Most were spinster nurses that Mother had worked with just after the war. There was Phil, short for Philomena, and Biddy, both of whom worked at Queen Mary's, Roehampton, and Maureen and Aunt Mary. Aunt Mary was a distant cousin of my father's, a shambolic, forbidding old party whose grey hair was as curled as the Gorgon Medusa's, and who was everlastingly kitted out, winter and summer, in a chunky-knit cardigan and a fat amber necklace. Her house in Putney always smelt of mould and wee. Madelyn and I dreaded being summoned to say the Rosary in Aunt Mary's gloomy parlour, because we would have to pray kneeling into a chair she'd recently sat in. She had a glass-fronted bookcase filled with old, probably original, Penguin paperbacks, the classic Mystery and Crime whodunits in their severe green-and-cream striped livery. I wasn't reading much in those days, and I took them to be impossibly recondite works of high earnestness, with not only no pictures or conversation, but not even a cover to speak of. Mary was a retired nurse with an irritable streak. You could see traces of the former nursing sister in her flashes of rage with the children. Once, when my sister and I had been mucking about with driftwood by the Thames at the end of her road, and got our feet soaked, I remember hearing her recommend to my parents that we get a ferocious thrashing. 'Oh yes,' she said, lips pursed, 'They have to be told.' She carried about her an air of dark disappointment with the world – disappointment that it had, somewhere along the line, decided she warranted no better than retirement in a dingy house near the Thames, sitting there getting older by the day, waiting for news from home.

Her closest friend was called Bel, a handsome younger woman, also a nurse and also a spinster, who incurred Mary's wrath by stepping out in her fifties with a man. There never seemed much prospect of marriage on the horizon, but as Bel spent more time with her unexpected boyfriend, she saw less of her Putney colleague. Mary was furious at such a betrayal, the way a child might resent having to share its best friend with another. She told my mother that Bel was making a complete fool of herself, and that her mind was befogged by her discovery of torrential sex, night and day. My mother blinked at the idea of the wholesome and nunlike Bel, with her support stockings and rosary beads, as a newly-fledged wanton, and upbraided Mary for thinking badly of her old friend. Mary flew into a rage and accused Mother of taking Bel's side. They parted badly, and none of the combatants ever spoke to the others again.

This was a characteristic of my parents' Irish friends – how vividly close they seemed, yet how equally likely to blow apart at any moment, abruptly terminating a long-standing relationship because of a word out of place. It happened again and again. It happened with yet another nursing pal called Esther, a woman of unbelievable silliness. She called everybody 'kid' and spoke in a studiedly modish slang, which might have been the last word in fashion in thirties Cork but had lost something on the journey to London. She would describe raucous parties she'd attended, and plays she'd been to with allegedly dashing young men, and new movies of staggering explicitness ('very x-y, kid, but you know what I'm like . . .') and her voice had a kind of choking sob in it, that gave to her most banal pronouncements a note of tragedy, like the Walrus in *Alice in Wonderland*. She was condescending to my mother, whom she treated as a hopelessly becalmed stay-at-home housewife, a dozen grades below her own ritzy, party-animal status.

I used to look at her, clad in pleated skirts, with a fox fur around her neck, and wonder how anyone could stand listening to her for fifteen seconds, let alone escort her to posh concerts at the Albert Hall and dinner at the Casa Pepe. Despite her full social diary, she always seemed rather solitary when she called on us. Once or twice she even arrived for Christmas dinner at our place, full of stories about exotic invitations she had selflessly turned down just to bestow on us the inestimable gift of her company. My mother listened to all of Esther's tall tales with fascination and clucks of disapproval; it was a window on a world which she had left behind, the world of Christine and the gentlemen who might buy you drinks in Soho if there were a hotel nearby. Her experience among the gentry meant she didn't need Esther to tell her about the *comme il faut* among smart modern English people. Then one day, the two old friends had a blazing row in the kitchen, to which I listened in surprise.

'Don't you dare speak to me like that,' snapped Esther. 'Or I shall feel I'm not able to visit you any more.' The sob in her voice made such an eventuality seem shocking, like being denied oxygen.

'Don't bother your head,' retorted my mother. 'Sure, the only times you ever come near us is when you want something.'

You could hear her former friend wince. I was surprised by this exchange for one reason. It sounded for a second as if my mother were defining a difference between the utilitarian and the emotional sides of friendship, when her attitude most of the time tended towards the former. Mother seemed puzzled all her life about the idea of friendship. She appreciated constancy, gossip, support, exchanges of information, errands, favours and keeping in touch, but not the glue of empathy which links friends together in the first place. Later, when I was a teenager, she would look at the squad of acned, pigeon-toed, long-haired visionaries with whom I insisted on hanging out, and say: 'Who are these great people? Who are these people you call your friends? What would they ever do for you?' I'd explain that it's not like that, Ma, it's not about being useful. It's a hanging-out-together-and-making-each-other-laugh thing. She wasn't impressed. Friends, in her tribal understanding of the concept, were useful, were obliging, were a support system and a prayer circle in need. They weren't supposed to be objects of affection as well.

And so I gazed on the exiled Irish as they all came drifting by our Battersea retreat, wave upon wave of them, some with English spouses, some with Irish, some red-faced, sportive and shouty, some thin and intense and seemingly embittered, some with wholly acclimatised English children, some with confusedly half-Irish offspring christened Breffni or Aoife. The Shelocks and the Lynches and the Ryans and the Sheerans, the Collerans, the O'Sullivans, the O'Briens and the

Graineys. My sister and I, knowing hardly any English people beyond our schoolfriends and what little we saw of their parents, accepted Irish behavioural patterns as normal. It was normal for a dinner party to go on all night. Normal for an outbreak of singing and dancing to punctuate the latter courses of dinner. Normal for all the guests to scramble to their feet when a Jameson's-emboldened patriot would sing the Irish national anthem. Normal for grown-ups to modulate their conversation into a stuttering flood of Gaelic, punctuated by winks and nudges, to conceal the nature of the chat from the children's ears.

I wasn't aware of it being a typically Irish way of conducting oneself, though of course I recognised the Irish components in this hospitable stew. Nor did I consider my own role in all this, or how peculiar I sounded, how correct and pedantic my voice seemed when I attempted to sing or to recite or just to talk among these bellowing roustabouts and cackling matrons. Most of the time, I had no idea what they were on about, just as ten-year-olds everywhere tune in and out of adult conversation. But I think I absorbed, by some silent osmosis, the information that these people were all fuelled on perform-ance. None of them was quiet for very long. Sitting in the kitchen taking tea with my mother, they spilled the beans like jailbirds unexpectedly let out of solitary confinement and given one afternoon to download their life stories. In the dining room, they told stories rather than exchanged views, tales about people and families they knew, updating the general database about who was doing what in Canada or Detroit or Cornwall, and which of their sisters was trying once more to be a nun, but had been up to her old tricks, (the rest of this story would be conducted in a flood of secretive Gaelic). I got the impression that performing was mandatory. Everybody was supposed to do their best, or just do something, to entertain the company. It was simple politeness, a small recognition that the ball had to be kept rolling, or the community would dwindle into a silent mass of bored islanders.

But the inference I drew – that it was simply polite to show off in company – affected me deeply. Only later, out in the grown-up real world, did I wonder how English people got by without saying anything (or anything very colourful) for hours on end. Had they some special dispensation that let them off? Was it that, although they had nothing with which to entertain the company, they harboured some special ancillary skill or accomplishment that made them interesting guests? Occasionally one heard about social casualties among the Irish – of someone who was peculiarly silent in company – and the same explanation would be offered. 'Does he ever open his mouth at all?' one would ask. Someone would invariably reply, 'Ah, Jack has a very dry sense of humour,' and my father would clinch it by saying, in a well-rehearsed sort of way, 'Jack doesn't talk much – but when he does, he says a lot.' Note the distinction between 'talking' and 'saying' – one activity noisy, phatic and content-free, the other quiet, expository and full of meaning. Among the English, the two words are close. Among the Irish they're as distinct as music and lyrics.

As for myself, I felt uncomfortable when addressed by friends of my parents – but not through shyness, so much as having the wrong voice with which to speak. All the Irish voices that nagged and neighed and trumpeted across the table had a conviction about them, a twang of passion, an explosive certainty that just rolled over my own puny attempts at conversation. I writhed with Englishness. I sounded adenoidal, stuffy and slow beside their quicksilver, allusive chat. I knew one had to perform; but if I couldn't do it their way, I wasn't going to do it at all.

But across the Common lived a family who changed all that. They were the Fitzpatricks, who hung out on the West Side, a London-Irish family of six children and one parent. Jo Fitzpatrick was a thin, golden-haired, elegant woman who held court at the kitchen table. She drank red wine and chain-smoked untipped Players and hoarded the newspapers every day after she'd read them, so that there was always a small mountain of newsprint under her feet. When I say she 'held court', I mean it as literally as possible. She was always in the same chair, in the same attitude, wine glass and cigarette in her hands, looking up with a sleek, sophisticated, actressy smile to see who had now arrived to amuse her.

I don't think she herself ever, even once, opened the front door. Visitors were ushered into her presence by one of her children, and she had a way of greeting you as if both you and she were on stage – she the exquisite chatelaine of a stately home, you the awkward and shuffling hick who needed to be put at his ease.

'Dah-leeng,' she would coo, 'how *lovely*. Come and have a drink and tell me everything.'

It was heady stuff being offered 'a drink' at the age of twelve by this piss-taking socialite. And as I sipped my Ribena, I knew she was only pretending that I was an adult. Her manner was so engagingly Gertrude Lawrence, so enterprisingly camp, it was clear to me that she just liked people to play up to her queenly desire to be amused.

So I did. I began to talk nineteen to the dozen under Jo Fitzpatrick's wicked eye. She wouldn't ask about my school or my hobbies or the stuff other grown-ups seemed boringly keen to know about. She would, rather, encourage you to embroider a tale, to put in jokes and spin things out and fantasise and dress the whole thing up in a cloak of self-abasement. She would extract from me stories of embarrassment or discomfiture, of something going wretchedly wrong on holiday or at Mass, of some mortifying encounter between my mother (whose draconian qualities she appreciated as a similar form of theatrical display) and one of my father's patients. Jo would sit there, her glittering eyes narrowed in the smoke from her eternally-smouldering Players, and laugh with her head thrown back. She was the perfect audience for a boy uncertainly poised between English reluctance and Irish excess. Though she was as Irish as buttermilk (she was born Nora Josephine Murphy, her family from Cork), she was a long way from being a colleen or a Catholic matron. Her voice was a cut-glass Kensington vase with a large orchid of theatricality inside it. She was a self-invented English-Irishwoman – posh, bohemian, hedonistic and brittle, with a self-destructive streak that made her all the more attractive.

The rest of the family was pretty spectacular too. The eldest girl was Kathrina (though sometimes they pronounced it Catriona, like the Stevenson heroine), a tall, angular beauty with spectacular cheekbones and a watchful disposition. Her younger sisters, Georgina and Fiona, were, respectively, a green-eyed twenties vamp with alarmingly long crimson fingernails and endless ropes of chestnut hair like Waterhouse's Lady of Shallot; and a volcanically sexy coquette with a sweetly innocent smile and an air of incredulity about the stupidity of men. The boys were Patrick, Anton and Finian, all of them tall and funny and wayward. Patrick, the eldest, was impossibly handsome and rather devious, and he never looked at you while talking to you. Anton was thin, moody and introspective, and had a drugged, internalised quality about him; Finian, the baby of the family, radiated optimism and cheerfulness and plotted to be a published writer by the time he was twelve.

With such a line-up, their house on the west side of the Common offered the best time to be had for a pre-teenager. My parents and my sister and I would go round in the evenings, the grown-ups would talk and the children would play games – but at some point, unlike in any other house, the age groups converged. Jo would switch on her battered gramophone in the hallway and put on some Greek bouzouki music, and she and my father would strike fanciful Hellenic poses and dance in and out of the doorways. Sometimes she would extend a languid hand to me and, with arms round each other's shoulders, we would attempt a Zorba's dance routine that gradually speeded up until we fell over together. The living room would degenerate into a heap of cushions and spilt drinks and fallen dancers. I would watch my parents with interest during these occasions. My mother would be in one of the awful trouser-suits she imagined to be all the rage in the mid-sixties, stopping her alcohol intake after two sherries, watching the accelerated dancing with a just-indulgent smile, looking at my father's ecstatic, sweating face as if overseeing a hyperactive child burn itself out before bedtime. My father would have no time to consider any impulse of restraint. He was lost in a frenzy of delight, 'euphoric and fatuous' as he would say, up for anything, unable to refuse another gin and orange, away with the fairies. If my mother was the still point, he was the turning world.

It seemed obvious to me that Dad was half in love with Jo, and I suspect my mother thought so too. Jo was, after all, separated from her husband, George, whom I knew only as a burly and slightly threatening shadow, a large powerfully-built businessman with a Jaguar. Jo had extricated herself from under his flattening thumb and her raffish lifestyle was partly a kind of therapy, a shutting out of the nastier elements of life, like husbands. But it meant she was, technically, available. Might she and Dad have got it together? Not a chance. They were allies, Mum and Dad and Jo. They'd protected her when she was splitting up with George. She and my mother gossiped about everyone – dubious husbands, bad marriages, sexual waywardness – and she and my father danced and drank and flirted; but it was imposs-ible for them to change the hand fate had dealt them. I don't think it would have entered my father's head to leave my mother for Jo, or anybody else. Like most Irish people of his generation, he had a Catholic sense of foreclosed destiny. He believed you were headed one way, and that's the way you had to go. 'You have made your bed,' he would say, with an interrogative lilt that drove me mad in its dumb acceptance, 'and now you must lie on it.'

When I was older, we went less often to the Fitzpatricks' house. The days of the Greek dancing in the hall were, like the days of the Kerry dances, 'gone, alas, like our youth too soon'. But my youthful infatuation with Jo had matured into a more grown-up affection for the whole household. With my sister away at university, and weekend afternoons stretching before me in a great Gobi Desert of boredom, I used to escape to the Fitzes' after lunch every week, and find them all sitting al fresco in the garden finishing their fruit and cheese course. Jo would wave her cigarette in greeting. 'Come and sit beside me this minute, dahleeng, and tell me everything. How did it work out with the girl from Arding & Hobbs carpet department?'

As the others resumed their conversation, and we whiled away the afternoon, I would steal surreptitious glances at Kathrina/Catriona who, in those days, affected a wide-brimmed straw picture hat with cherries on the side, a gorgeous frame for her Maud Gonne beauty. Kathrina and Georgina and Fiona were like three essences of Biba Girl, sitting amid the debris of lunch crushing a last strawberry against their perfect teeth while their cool, rackety brothers lit fags in the sunshine whilst they talked about boats and holidays and played Rolling Stones LPs.

It was perfect. I so wanted to be part of it. Later, when I read Philip Larkin's 'I Remember, I Remember', it was with a jolt of recognition. In it he itemises all the things his childhood was not, the places he didn't go to, the girls he didn't take out, all the clichés of a happy childhood that he never shared. One of them was:

And here we have that splendid family,
I never ran to when I got depressed,
The boys all biceps and the girls all chest,
Their comic Ford, their farm where I could be
'Really myself'.

Poor Larkin never had them. But I did. And it was both their un-English hedonism and their un-Irish sophistication that drew me towards them and held me there. Their neither-one-thing-nor-the-otherness. Their mixed-upness. Their English-Irishness.

IV

SINGING THE GREENS

FOND MEMORY

It was a school where all the children wore darned worsted,
where they cried – or almost all – when the Reverend Mother
announced at lunchtime that the King had died

peacefully in his sleep. I dressed in wool as well,
ate rationed food, played English games and learned
how wise the Magna Carta was, how hard the Hanoverians

had tried, the measure and complexity of verse,
the hum and score of the whole orchestra.
At three o'clock I caught two buses home

where sometimes in the late afternoon
at a piano pushed into a corner of the playroom
my father would sit down and play the slow

lilts of Tom Moore while I stood there trying
not to weep at the cigarette smoke stinging up
from between his fingers and – as much as I could think –

I thought this is my country, was, will be again,
this upward-straining song made to be
our safe inventory of pain. And I was wrong.

Eavan Boland

71

You had to sing. Singing was mandatory. If you had any kind of voice at all – choirboy falsetto, basso profundo, sharp counterpoint, flat descant – you were expected to sing. Unless you were utterly, blankly, un-get-past-ably tone deaf, you had to have a song with which to regale the company. Not to sing was to be English. Refusing to sing was making yourself too good for the company, too posh for your elders and betters, too stuck-up to fit in with the tribe. My father had a phrase to confront the moment when you refused to sing – if that's the right word for the moment when, standing in your pyjamas and dressing gown, by the dining room door with the thick red plush curtain hanging down to keep out draughts, regarding the flushed and hilarious gathering of Irish friends around the smoke-obscured rosewood dining table, all the faces twisted round in their chairs to look at the curious little phenomenon that was your pathetic young self, ablaze with self-consciousness, a-twitch with mortification, embarrassed beyond death by your uncertainly piping childish treble – the moment you were invited, in a great paternal shout, to perform a Bing Crosby number.

'No,' I would wail, 'I can't sing. I don't want to.'

'Go on and sing,' my father would shout. 'And don't be making a compliment out of it.'

What did he mean? It was a mystifying injunction. The others would laugh, leading me to suspect that their fathers had said it to them in their turn. It meant, I now see, that if they had to ask you once more to sing, or offer you reassurance about the loveliness of your voice, it would count as paying you a compliment, and that would never do. Tribal elders do not demean themselves by congratulating the juniors.

And so one would begin:

In a town on the sea by the Castle Doneen
The fairest of all was the maiden Eileen.
The bloom on her cheeks was as fresh as the dew
And her heart to a young fisher laddie was true . . .

It wasn't the greatest song in the world. The Castle Doneen sounded like a prop, included for the sake of the rhyme. The first line bristles with prepositions ('*In* a town *on* the sea *by* the castle . . .') until you wonder – if you're being *that* precise about the place, why not just tell us its name? There's something mildly rebarbative, too, about the young fisher 'laddie'. His presence makes the line more musical than would the words: 'to a young fisherman was true', but it seems like an eruption of Scots colloquial into an Irish landscape and never sounds right. But then neither did my imitation of the Crosby delivery: making the start of the second line a non-specific mumble ('The-huh fairest of all . . .' or sometimes 'Huh-the fairest of all . . .' in a spooky echo of Elvis Presley) and pronouncing the dew 'the doo' until my father put a stop to it, and made me pronounce it the Irish way: 'fresh as the Jew.'

It's a terribly sad song, glum as a flounder, murky as the Castle Doneen moat. The narrative is simple: the fisher laddie pledges to make an honest woman of the dew-faced maiden, but ill-advisedly sets off 'with the tide' the morning before their nuptials. With a certain inevitability, he dies in a storm, and Eileen, back home, expires from a broken heart. Her friends carry her corpse down to the beach where she used to wait for the defunct angler's return, and bury her *by* a rock, presumably *in* the sand. To this day you can hear the stricken fiancé's voice singing softly on the wind as the song cheerfully concludes: 'Eileen, my Eileen/ O wait for me, wait . . . Eil-ee-heen.'

It is extraordinary to think of myself standing there in my night attire, giving the last note a lilting flourish and doing a final little shake of the head, as if I were overcome, at the age of nine, by *lacrimae rerum*. In the world out there Beatlemania was just starting. I was aware of the Fab Four, but in a slightly disapproving way (taking my cue from my parents' fear of social upheaval). They could not yet eclipse the Irish songs that had been filling my head for years.

Every Saturday and Sunday lunchtime the family gramophone would spill with music; it had a spindle on which you could stack four or five long-playing records, each crashing down on the exhausted vinyl of the previous disc, presumably to keep the party going without the need for any human intervention. My parents loved show tunes and enthusiastically joined in the late-fifties vogue for Caribbean calypsos, mostly by Harry Belafonte. The rest of the time they played (exclusively) Irish music. The dining room reverberated to jigs, reels, ceilidh bands, soupy ballads and 'novelty' joke songs about donkeys, goats and hoolies in the kitchen.

There were many songs of exile, like 'The Old Bog Road' with the gorgeous, yearning bend-for-home at the end of each verse:

73

My feet are here on Broadway, this pleasant harvest morn,
But O the ache that's in them for the spot where I was born.
My weary hands are blistered from working cold and heat,
But O to swing a scythe today through fields of Irish wheat.
Had I the chance to journey back or rent a king's abode,
It's soon I'd see the hawthorn tree down the old bog road.

And terribly kitschy songs of coming back again, written for sentimental Americans:

With me shillalegh under me arm and a twinkle in my eye,
I'll be off to Tipperary in the mornin',
With me shillelagh under me arm and a toora-loora-lye,
I'll be welcome in the home that I was born in.

There were accordion-driven songs of courtship such as 'The Bridal Path' and 'Johnny Gray', full of innocent colleens sporting with likely lads, watched over by benign priests. A woman called Bridie Gallagher used to sing them. She could put a catch or a sudden lilt into her voice, as if she were overcome by laughter (a little like Alma Cogan, of 'How Much Is That Doggy In The Window?' fame, only Ms Gallagher managed to sound incorrigible, quite the naughtiest girl in the school).

I went to the chapel on a Monday,
My prayers all for to say,
But when my Johnny smiled at me,
Me prayers all ran away.
And me Father Dan gave a sermon there
In his good and kindly way –
And I know it was a sin but I never took it in
All because of Johnny Gray.

There were hugely moral songs which tended to follow the same trajectory: a chap from an Irish village leaves the warm embrace of home and parents, and hits the big city, where he soon finds himself heading for 'the tavern' and a one-way ticket to Palookaville. He falls in with gamblers, women, Protestants (you assumed they were Protestants, if not worse), and all manner of thieves and murderers.

Then one night, as he approaches the swing doors of the den of vice once more, his mother appears to him in an apparition, and says:

Don't go — don't go. Don't go back to the tavern and sin,
Don't go — don't go. Don't go back and start drinkin' agin.

A less glutinous moral dressing featured in the most popular Irish song of all, 'The Wild Rover', with its foot-stamping chorus of 'An' it's no nay never/ No, nay, never no more . . .' which at least carries a hint that the crazy galoot singing the song will not be reformed as easily as he seems to suggest: 'I'll go back to my parents, confess what I've done/ And I'll ask them to pardon their prodigal son.' We had a version by The Dubliners and another by the Clancy Brothers, both of whose records crammed the gramophone spindle. My mother disapproved of The Dubliners because they had great bushy beards and were always photographed with pints of Guinness in their hands (though at least one of them was a pioneer) and their singer Ronnie Drew had sad bloodhound eyes and sang in a gravelly, don't-give-a-shit voice, 'like glass' — everyone said — 'being crushed under a door'. He was a bit common and vulgar for Mother's taste, not a nice man at all. The band's subject matter gave grounds for concern too. They favoured bad-taste ballads like 'Weila Waila', about rustic infanticide:

She stuck the knife in the babby's head,
A-weila weila waile
An' the more she stuck, the more it bled,
Down by the River Saile

or 'The Old Woman From Wexford', about infidelity, visual impairment and attempted murder, with its edifying conclusion:

O feeding eggs and marrowbones can make yer old man blind,
But if you want to drown him, you must creep up close behind,
With me rightful lithera-layral and me rightful Laura Lee.

The Clancys were the antithesis of The Dubs. They were clean-shaven, strapping, outdoor types with ruddy complexions and ringing voices, as wholesome as *lederhosen*. You could imagine them drinking a few pints, but only in the course of a protracted hiking holiday.

They wore matching white Aran jumpers, with the sleeves pushed up to the elbow. They played guitars like lumberjacks sawing wood, and their whippet-faced chum Tommy Maken played the tin whistle. They sang incorrigible-colleens songs ('I'll Tell My Ma When I Go Home'), and bridal songs (like the Scottish 'Marie's Wedding') and shouted 'Fine gerrl you are!' after the chorus of 'The Holy Ground'. They were uncool to a phenomenal degree. But now and again they did something good. I remember the shiver that used to go through me when I listened to the opening strains of 'Shoals of Herring':

In the darkness and the deep we're faring,
On the wild and wasteful ocean —
It's out there on the deep that we harvest our bread,
As we hunt the bonny shoals of herring . . .

This opening is sung *a capella* with a passionate, stretching, swooping vocal line that suddenly has your imagination flying over the dark sea, going up, up, up, on (paradoxically) the word 'deep', then lapsing down again in a spiral of vocal curlicues, like a spent firework. Then the guitars kick it into a jaunty ballad, the kind that you could dance to — until the penultimate verse, which slows the action once again. The instruments stop dead and Liam Clancy's voice strays in from the dark, haunted and reflective:

Night and day we're faring
Come winter wave or winter gale —
Setting our course, growing up, growing older,
As we hunt the bonny shoals of herring.

It was this adventuring quality, this cold, flinty, onward drive to maturity that tugged the heart. It's such a grown-up song, such a lonesome passion for something as mundane as fishing. It went into my head and stayed there, in a way that Cilla Black's 'Anyone Who Had A Heart' (which my father bought the same year) didn't.

English pop music was starting to cascade into the house. There was always a radio on somewhere, whether the big wireless in the kitchen, or a transistor in the bedroom or the study, relaying the Top Twenty ('Hi there, pop pickers!') to our fascinated ears. You could remember the words to lots of the songs, as the tunes went round and round your head, but the words didn't really matter in those days. Nobody stopped to wonder what exactly was the narrative sense of 'Good Vibrations' or 'I'm a Believer', they just liked the hook. But in the Irish songs that played in the background of your life – the second chamber of your burgeoning sensibility – the words were important.

Irish songs seemed to be fixated by place. Just as I was beginning to get a sense of the mysterious neighbouring land where everyone talked in my parents' accents, where everybody seemed to be called the same kind of thing (Connolly, Colleary, Colleran, Cahill, O'Neill, O'Brien, O'Rourke, O'Dowd); where ridiculously fanciful place names like Ballydehob and Borris-on-Ossery and Dingle and MacGilli-cuddy's Reeks and the Knockmealdown Mountains co-existed along-side ridiculously blank, go-away names like Gort and Tuam and Moate and Cong and Binn and Clones, like a tribe of recklessly romantic Cavaliers hanging out amidst a platoon of stern, monosyllabic Round-heads; where tiny, elaborately-bearded and chronically fraudulent elves with miniature shovels allegedly looked for gold at the end of rainbows – just as I was working out what and who represented the essence of Ireland – I was given a rapid crash course in the Irish obsession with land, place, ownership and territorial possession through the songs that my parents and their friends used to sing.

Every song seemed to have a place name in the title. Sometimes it seemed that every town in Ireland, every village, every Monaghan hamlet, every Kerry boreen, had a song of its own. I listened to rapturous evocations of 'The Cliffs of Doneen' ('But of all the fine places that I've ever been/ There is none to compare . . .') and 'Lim-erick the Beautiful' ('O Limerick is beautiful, as everybody knows', a questionable judgement in the fifties and sixties), of the 'Sweet Vale of Avoca', of 'The Banks of My Own Lovely Lee', of 'The Rose of Allendale', 'The Rose of Tralee', 'The Rose of Mooncoyne', 'The Maid of Bunclody', 'The Bard of Armagh'* and 'My Lagan Love' and 'The Star of the County Down', 'The Galway Shawl' and 'The

---

* Which has a weirdly moving final verse that begins: 'And when Sergeant Death shall with cold arms embrace me' – an unsettling image of the Grim Reaper as a fond Irish policeman, although of course the image is from Shake-speare, where the dying Hamlet cries 'this fell sergeant, death/ is strict in his arrest'.

Queen of Connemara' (who turned out to be a boat). I heard all about 'The Boys of Killybegs', 'The Boys of Wexford' ('who fought with heart and hand') and 'The Boys of Kilkenny' (who 'are stout roving blades'), of Kelly the Boy from Killane and Sean South from Garryowen and a hundred other temporary heroes whose exploits once merited a song.

And it seemed that when the ballad-makers ran out of places to celebrate, they turned to people's names alone. Thus I learned about the exploits of 'The Bould Thady Quill', and 'Bould O'Donoghue', both apparently famous as serial Lotharios but nothing else, and about the 'darling boy' Teddy O'Neill, and a seafaring renegade called Dainty Davy, and Roddy McCorley, the idealised, Christ-like ('About the hemp-rope on his neck, the golden ringlets clung') Antrim hero who led a rebellion and went off to be hanged on the Toome bridge, beside where Seamus Heaney noted 'headphoned soldiers standing up in turrets' fifty years later, and Kevin Barry, the eighteen-year-old Republican, hanged by the British in 1920. And this list only hints at the multitude of Irish names and places that dinned into my ears. By sheer numbers and repetition, they presented the Irish as a people passionately, one might say inordinately, proud of their respective home towns. Nothing else could excuse the reiterated trope that, despite much travelling in foreign lands, the singer reckons his back-yard is *the* place to be. And the titular villages, towns and cities were not just praised for their beauty – the fairest spot and the finest sight anywhere in the whole world, in the singer's humble opinion – they were celebrated as the place where the noblest, bravest race of people anywhere in Europe were to be found. Such vainglory. Such self-regard. Such bathos!

Ye may strain your muscles
To brag of Brussels
Of London, Paris or Timbuktu,
Constantinople, or Sebastople,
Vienna, Naples or Tongataboo,
Of Copenhagen, Madrid, Kilbeggan
Or the Capital of the Rooshian Czar,
But they're all inferior to the great superior
And gorgeous city of Mullingar.

Mullingar, eh? But if you think that highly of Mullingar, what will be left to say when you encounter Venice? It wasn't, of course, a matter of guide-book plausibility. These were songs of local pride, of patriotism in miniature, of small-town beauties and neighbourhood local rows elevated to epic proportions. Thus when in 'Spancil Hill', a Californian exile dreams of his home town and imagines himself landing there 'on the 23 June':

The day before the fair —
When Ireland's sons and daughters
And friends assembled there,
The young, the old, the brave and the bold
Came their duty to fulfil
At the parish church at Clooney,
A mile from Spancil Hill.

The exile isn't assuming the whole population of the Irish Republic will be at the Spancil Hill fair, he's just modestly presenting the population of his old home town as the flower of Ireland's children.

In his poem 'Epic', Patrick Kavanagh explained the rationale of dealing in the particular, and choosing between writing about the Munich crisis or the fight between the Duffys and the McCabes, about which battling family had the ownership of 'half a rood of rock':

I inclined
To lose my faith in Ballyrush and Gortin
Till Homer's ghost came whispering to my mind.
He said: I made the Iliad from such
A local row. Gods make their own importance.

But some of the 'rows' recorded in the songs were more than local barneys. They were historical battles, mostly if not exclusively against the British, and the songs that memorialised them were living testaments, like campaign ribbons or football club pennants. Unfortunately, the occasion for and the outcome of the battles themselves were often obscured by time. You had to guess at what had happened. There was a fantastic epic song called 'The West's Awake', a potted history of Irish derring-do when faced with the invader, the conqueror and the perfidious Brit. I loved the sound it made, its serious, low, rumbling chronicle of hard-fought heroism, without ever having the faintest idea of what it referred to.

> For often in O'Connor's van,
> To triumph dashed each Connaught clan
> And fleet as deer the Normans ran,
> Through Curlew's Pass and Ardrahan.
> And later days saw deeds as brave,
> And glory guards Clanrickard's grave,
> Sing O! they died their land to save
> At Aughrim's slopes and Shannon's waves.

The point of the song seemed to be the rebuttal of an inter-tribal insult; through some congenital ennui that affected everyone west of Athlone, the tribes of Connaught were sleeping, dulled, uninterested in keeping Ireland safe from danger of invasion. 'Alas and well', runs the opening, 'may Erin weep/ When Connaught lies in slumber deep'. By the end it's clear that, on the contrary, the West is supremely alive to the threat from across the water, (whatever the exact threat might have been at the time) and, excuse *me*, will 'watch 'till Death for Erin's sake'.

When you're singing it yourself, its passion is unmistakable. Its power to move the singer – especially when the singer is, to all intents and purposes, English, cynical and clueless about Irish history – is wholly unexpected. By the final lines, which are, 'Sing Oh, hurrah! Let England quake!' you are right up there charging the redcoats, pike in hand, desperate for glory.

My father's favourite song was 'Boulavogue'. He would sing it in pubs and living rooms, in hotel lounges and at weddings, with his eyes shut and his head tilted back. It was published in 1898 by one P. J. McCall and celebrates a rebellion of the Irish peasantry in May 1798, led by a Wexford priest called John Murphy, the parish priest of Kilcormack. Fired by his eloquence, the locals rose against the 'yeomen' soldiers of the English king who kept them landless, vote-less and all but enslaved. They defeated the redcoats in a series of skirmishes but were finally put to the sword. The lyrics of the song are obscure to modern ears, but oddly resonant. They're full of names: Boolavogue, Shelmalier, Kilcormack, The Harrow, Camolin, Enniscorthy, Slieve Kiltha, Tubberneering, Ballyellis, Vinegar Hill, the Slaney river,

Tallow . . . On a modern map you can locate Enniscorthy, Tallow, the Vinegar Hill battleground and The Harrow, but, frustratingly, not the place where the rising – and the song – began. Of Boolavogue itself, there's no longer a trace. The song is a simple chronicle of a rebellion, full of stirring battle cries ("'Arm! Arm!" he cried, "For I've come to lead you/ For Ireland's freedom we'll fight or die"'), and a bravery that signifies tribal glory and proven manliness ("'Twas at the Harrow the boys of Wexford/ Showed Bookey's regiment how men could fight'). It combines the epic and the domestic, nailing down towns and rivers as if marking territorial flags on a map of glorious, unforgotten names, speaking one minute about the local farmers, and the next about a fiery insurrection across the whole country:

> On Boulavogue, as the sun was setting
> On the bright May meadows of Shelmalier,
> A rebel hand set the heather blazing
> And brought the neighbours from far and near.

Bringing 'the neighbours' over, rousing the community, is a serious Irish trope, however much it may sound, to British ears, like a lot of friends popping in to borrow sugar. The neighbours are the nearest representatives of the whole nation, the first ones whom, vitally, you have to impress in order to get something done (such as a revolution). After years of living under the British yoke, it took an act of considerable leverage to stir the cowed locals into action, and Father Murphy (who makes no appearance in any Irish history books I've read) managed it with his fiery eloquence. 'Set the heather blazing'*, is a slight and moving image of a backyard uprising, a modest elemental phenomenon like a grassy field catching fire. The song's pre-climactic verse sounds a warning:

> Look out for hirelings, King George of England,
> Search every prison that breeds a slave
> For Father Murphy from the county Wexford
> Sweeps o'er the land like a mighty wave

* Which became the title of Colm Toibin's second novel, *The Heather Blazing* (1992).

And you notice that, although the rising started and finished in County Wexford, it has now been imaginatively expanded to sweep not only across rebellious Ireland, but across England as well, putting fire in the belly of Irish prisoners and itinerant Irish workmen, even trying to scare the mad monarch George III into looking under his brocaded bed in search of bolted Irishmen lurking there, with flintlocks and arquebuses at the ready.

This, and 'The West's Awake' are the quintessence of the Irish song tradition which teaches you courage, moral bravery, patriotism, constancy, love of home, respect for traditional ways, abstemiousness and chastity – but which also suggests that to utterly flout or reject any of these sterling values is not an unheard of state of affairs and may be just about forgivable (see 'The Wild Rover'). The songs deal in a whole moral universe, dressed up in swaying ballads and hot little dance rhythms. They make you sing – quite against every normal prompting in your English cultural make-up – about your country's history and imbibe its lessons subliminally but passionately. They make you sing yourself into becoming Irish.

V

KATY WILTHO AND TOMMY G'MOTH

'You,' my father used to say, 'were either nurtured in depravity or are haunted with ignorance. You were bred, born and reared in a pigsty.' It was his common response to a minor transgression, like being cheeky to one of the priests or failing to brush one's shoes on a Sunday morning before Mass. He didn't mean it seriously. Nor – given the self-reflective nature of the insult – did he mean to blame himself and my mother for producing such a savage as me. It was a quotation from the historical back of beyond. It was one of the insults routinely hurled at his generation of boys by the priests of St Jarleth's in Tuam, Co. Galway, where he went to school. I was hearing the authentic voice of the western Irish clergy, circa 1924.

In his sixties, my father still had a total recall of the formal language of his schoolmasters. The words had fallen on his Irish ear like a foreign language, a strange, noble music quite unlike the chat he would have heard at the family hearth. He once tried on my sister and me a spelling test he'd been given at the age of ten, in the form of a single stodgy English sentence: 'An embarrassed pedlar met a harassed cobbler engaged in the gauging of the parochial cemetery with unparalleled ecstasy.' It had stuck in his mind, not just as a handy mnemonic of the hardest-to-spell words in the English language, but also, I'm sure, as an exotic picture of the race beyond the sea, where shoemakers and ribbon salesmen, both in a highly emotional state, were given the apparently delightful task of landscaping the local graveyard. What kind of country, I imagine him wondering, had encounters like that, couched in language like that?

Most of the time, though, his school-derived sayings were insults. 'Look at you,' he'd say as I appeared on the stairs, aged fourteen, with hair creeping anarchically over my collar, 'you'd disgrace a field of tinkers.' Invited to comment on the spectacle of The Crazy World of Arthur Brown, performing their hit song 'Fire' complete with flaming helmet and draggled eye make-up on *Top of the Pops* in 1968, he only shook his head and went back to reading the *Telegraph*. 'It'd turn an ass from his oats,' was his laconic reply.

I didn't know anything about asses or oats – or about the disgrace of resembling tinkers, beyond the fact that tinkers were like gypsies and thus outside polite society. But I soon realised that ignorance was the thing that was to be most avoided. 'Ignorance' held a special place in my parents' lexicon of disapproval. On their lips it didn't mean stupidity, or lack of knowledge. It meant bad manners, rudeness, lack of consideration. It was a class thing, a terrible put-down about someone's social standing, their education, their place in the social nexus of the Irish village. My mother would apply it to yobs in the market who shouted raucously to each other as she wended her courtly way – the doctor's wife on a royal progress – down the street. She applied it to men who pushed through the door of a shop without holding it open for her, or to women who swore in front of their children.

These, though, were mostly English people, to whom the word was directed more in pity than contempt. She reserved the greatest vehemence for her own countrymen. One day, in the kitchen, she served tea to one of my father's Irish patients who had arrived with a rota of church cleaning or flower arranging for my mother's scrutiny, and had brought along her husband as a kind of wretched bonus. The husband was a silent, bewildered-looking man, a retired council gardener, and he held my mother's china cup and saucer like an unwelcome prize in his enormous hand. As the ladies talked he looked about him, tried his tea, recoiled with pain (my mother's tea somehow always came out of the pot scalding, as drinkable as molten lead) and, to my delight, poured half of it into his saucer and sucked it noisily off the rim. *Schhlllooop*. My mother was in mid-sentence ('and there's no point in asking Mrs Gallagher to do the floors, and her with the desperate varicose veins . . .') but I could see her flinch as if she'd been coshed on the back of the head. Soon afterwards, the lady patient and her horticultural spouse were escorted firmly out the back door. Mother came back into the kitchen. 'Jeesus, Mary and Joseph,' she said with feeling. 'Can you believe the ignorance of some people?'

All the man had done was behave as he might have done in his own kitchen. To my mother it was a sin as heinous as dropping his trousers. It was ignorance, pure and simple. Nobody had told him right from wrong, no one had explained the rules for behaving in public, particularly in front of the doctor's wife. My mother, who was bred, born and reared in a simple farmhouse in Tubbercurry, and had received no formal training in the social graces, came on like Gloria Vanderbilt in matters of correct form. Hers was a fierce, Victorian-English kind of mortification, the kind that was satirised in H. M. Bateman cartoons, in turn-of-the-century *Punch* and in the novels of H. G. Wells. But the word 'ignorance' – 'ig' stressed with a ferocity that threatened to choke her – was a specifically Irish usage, derived from schooldays when it was a terrible accusation to have hurled at you. The nearest English equivalent would be to say: 'Don't be so common' or 'He's so vulgar,' which nobody says any more because it sounds too genteel.

The word 'reared' was itself a landmine always waiting to go off. It exploded regularly through my childhood. I'd hear Mum telling Dad some scandalous tale of a family whose daughter had given birth to a child out of wedlock, and the girl's parents had 'reared it as their own'. American parents 'raise' their children. English parents 'bring up' their children. The Irish usage carries businesslike connotations of fattening cattle or plumping game birds for the market. It treats the concept of bringing up children, not with any modern nonsense about self-expression, but as if it were a kind of organic manufacture – a process of germination, construction, injection moulding, watering, pruning, caring-for, planing down, toning up, buffing and cleaning and servicing, along with a lot of stern disciplining and a sheepdog-like harrying of the finished product until it has learned to be right, decent and proper and a credit to its maker. In its Irish finery it means making your children into something. It was recognition that, for an Irish mother, it's all you're going to be known for; your children are the advertisement of your virtue or its opposite. To please my mother, one of her friends would look at me (or more likely Madelyn), and

85

say: 'God, Anne, I'd love to have rared a child like that,' and my mother would beam because it meant she had done her job well.

But the word had its negative aspects. The voice of class contempt was never more waspish than when my mother, at Mass in Athenry, spotted a fortyish woman going up to receive Holy Communion in an enveloping musquash fur coat. Her eye fixed on the coat like a heat-seeking missile and on the woman's thin red tongue as it darted out like a hungry gecko's to receive the blessed host, and on the demurely downcast eyes of the woman as she regained her seat and sat, praying away in an ecstasy of devotion, the living image of the comfortably-off, classy Irish bourgeoisie.

Outside, her friend Rose asked her: 'Anne, wasn't that Kathleen O'Brien, Aggie O'Brien from Charlestown's daughter, sitting two rows up from you?'

''Twas,' said my mother shortly.

'The Aggie who was at school with you in Sligo?'

'Indeed it was,' said Mother, 'the very same.'

'And did you,' Rose persisted, 'see the lovely coat Kathleen had on her?'

'Oh now,' said Mother, 'I tell you, 'twas far from *that* she was rared.'

When my mother said, 'Oh, now . . .' a lifetime of regret, an anthology of unsayable things, hung in the air. Those two words were enough to imply, 'Don't start me off about the iniquities of that man, because if I were even to begin to hint at the suffering he has caused his unfortunate wife and children, his friends and family and all around him by his drinking, his wild ways, his night-time debauches spent indulging the most depraved and perverted appetites since the time of Petronius with the kind of people that would need a stepladder even to reach the gutter let alone climb above it; if I were to mention just a fraction of the things I know for certain to be the case about the personal, social and municipal criminal activities with which he has besmirched the name and reputation of Irish manliness, you would surely soon retire to your bed, appalled and thunderstruck by the vileness ringing in your ears, and never rise again, at least not until I had drawn breath enough to venture on a second instalment.' She put a lot into it.

She had a real gift for abuse. The only Irish words I remember her uttering were insults. That man was an *omathaun*, meaning idiot or simpleton (as in the Irish *omadan**). That woman was an *oanshaugh* or fool. Some of her words were spectacularly onomatopoeic, as when she called an unpleasant neighbour 'a right schleemathore' (it meant someone who is both thick and obnoxious together). Just as puzzling to English ears were her gnomic dismissals.

'That fella,' she'd say after someone had just departed, 'would leave you with one arm as long as the other.'

'But Mama,' you'd say pertly, 'surely that is a perfectly desirable condition.'

'I mean, John,' she'd reply, 'there's no danger of being left weighed down with gifts after he's come a-calling.'

Of a noisily self-delighting visitor she would say, 'George has great welcome for himself,' a crushing put-down to come from a culture where 'welcome' – the famous Irish *failte* that greets you a hundred times at Dublin airport – is a defining condition of existence. Without welcome, and the need for and assumption of welcome on every threshold, the people are divided, incohesive, solitary, disparate, scattered and incomplete. The social glue of Irish community is missing.

By the same token, nothing in the annals of human sympathy, no sound, from the piping of thrushes in May to the late Quartets of Beethoven can convey the tenderness with which she'd say 'Look off' when watching a child toddling down the garden path. She'd interrupt serious and important discussions with – 'Ah, look off . . .' – and it held great oceans of appreciation, of feral love for the cubs of the tribe and their wobbly attempts to grow. You could almost hear the pupils in her eyes grow larger as she directed people to see what she saw before her.

Some of her phrases baffled me. Like the way, after confiding a secret, she would say, 'Here comes your father – now, don't pretend you know anything.' Don't pretend? Why I should I pretend to know something? Keeping a secret, keeping, as it were, mum, was different from affecting to know something you didn't.

Years later, when I was studying Synge, I discovered two different usages of the verb on the same page. In *The Shadow of the Glen* (his one-act play written in 1902), a tramp knocks on the door of a lonely

* A slightly puzzling transliteration of the word forms the title to Mike 'Tubular Bells' Oldfield's record *Ommadawn*.

farmhouse on the road from Dublin to Galway, is greeted and given a drink by the woman of the house, and notices there's a corpse laid out on a bed by the wall. The woman complains about her loneliness in the cottage, and the coldness of her husband by day and night, and mentions a young man she hopes to meet outside in the glen. When she has gone, the tramp is startled to see the corpse look out from under his winding sheet. He explains that he's pretending to be dead in order to spy on his unfaithful wife. 'I'm thinking it's not for nothing,' says the tramp, 'you're letting on to be dead.' Four speeches later, Dan, the corpse, hears his errant wife returning and tells the tramp, 'be falling to sleep now and don't let on you know anything', meaning something quite different – don't reveal the secret, don't give away the pretence, don't *un-pretend* me. In Irish, the verb for 'pretend' also means 'reveal', as if they were interchangeable; hence my mother's baffling directive.

As she got older, Mother reverted to odder forms of Hiberno-English expression. Confronted by signs of teenage rebellion – when say, my sister and I decided to go to the movies on Good Friday instead of the Passion – she'd produce an odd expletive: 'Werthatchamay', an incomprehensible portmanteau word, and we'd look at her as though at a foreigner. She was saying, 'Well, *that* you may . . .' an ancient, subjunctive wish–cum–threat, anticipating trouble: 'Oh, that you may just bloody try it and see what you get.'

My father tried to teach my sister and me a bit of Irish, to match the smattering of textbook vocabulary he and Mother had learned at National School in Tuam and Charlestown in the 1920s. Since Madelyn and I were already wrestling with Latin, Greek and French, we didn't take kindly to this hawking, seething, hyperguttural, strangled-cat language. Latin was formal and mechanical, and everything in it matched and fitted. French was rhotic and liquid and everything sounded like it was meant to sound: '*Longtemps je me suis couché de bonne heure*' meant 'for a long time I used to go to bed early' – even '*heure*' and 'early' matched up, even though they weren't synonyms. Irish, on the other hand, always sounded wrong; everything seemed too sharp or too sibilant. Words of love or domesticity, even simple conjunctions like *agus* ('and') and *areesh* ('again') sounded like cries of battle. The rhythmic flow of a sentence never seemed to match the look on the speaker's face. But my father did teach us to say, 'how are you?' And to reply 'just great now, how's yourself?' The phrases went, respectively:

'Kay-hee wiltho?'

'Thahmay go-magh. Kayhee wiltho hain?'

They were just words, but in my head they became people, Katy Wiltho and Tommy G'Moth – a nice old couple, walking the roads around Galway together, taking a sup of milk here and a slice of soda bread there, and greeting people and being greeted in return, the essence of Irish companionability.

Giving up our lessons as a hopeless venture, my father substituted a fondness for Hiberno-English phrases and humorous bombast. 'Call home those roving hooves,' he'd say jovially, if my long teenage legs accidentally kicked him under the breakfast table. When I went to live in Dublin for a year, he warned me solemnly against the *jackeens* of the capital and how they would treat a London *naif* such as myself. 'They'd make a nest in yer ear and fly away,' he said, 'and you'd never notice.' Unreconstructedly sexist in his appreciation of women, he would gaze in awe as some mini-skirted young lovely in Carnaby Street threads trit-trotted down Battersea Rise. 'Will you look at that,' he'd say to his spotty, virginal son, 'She'd give you a bar that'd lift an ass out of a sandpit.' He invented humorous medical conditions. 'That poor man,' he'd say to a visitor about say, Reginald Maudling, during the television news, 'he must suffer from Ano-Cubital Ignorance Syndrome.' What? 'He doesn't know his arse from his elbow.' He revelled in picturesquely rude metaphors. He remembered a pert young woman from his teenage days saying: 'Jeesus, Martin, I'm starving. I swear to God I'd eat a reverend mother's arse through a cane chair.' I remember his delight at hearing from his nephew, John, a GP in Donegal, about an old woman patient, who, on being asked about the state of her stool, replied: 'Arrah there's days, Docther, you could bolt the door with it and days you could sup it off the end of a spoon.'

There was something of the schoolboy about the way he called people 'hoor'. The word is used by the Irish, indiscriminately, about men and women, as if it were almost too offensive to apply only to women. When referring to men, the etiquette runs, you qualify it with the word 'cute', not meaning sweet or mignon, but 'acute', meaning sly and cunning.★ A 'cute hoor' is a definition of a particular

★ As Leopold Bloom is called 'cute as a shithouse rat' in the 'Cyclops' episode of Joyce's *Ulysses*.

kind of Irishman, who has gone abroad to make a packet, and – cute enough – only comes back home to Kerry or Athlone for holidays to parade his wealth rather than actually spend it in his homeland. If you weren't obviously referring to a man, it was a word you fastidiously covered up, as in my father's tried and tested joke at parties: 'there's some hoor singing – and some who're not'.

'Hoor' rather than *whore*, 'shite' rather than *shit*, 'feck' rather than *fuck* – part of the sidelong Irish gloss on everything English was that the most popular Anglo-Saxon swear words were recast by Irish voices, adding a vowel here, shifting one there, and even changing the sense without any semantic logic. Through my father and his friends, I learned about the multiplicity of the word 'feck'. It had a life way beyond the dictionary. You could be caught fecking apples off the trees. I heard about the unorthodox priest who, wearied by the liberal pronouncements from the Vatican of the mid-sixties, started to read in the pulpit from a papal encyclical, disliked the drift of its comments and, 'without any warning he said: "that's quite enough of that stuff" and didn't he feck the little book over his shoulder and start on about somethin' else?' It meant *steal*, it meant *throw*. What 'feck' did not mean, apparently, was 'have sex with'.

Also, I noticed in my teens that very few Irishmen said 'cunt'. Even after undergoing the inevitable Irish vowel-shift into *cont*, it wasn't a popular usage, even among the rough-diamond contingent of my father's mates. It just wasn't done. I remember how my father responded to the word one day in the 1970s (and incidentally saved me from being bashed up). We were going to a hurling match together in Tuam. I was wearing a summer jacket in green and pink candy stripes, a little touch of the King's Road, Chelsea amid the beige slacks of north Galway. I was ordering drinks from the bar before the game, when a man who was already on the dangerous side of eight pints of Guinness lurched up to me.

'Fancy fuckin' jacket,' he sneered.

'What *this* old thing?' I said archly, the way you do when offered fashion critiques by pissed strangers in pubs. My father stiffened, like a dog expecting trouble. The man steadied himself, looked more closely into my face (from which the blood was rapidly draining) and rasped:

'I said, that's a fancy fuckin' jacket, ya *cont* ya.' Whereupon my father strode forwards, determined as a cop, and pushed him hard in the chest with both hands.

'You'd better watch it,' he said, pointing a finger between the man's eyes, 'Usin' language like that round here.' The man, to my amazement, backed off.

Anybody who's been to Tuam would find it hard to believe that any agreement exists among its citizens banning the use of foul language on grounds of taste. But that's what my father was subtly implying. He was issuing a linguistic challenge, a Locals vs. Outsiders challenge: 'We don't talk that way, only gougers, bowsies, thimbleriggers and street-corner boys use language like that; you do; you must be a gouger, bowsie, etc; you're not one of us anymore and we'll run you out of town.' I suspect that nowhere except in Ireland would you have such a language-based confrontation in the street.

But the word I most associate with my father is 'beyond'. When in London, he used to say the word with inexpressible wistfulness, to mean Ireland, almost as if saying the name of his native land was just too much to bear. 'When next I'm *beyond* . . .' he'd say, or 'Gerry was in Liverpool for a time, but now he's back livin' *beyond*.' You could almost imagine he was talking about death and the afterlife, beyond the grave, but all it was *beyond* was the Irish Sea. The sea did not itself represent an insuperable burden to an Irishman who had access to a timetable and the phone number of a ferry company, but in my father's use of the word hung many complicated layers of regret and denial and compromise. How he could never get back to the Ireland he had left behind, which was changing perceptibly in his absence. How impossible it was for him to now forge a life in his own country, which he'd had to leave in order to find meaningful work. How he liked England well enough but knew it could never mean as much to him as Ireland, not if he stayed for six hundred years. And how tantalising it was that neither his London nor his Irish home – two radically different cultures separated by a small stretch of sea – would ever be enough for him. He was always going to be pulled between the two, unable to land.

The curious thing was, he also referred to England as 'beyond' when he was in Ireland, but with a harsher intonation. The English 'beyond' was accompanied by a hand gesture, a vague flapping at the horizon 'over there', where work got done, money got earned and children got reared, where serious professional concerns were performed. It was the grind of routine and mundanity, a million miles (and one sea) away from the Land of Youth and Laughter and Forgetting.

That was my parents' Hiberno-English lexicon, from which I heard selections when I was young and baffled, and later when I was older and understood more. But there were other Irishisms that I took on board. If I didn't use them myself, they stayed in my head as a signifier, a code or tribal rallying cry that one was in the company of an Irishman. Today, if I meet a doctor who waves me towards a chair with the word 'grand', if I meet a barman who sets a pint on the bar with the word 'now', if an impeccably English-accented woman refers to there having been a 'great crowd' at the party the night before, or to some acquaintance as 'your man', or to somebody being 'on the tear' – why (as Coleridge said of certain lines of Wordsworth's verse), if I met these words galloping around the deserts of Arabia, I should say: 'so you're Irish. Which part?'

What the Irish do to the question 'why' is (as Mother used to say) nobody's business. Ask any Irish person, large or small, why they have pursued some course of action and they'll say: 'why wouldn't I?' and that's the end of the matter. After a while you start doing it yourself, but it sounds less impressive when done with an English accent: an Irish voice makes it sound pert and cheeky ('Why wouldn't I marry P. J. O'Leary/ holiday in the Bahamas/ drink ten gin and tonics in the evening?'). An English voice makes it sound rather dim and clueless, like Bertie Wooster ('Oh, you know, why ever not?').

More alarming is the construction I first heard on the lips of a telephone operator. I was standing, aged eighteen, in a phonebox in Killaloe, Co. Clare one winter's evening. Penniless and desperate, I tried to ring my parents in Galway.

'Hello operator,' I said. 'I'd like to make a reverse charge phone call to Athenry please. The number is 091 . . .'

'Well you can't,' she said with amazing bluntness.

'Sorry,' I said. 'I can't what?'

'Reverse the charges.'

'But they'll be happy to pay for the call at the other end. They're waiting to hear from me. Ring this number and ask if they'll accept . . .'

'I'm sorry,' she said firmly. 'You can't do that.'

'But why?'

'Why?' she said. '*No* why, *every* why, *that's* the why.'

This was a linguistic impasse, explaining nothing yet making it impossible to continue the conversation. But I discovered later that it's a construction used to silence querulous Irish children. It puts you in your place, lands you back squarely in the nursery where even an English child knows it's being patronised.

At home I was the small Englishman, regarding the Irish hordes with curiosity and some alarm. At school, by contrast, I was the class 'Mick'. In my pale blue uniform and slicked-down hair, I don't suppose I looked any different from every other short-trousered boy kicking a tennis ball around the playground in Wimbledon. But sometimes I sounded different.

When I was small, I had a Galway accent as thick as turf. By the time I was eight or nine, it had mostly been flattened. The process that takes small boys from a score of different backgrounds and pestles them together until they emerge as homogeneous alumni of the English education system had worked its way with my accent; I now spoke a charming, rather highfalutin' English from which most traces of shebeen and shamrock had been eliminated. But some traces remained. I said 'bath' to rhyme with 'Kath' and 'dance' to rhyme with the first syllable of 'fanciful' and 'can't' to rhyme with 'rant.' The last led to trouble, as follows:

Teacher: 'Walsh, can you be sure to come along to Second Fifteen Rugby practise on Saturday morning at 11 o'clock?'

Me: 'I cant, sir.'

Teacher: 'Good. And don't forget your kit this time. As for you, Musgrave . . .'

Me: 'No, I cant sir. I have to go to a wedding with my parents. I cant go to rugby practise, sir.'

Teacher (turning back to me): Make your mind up boy, either you can or you caaant. Which is it to be?'

Me: 'I cant sir. It's not possible.'

Teacher: 'Do you mean you can but you don't want to? Or are you simply unable to say "caaant?" '

I was crushed. How could he think it was just a matter of inability? The trouble was that the word 'caaarnt' sounded so silly, so fake-posh, you couldn't say it without laughing. Nobody would take you seriously if you went around affecting the languid drawl required to say it. Learning to choose between one pronunciation and the other became a phonetic battlefield. Next year, in Lower Elements, the class that took the 11-plus, my teacher, a formidable woman called Miss Stacey, put me up for an elocution competition because of my uniquely precise and fluting delivery.

The poem I chose to recite was a humorous work called 'Who Stuffed That White Owl?' from the *Golden Treasury of Poetry*. It concerns a self-important and pretentious young man sitting among the hirsute classes, waiting their turn in a barber's shop. The man makes the titular enquiry and, to the utter non-interest of all present, complains about the ineptness, the taxidermal enormity, of the badly-stuffed bird perched high up on the wall. He rants and raves about its lack of verisimilitude, of proportion, of colour, the absence of a single life-like quality about it. By the end, of course, the bird turns out to be real. But at one point, when the young man is banging on about Audubon, there's the line:

'He *can't* do it. It's against all bird laws', in which the 'can't' is emphatic, climactic and unconcealable.

I still pronounced this one word à la Galway – 'He CANT do it . . .'

Miss Stacey stopped the recital. 'No John,' she said. '"He caaarnt do it." Try it again.'

I tried. I tried rushing at it, shifting the emphasis to become 'HecantDO it, it's against all bird laws,' but she pulled me back. 'You mustn't say "cant"' she said shortly.

'But I always talk like that.'

'Yes, well I'm sure it's very nice and regional and it's fine to sound like that at home. But it's just not good English. You wouldn't find the people who read the news saying "cant" . . .'

'But I don't want to say it in an English way. It doesn't sound like me.'

'John,' she said with finality. 'This is an elocution competition. Do you want to win it or don't you?'

'Yes.'

'Well then say it as I tell you to. Say caarnt.'

There was a silence for fifteen seconds.

'He *caaarnt* do it,' I said, pulling out the drawl to its fullest extent. 'It's against *awwwllll* bird *lawwwws*.' It sounded ludicrous, but it didn't feel like something you could laugh at. It felt as if I'd put on a different uniform; as if I'd just changed sides in a battle.

I compensated later by absurd displays of Irishness in class. St Patrick's Day, 17 March, gave me an opportunity. Aunt Peggy from Monivea, Galway, would send some shamrock over in an envelope, and I'd set off for school with a sprig pinned to my blazer. At school, where any display of differentness was greeted with whoops of derision, the class fell about laughing.

'Are you proud, Walsh,' asked a snooty piece of work called Jeremy, 'to think that your national flower is a weed?'

'The thing to be proud of with shamrock,' I retorted, 'is that it doesn't grow in England.'

But then Jeremy had a French mother. Only the half-English could give themselves such prattishly English airs. Jeremy and I later resumed being friends, and I began to notice that my closest buddies were likewise half-breeds – Paul's forbears were French, Harry's mother was Dutch, Tony's father was Polish. In their cases, however, the families were thoroughly assimilated. They didn't feel any need to wear badges (or weeds) of national pride, to insist on their differentness. They didn't talk with an accent, nor endure a score of stereotypical jibes about stupidity and drunkenness. (I don't think we knew what the stereotypes were for French or Dutch or Polish people; we never claimed that Paul was pretentious, Harry was mad about tulips and dykes and Tony's only function was to hold up telegraph wires.)

A year after the shamrock episode, on the next St Patrick's Day, I received two greeting cards from the Galway relations, both bearing green-white-and-gold detachable cardboard harps on the front. My mother had acquired a wet mass of shamrock from one of her little men around the corner. Which should I choose for school? Fired by an impulse to show off, I wore the whole lot, and went off festooned with national symbols like a Shannon gift shop on the move.

In a class of New British twelve-year-olds, it was waving a green rag at a field of bulls. I don't know what possessed me; it now seems eerily cognate with the Orange Lodge in the late nineties, kitted out in sashes and bowlers, determined to walk down the Garvaghy Road surrounded by deadly enemies. I was a one-boy identity protest, asserting my Irishness in the midst of this Anglo-Saxon throng, putting into action what I'd learned about the perfidious Brits from a hundred songs and a thousand glancing references in my parents' conversation. I wanted to wind them up, to provoke a reaction from the stiff little Englanders who were, at most other times, my friends.

Amazingly, I didn't get beaten senseless for the harps and shamrocks.

I just encountered a lot of cries of 'stupid Mick' and at break-time the class went outside and pulled up handfuls of grass and stuffed them into their collars and breast pockets, so that, by the time the teacher arrived for the next lesson, he was greeted by the sight of twenty pre-pubescents sprouting acres of greensward from their necks.

VI

THE DANCING PRIESTS

For most of the inhabitants of Battersea in the sixties, the core of their revels may have been the newly-trendy Clapham Junction, the clanging, mould-scented gateway to the big city via the major termini of Waterloo or Victoria; they may have been taken by Battersea Fun Fair in the wide leafy park between the Battersea and Albert Bridges – one of the few reminders of the 1951 Festival of Britain left standing, with its spectacular Guinness Clock still in working order – or by the nationally famous Dog's Home, or any of a dozen other landmarks that prompt what passes for civic pride in South London. But for the Irish Catholics of Battersea, the twin peaks of our socialising were the local churches.

St Vincent's was, and is, a bleak little church in Altenburg Gardens, one street away from Lavender Gardens. As churches go, it was modest to the point of invisibility. It had a lady chapel, a choir loft with an organ, and a hellfire-preacher pulpit, but there was nothing about it that would occupy more than a tiny paragraph in Pevsner's *Great English Churches*. It always needed a new coat of paint, a new heating system and some new unchipped statues. An air of mystery or solemnity or wonder would have been nice too, but instead it radiated a crouched atmosphere of dogged survivalism, embodied in the faces, the stance and the horrible clothes of the elderly ladies who made up the bulk of the congregation. My parents attended church all the time and my sister and I had to accompany them. Neither of us ever felt we fitted in. From being an altar server I rose through the ranks to become 'MC' – the top job, the dizzying senior posting of the serving fraternity, the seraphic panjandrum who stands by the priest's right hand at High Mass, turning the pages of the giant missal with its illuminated text, its singing passages marked in square black crochets and minims, its little leather tabs on the side of key pages to alleviate the wear and tear on the sacred paper when we were about to embark on the Offertory or the final Blessing.

You weren't, of course, much of a 'master of ceremonies' like a ringmaster or a gavel-bashing Leonard Sachs, merely a smoothly efficient civil servant to the priestly minister in the fancy chasuble presiding over the mysteries. This privileged proximity to the central rubric and rituals of church life didn't turn me into a convincing candidate for the seminary, however; the baser elements of puberty, rock 'n' roll and intellectual snobbery kept me longing for the greater world out there, beyond the dull sermons on chastity, the hopeless little inspirational magazines on sale in the porch, the headscarves and umbrellas, the bronchitic explosions and quavery hymn-singing, the queue for Communion, made up of dismally unexcited, defeated-looking people whose ranks I was extremely loth to join. I believed in God – for a cradle Catholic, belief arrives along with your mother's milk – but I couldn't stand the Church. Almost from the start, I wanted out. And once you left the precincts of St Vincent's and headed home, you could leave all that glum religious hierarchy behind, couldn't you?

Actually no, you couldn't. The priests came along too.

My childhood was filled with priests. They invaded our household, from morning to night. Wherever you went there seemed to be priests – in the kitchen, the dining room, the upstairs 'lounge', the bathroom, the garden – taking their ease, making themselves at home. And with the sole exception of Father Bernard Smith – the parish priest of St Vincent's, a large, irritable, academically-minded man spectacularly miscast as the pastor of a sad, low-brow, intellectually zomboid congregation, wholly uninterested in his weekly exegeses of the New Testament – they were all Irish.

Immediately upon moving to Battersea, my mother announced her presence round at St Vincent's, informed the parish fathers (namely Father Smith, his housekeeper Miss Rayer, and – some way below them – the curate), that she was, in effect, open for business. She invited any priest who cared to try some alternative hospitality to call round. Once a timid curate had crossed the threshold, he was sunk. She drenched him with tea, plumped him with barm-brack, saturated him with gossip, carpet-bombed him with an attention that was half-motherly and half tinkling Irish sophistication, hung on his every word and insisted that he become 'one of the family'.

More practically, she gave him the key to the house. She had special back-door keys made for the exclusive use of the young Irish clerics who fetched up in Battersea, some of them just out of seminaries in Maynooth or Galway, pink-necked, far from home and understandably appalled by the grim inner-city society in which they'd landed. Any time you fancy, she would tell them, you just let yourself in through the back door, make tea, carve a hunk of cold chicken or roast lamb, sit down, take the weight off your feet, read the paper. If she was home, with friends in the kitchen, the priest must never be shy of joining the company – after all, back in Sligo, to have a priest drop by on a social visit would be thought a compliment to the household. Never think twice, she told them, about making this your second home.

And they didn't. No temporary curate in Altenburg Gardens could resist my mother's worshipping embrace for long. For some of them, our house in Battersea Rise became their first home. They could weigh the merits of Miss Rayer's silent and purse-lipped Eastbourne-landlady ways, or the problematic bliss of an evening spent listening to Father Smith assaulting Scriabin on the parlour Bechstein; they could balance such bleak joys against Mrs Walsh's insatiable chat, the constant soap opera of her dealings with the patients and the ladies of the parish, my father's conspiratorial jokes and quadruple gin-and-oranges, the endless provision of food, television and songs. It wasn't a tough decision. If they could have slept there, I sometimes felt, they'd have done so, rather than slink out into the night at 2 a.m., back to the lonesome bedsit life of the exiled Irish cleric in London SW11.

If they could have slept with my mother – now there was something unimaginable, yet as I grew older I sometimes felt it in the atmosphere. My mother was a handsome woman in her early fifties, huge of bosom, slender of legs, lightly tactile with men and impressed by any sign of sacerdotal gravitas. She flirted with priests all the time, unconsciously but palpably, as many Irish women do. She treated

99

them as heroes of a nameless war, soldiers on leave from the front, men whose most mundane utterance was back-lit by the fires of some tremendous battle, as if a hundred wise and serious things were being left carefully unsaid, but understood by her and by them alone.

These were men who appeared before us twice or thrice a week on a stage or altar, in white surplices and gem-encrusted chasubles, their hands raised in intimate supplication to God. At certain times in the church year, during an Exposition of the Blessed Sacrament, they walked in awful, slow majesty up and down the nave of the church carrying a wondrous, spiked, gold object inside which, through round glass portholes, you could see a large sacred host, clamped by angel wings. The golden vessel was called a 'monstrance': even saying the word pitches me into a state of respectful awe. It was like, literally, a monster passing by. The words sit beside each other in the dictionary (one comes from *monere*, meaning to warn, as of a gross and portentous presence, the other from *monstrare* meaning simply to show, as in demonstrate) but they seemed alarmingly similar to me. Technically, you weren't even supposed to look at the thing, as it passed by your pew in a processional fog of incense and the scuffling feet of the altar servers. But as I risked a glance, through the little windows at the circle of unleavened bread within that was the core of all our adoration, it seemed to me that I could see something in there, something else besides the host and the metal clip, some odd, flickering presence that waved tiny hands and made you shiver all over . . .

When you met priests on the home front, therefore, in their ordinary dark suits and dog collars, you had to make some instant mental adjustment to the fact they were, basically, ordinary men – like my father's patients or Pat Hines, the roofer. To my mother, they were never ordinary. They were always secretly on duty, being holy, guarding the mysteries, knowing not just where all the parish bodies were buried but where they'd all gone afterwards. Her attitude to them was subservient and genuflectory, with occasional eruptions of girlish intimacy.

Sometimes, at parties, she would dance with them and I'd watch her with interest. She had a curious little habit when dancing with some men (including me). In a waltz, whichever man was leading her would naturally hold her right hand with his left, both arms out-stretched in formal rigidity, as the dancers twirled about the floor. But if things slowed down, my mother would suddenly bend her elbow and bring her partner's hand back towards her shoulder, clasping it to the soft flesh bisected by the strap of her gown – a gesture of un-get-pastable togetherness. It was as if she were pulling her partner into an embrace of frank complicity. Heaven knows in what Tubbercurry dancehall she picked it up, but it was undeniably flirtatious. My mother was a farm-reared woman, and her grip was as strong as a man's. It meant she was, effectively, leading things from now on, moving from passive to active, drawing attention away from the formality of the stiffened arms and correct placing of feet, to the thereness of her face, her eyes and mouth and bosom. She would dance like this with favoured men whom she trusted. Since priests were bound by laws of celibacy and chastity, since they were 'practically family', and the recipients of a million other little attentions in the kitchen, of hugs and kisses on arrival and departure, it was only a natural extension of Catholic hospitality. But the dancing priests would not, I suspect, have ever encountered anything like it in a hundred parlour visits, this warm, do-it-my-way engagement with my mother's body. If it disconcerted them, they would never have admitted it; they merely basked in the heady whiff of Balenciaga Le Dix that emanated from my mother's matronly chest.

These were, of course, the days of innocence, before the Catholic church was riven with sex scandals, paedophile rings and the revelation of Bishop Casey of Galway's teenage love-child. The priests were holy men, deserving of respect, walking embodiments of moral virtue, modestly dressed in black, endlessly cheerful and slightly world-weary from their afternoon encounters with the sick, the dying, the addicted, the lonely, the desperate and the confessionally disposed. We looked after them all. We joined in our mother's passionate regard for them. There was Father Shannon, a bluff figure with a silvery bouffant and a big laugh, who'd make jokes about his curate, Father Dove, an ascetic Englishman ('Sorry I'm late. Took ages getting ready. The Dove was in the bathroom. He was moulting, a-ha-ha-ha') and Father Frank Moran, an ebullient and genuinely kind chap who acted like my big brother, took me on the golf links at Richmond, took me to the cinema to see 2001: A Space Odyssey, and asked what I thought about current affairs.

There was Father Sean O'Malley, from Oughterard on the edge of Connemara, whose aunt had once, during the Irish Civil War, concealed the family revolver from visiting Black and Tans by hiding it in a beehive aswarm with irritated hymenoptera; despite this impressive pedigree, he was a sweet innocent twentysomething with wavy hair, a recent graduate from the seminary. Madelyn grilled him about the doctrine of the Trinity, and argued with his stumbling explanations, until he'd say in desperation, 'Well, if you don't believe in it, you're no Catholic, that's all I can say,' upon which she tossed her ringletted head and left the room in triumph. And Father Jim Furlong, an aptly-named sporty bloke with no time for teenage argumentation, and Monsignor Pat Keaveney, an intelligent, blandly handsome man in his late forties who first demonstrated to me what the word 'charisma' might mean through the effortless superiority with which he arrived, spoke, ate and departed.

My father's special pal, Father Bill Sheridan was an enormous, mighty-voiced, thrillingly dramatic man, who, had he been English, would have surely forsaken his vocation to build hydro-electric dams, with a cast of millions of cowed locals, in some African wasteland. He would arrive in a flurry of activity, as if he had an entourage around him bearing steamer trunks, and would depart in a swirl of greatcoats and scarves. He once stunned me, as we crowded round the back door to see him off, by seizing my mother in a burly arm, and landing a dashing, Douglas Fairbanks kiss on her upturned face that left her visibly swooning. Some of the priests were Olympians, like him; some were unconvincing pastors who left the priesthood some years later to find jobs in the civil service.

They were all Irish. They brought over with them, like luggage, a lot of songs, stories, family gossip, political opinions about De Valera or Terence O'Neill, strong views about the Pope or the Kennedys or Grace Kelly in Monaco or Dana winning the Eurovision Song Contest with 'All Kinds of Ev'rything', or the shocking nerve of Dave Allen, to be making jokes about Extreme Unction and contraception (my mother would tut-tut along; my father would store up the offending gags for later use). They never, in any of my memories, talked about London, where they lived, or the wider hinterland of England, which they seemed never to visit, or the burgeoning counter-culture of drugs and hippies and alternative lifestyles.

Once, my father, who had a child's enthusiasm for the new and the odd, came home late from his post-surgery visits. It was after 10 p.m., and my mother had started to worry about him. He arrived full of chat about a family to which he'd been called out, to deal with a sick child in a flat off Lavender Hill. The parents were young, middle-class and idealistic proto-hippies, both aspirant painters, who lived on a macrobiotic diet and had been feeding their eighteen-month-old son on brown rice and tofu curd.

The infant was suffering from malnutrition, was listless and dull-eyed, and Dad had recommended a more balanced regimen of food. But this would mean a radical change of lifestyle for the couple, a complete re-thinking of the purity to which they were committed. He could either harangue them into eating meat and potatoes, like decent Western citizens, or could try to persuade them that their child would never thrive on the fruits of their macrobiotic obsessions alone. Typically, he chose the latter. And in talking to them about hunger and need, and purity and ingestion, and enzymes and vitamins, he found himself in the most absorbing dietary discussion he'd encountered in years. No wonder he'd stayed out late, looking through their fridge, drawing up calorific tables, even inspecting their paintings. He was keen to find out why they lived as they did, and wouldn't condemn them for their holistic impulses.

Back home, he regaled us all (Father O'Malley included) about this brave new world that had such difficult purity in it. They were at the cutting edge of organic living, and he'd been fascinated to learn about it all. He hardly drew breath for thirty minutes. At the end, my mother looked at the priest. 'Fat lot of good it'll do them with all their fancy ideas, when they have a dead child on their hands,' she observed, ever the practical ward sister. My father looked crushed. Father O'Malley spread his hands in a gesture that said he couldn't fathom the iniquities of the modern world. If that was the future, you could keep it.

The only English cleric who ever came through the front door was Father Smith, the parish priest. He came only once. He was not part of my mother's general invitation to the young Irish curates. He represented, for her, something altogether too English, too serious and academic. He would be no fun. The day he arrived was the scene for one of the most alarming encounters of my childhood.

It was a Saturday. The steeped-mutton pong of Irish stew hung over the hall. When the doorbell rang, my parents were upstairs having an afternoon nap, and were not to be disturbed. Madelyn and I were doing our homework in the kitchen. Father Smith came in with awful majesty, his long black cloak with its lion's-head clasp sweeping off his shoulders. He had taken an interest in me as a potential keyboard scholar and decided that I should be taken in hand and personally groomed as a future performer on the church organ. I ushered him into the dining room and sat him down. The grand salon, scene of a thousand Irish hoolies, seemed suddenly paltry and trivial, diminished by his awesome bulk. The china figurines of dogs and swans on the mantelpiece seemed to bury their noses and beaks deeper in their porcelain fur, cowed by his distinguished presence. Madelyn went off to make tea and to butter some slabs of sliced fruitcake, and I tried some ten-year-old small-talk on this deeply unworldly and buttoned-up man.

'I like "Jesu, Joy of Man's Desiring"' because it never seems to end', I said airily, pinching a *bon mot* I'd heard on the radio from Frank Muir or Patrick Campbell. 'Just when you think it's stopped, it sort of starts up all over again.'

'Well yes, John,' said the parish priest judiciously, 'but the glory lies, I feel, in Bach's solidity, the iron quality of the slow singing line that asserts itself above the streaming counterpoint. Now Purcell . . .'

There was a ring at the doorbell, the second in ten minutes on this quiet Battersea afternoon. I decided to ignore it. 'I thought Purcell was mostly for trumpets,' I said.

Father Smith allowed himself a short, high table guffaw.

'My dear chap, when you've studied, as I hope you shall, the less, shall we say, canonical works of the great Purc–'

The doorbell rang again, long and insistent, as if a concrete pillar had been propped against it. It was hard to ignore.

'John!' yelled my sister from the kitchen. 'Can you get that? The kettle's just boiled.'

I excused myself, went out to the hallway, and opened the door.

Before me was a large, disreputable-looking man in a tartan shirt, with one outstretched hand on the door, leaning in, about to collapse on top of me.

'That *fookin'* bastard,' he said blearily. 'Oi'll fooking swing fer him, so I will.'

He tottered slightly.

'Erm,' I said. 'What can I do for . . . ?'

'Is this the docther's house?' he said. 'They told me Number Eight. Ohhhh . . .' A ghastly groan escaped his lips.

'Actually,' I said, 'the surgery isn't open now. You'll have to come back, er –' I thought fast. Saturdays were days of rest. Surgery was from 9 to 11 a.m., then nothing until Monday morning. It was dead time, lie-down time. As I stood wondering how to break it to this rough individual, in his corduroy jacket and unshaven chin, that he'd have to come back in thirty-six hours, he doubled over in pain.

'Aaargh,' he said. 'That *fooker*.' For the first time, I registered that his left hand was clamped to his stomach. Through his fingers, a dark purple oil was seeping.

'What's wrong?' I asked. The man's hand came away from his bulging abdomen and, to my horror, I saw a horrid red mess all over his soiled shirt. It seemed to bubble and gurgle and gush, just slightly. It was a knife wound.

'Jesus,' I said faintly, mindful of how such a profanity might sound to the elderly cleric in the next room.

'Fooker in the bookie's up the road,' said the man who was now standing, a ghastly Hammer horror vision in the family hallway. 'Nicked me wid his blade, de bastard. Wait'll I'm patched up and I'll fookin' kill'im.'

Suddenly there seemed to be blood everywhere. The man's stained right hand was searching for somewhere to rest or to lean. It sawed the air. Any minute now, our handsome hallway would look like the shower unit in *Psycho*.

'You'd better come into the waiting room,' I said politely.

I helped him onto a chair. 'Be right back,' I said, and ran to the kitchen. 'Mad,' I said, 'There's a patient in the waiting room. He's bleeding. Can you get Dad?'

'What about Father Smith?'

'I'll look after him. Where's the tea?'

As she fled upstairs, I took a tray of tea things and fruitcake impedimenta into the dining room. Father Smith was smoking a small cigar with an abstracted air, and looking about him like an ambassadorial grandee in a banana republic, well used to eruptions by local agitators. 'Ah, cake,' he said, comfortably. 'I'm afraid Miss Rayer's excursions into the culinary field do not, generally speaking, stretch to comestible sweetmeats. Fish is more her thing.' He picked up a slice of elderly barm-brack and surveyed the yellow smear across the top. 'Is this butter? How luxurious.'

From the room across the hall came a horrible groaning noise.

105

'That *cont*,' said the unseen patient in a muffled tone. 'Tha' fookin' . . .'

'I've never actually played a proper organ,' I said loudly, keen to return the conversation to the point and get the parish priest off home. 'Though I used to play a harmonium in the college chapel. You had to work it with your feet.'

'Indeed,' said Father Smith, pouring tea and stirring in sugar with a civilised tinkling noise. 'I think you'll find the church organ a deliciously *demanding* instrument in that regard. A wonderfully physical experience, combining delicacy of fingering with the glorious sustain of the pedals. The chordal structure of the organ, you see, is quite unlike the piano in its . . .'

'I'M FOOKIN BLEEDING TO DEATH SITTIN' HERE' came the intruder's voice, unignorably, from across the way.

Father Smith stopped, with a china cup halfway to his mouth. 'Did I hear the voice of some poor unfortunate . . . ?' He regarded the firmly closed living room door. 'Perhaps I could . . . ?'

'No,' I said. 'Have some more tea.' I disappeared through the door. In the waiting room, the stab victim was rocking back and forth on his little chair, singing a little song to himself. An agonised smile was on his face and his eyes were closed. 'The doctor will be right with you,' I assured him. 'Really, any second now.'

In the hallway again, I could hear Father Smith whistling an aria from Gounod's *Faust* on my right, while, from the left-hand door, sounds of distress emerged through a wrenchingly emotional rendition:

Shoot me like an Irish soldier
Do not hang me like a dog,
For I fought to free my country
On that clear September morn'.

Why, you ask, did I not get the priest to help the stab victim? How can you ask such a thing? I stood in the hall between two rooms that were far more than rooms. They were two worlds that could never be brought together. One was a correct and formal, well-mannered and tidy sort of place, where people glided about discussing books and floral displays and classical music, and made slightly obscure little jokes and laughed as if they were coughing. The other was a shockingly informal, pungent, hairy, large-booted, shouty-voiced class of establishment where the people never looked right sitting on chairs, their conversation made no sense and they seemed to come alive only in a crowd.

I couldn't ask the parish priest – a man as awesomely, severely English as Dr Johnson or Sherlock Holmes – to come and inspect the shameful sight in the waiting room. It was a huge family embarrassment that this rough fellow was to be found, swearing and bleeding away, under our roof: a real-life skeleton in the Walsh cupboard, a kind of unacceptable, folk memory behind all my parents' London–Irish sophistication. I stood there, stuck between the two worlds, at a loss about how to introduce one to the other.

Eventually a shriek from the eviscerated songbird on the left made my mind up. Shamefully, I fled back to Father Smith.

'Ah John,' he said, his chin ablaze with fruity crumbs, 'Perhaps this is an inconvenient time to call. If your parents . . .'

'No, no, everything's fine,' I assured him. 'About the organ lessons, I go to piano lessons already, on Saturday afternoons, but perhaps I could come along to the church just after lunch?'

'Possibly, possibly,' said Father Smith, 'although to use the word 'lunch' for Miss Rayer's unstructured collations of tongue and corned beef is something of an offence against exactitude. If we were to say, two-thirty?'

Madelyn's head appeared around the door. 'John, Dad's just getting up. I've phoned for an ambulance . . . Hello Father Smith.'

Startled, the parish priest, still chewing cake, rose to his feet.

'Good heavens.' he asked. 'Is there something wrong with your parents?'

'No,' I said, 'it's perfectly all right. Personally, I've always thought that the trouble with organ stops . . .'

'Not exactly, Father,' said Madelyn, taking charge in her annoying way. 'There's a guy from Kerry here who's been in a fight at the bookmaker's up the road, and he's been knifed in the stomach and is bleeding like a stuck pig in the waiting room, and our parents are upstairs and we don't quite know what to do, but I've rung the hospital and they said they'll send an ambulance over.'

Amazingly, Father Smith rose to the occasion. He left his tea, his fruitcake and our elevated discourse behind, and bustled into the waiting room, where the stab victim had gone back to cursing in a low growl, doubled over in his chair. Father Smith knelt before him and examined his eyes for signs of imminent death.

'Warm water, Madelyn,' he commanded, 'and some J-cloths.' He looked at me. 'Go upstairs and tell your father he has an emergency on his hands.'

I ran upstairs, freed from Irish guilt and English fastidiousness. I banged on the portals of the parental boudoir. My father appeared, looking dishevelled and I delivered the kind of line you only get to say once or twice in your life:

'Sorry to wake you up,' I said, 'but there's a guy dying in the surgery because this other guy stabbed him, and I thought he was all right because he was singing, but there was blood all over the place, so you must come. But he'll probably be all right because Father Smith is looking after him . . .'

My father never forgot that day either.

Of all the priests, the most interesting was Father Dominic Doherty, who came I think from Wexford, whom we knew as 'Father D' and whom my mother called 'Dom' to his face – a rather racy contraction, given her insistence that we showed respect at all times to priestly honorifics, but 'Dom' was a respectable familiarity, since it seemed to confer on him the temporary status of a Dominican friar. He was a young, lanky, brick-red-faced chap with a fake-humorous manner and a very short fuse. He was no great thinker on Catholic matters, I suspect, and channelled his intellectual shortcomings into a fierce adherence to the doctrine of the catechism – that hectoring little question-and-answer booklet about belief ('Why did God make you?' 'God made me to know him, love him and serve him in this world and be happy with him for ever in the next') which all Catholic children were required to learn by heart. He was not a man to curry favour with stroppy pubescents. They were to be moulded into God-and-Church-fearing adult members of the congregation, and, in the Papist homes of Battersea, to be endured as sulking irritants.

Father D was easily roused to anger. I once watched as he argued with Adrian, one of the choirboys at St Vincent's, who was trying to get out of choir practice the following week. Adrian said he couldn't make it because he had to go ten-pin bowling at his brother's birthday party next Saturday afternoon. He was sorry but he really couldn't miss it.

'Bowling?' said Father D. 'Bowling? This is the choir, you stupid boy. We are preparing for Easter Week. Nothing in the Church year is as important as the celebration of Christ's dying on the Cross for your sins, and rising from the dead on Easter Sunday. And you want to jeopardise its success to go . . . what is this bowling?' His voice was a tungsten wire encircling the neck of the truant chorister, about to garrotte him.

'It's a game, Father,' said Adrian. 'At that place in Streatham. There's like these skittles and you bowl a big heavy black ball with three holes in it for your fingers . . .'

'I'm not interested in the rules,' Father D shouted at him. 'I don't want to hear about these stupid places where stupid people idle their lives away. Preparing for Easter is far more important than silly games on a Saturday afternoon. You will be here at three o'clock with the others, and that's all there is to say.'

'But it's me brother's birthday, Father,' said Adrian, wavering a little. 'I want to go.'

Father D's face went from brick to terracotta. 'Do not defy me.'

'I'm not,' said Adrian. 'I'll be here the next week. It's ages till Easter.'

'If you're not here at three o'clock on Saturday, you can damn well stay at home in the future. I don't want you back here. You can just bowl your foolish life away from now on.'

I could see that Adrian was near to tears. He was just a twelve-year-old Battersea kid with nothing to do. Nobody paid him to be in the choir. It wasn't a vocation or a remunerative career. He just liked singing and messing about with the others. But anger flashed a sudden fin and he said an unforgivable thing.

'You can keep your choir,' he said chokingly. 'And your bloody Easter.' Whereupon Father D, my mother's champion, friend to all and benign presence in the Battersea Rise kitchen, raised his arm and delivered a slap across Adrian's face that rang around the church like a gunshot. We all, altar servers and choirboys alike, froze as if we'd just witnessed an execution. Adrian went to the vestry, took off his cassock and cotta, walked out of the church and never came back. For the rest of us, as if it had been an embarrassing event at school, we never referred to it again. We were very wary afterwards of this once-friendly cleric who drilled us in church ways. It wasn't his temper, which we'd known about already. It was the womanish slap across

Adrian's face, a moment of strange gender-realignment that made us seriously uncomfortable.

Oblivious to his irascible ways, Mother and Father D went on pilgrimages together. There's a photograph of them in Lourdes in July 1964, when they were at the height of their mutual absorption. They are standing in a group of pilgrims, some in wheelchairs, before the basilica of St Peter's, the flagstones under their feet slick with rain, standing together but looking spectacularly unconnected. Her hands are in the pockets of her sensible raincoat and she is looking away from both the camera and the priest, eyes fixed, self-consciously, on something off to her right. He is belted into a shiny grey mackintosh with all the charm of a holiday-wear Gestapo trenchcoat, smiling as if caught in the middle of some verbal pleasantry. Oddly, they are the only people in the twenty-four-strong group who have other people's hands upon them: behind Father D is a Continental-looking priest whose left hand sits on Father D's shoulder; behind my mother is a gnarled, elderly nun who has placed both her hands on my mother's shoulders, as if steering her. Thus we have one nun and one priest, presiding like bedtime angels over the figures of Anne Walsh and Dominic Doherty – both doing their best to look unconcernedly separate and who, in consequence, look fantastically guilty, like lovers at the start of an affair.

I wouldn't wish to suggest that any 'inappropriate' relationship existed between them. But undoubtedly there was an element in my mother's friendships with priests that transcended ordinary rules of engagement with men. And it was, I think, quintessentially Irish. They were male and Irish and Catholic and celibate, and in their foreswearing of sex and upholding of Vatican doctrines they achieved, in her eyes, a kind of über-masculinity, a heightened form of old decency that meant she would never question their views, their habits, their attitudes, even their emotional caprices. She became, in a sense, their handmaiden, their vestal virgin, no matter down what erratic paths they chose to lead their extra-pastoral lives.

I stood and watched in puzzlement as these odd and interesting men were elevated in front of me, like the host at Communion, into beings of utter moral authority. If a priest at dinner aired his exciting views on, say, the Profumo scandal or the Permissive Society, my mother was not above saying – actually saying out loud to the company ranged about the rosewood table with its fussy napery and its lovely brown soup tureens – 'Father is speaking. Let's all listen to this carefully', and I would cringe for her, and for my smiling, indulgent real father as well. Such total acceptance of priestly infallibility wasn't just a denial of the spirit of the time, it was a denial of the forceful, determined, tough-bunny, argumentative woman against whom I battled throughout my teenage years.

I couldn't understand the subservience with which she greeted the priests' mundane pronouncements. They seemed not to read books, or know anything about modern music, or have seen any new films, or to hold anything but the most jejune opinions about current affairs. And a curious condemnatory blankness seemed to inform their notions of culture.

If you said how much you liked *My Fair Lady*, you'd get a lecture on how many times Rex Harrison had been married and divorced. If you mentioned a pop group, my mother would assure you – she had friends on the nursing circuit and she knew these things – that this singer or that guitarist had been 'in and out of the Priory,' the famous drugs 'n' drink detox sanatorium in Roehampton. The priests would nod along. 'Desperate,' they'd say, 'oh desperate behaviour.'

My mother and I fought a lot, and all our rows were about morality. They were not philosophical discussions. They were battles of will. Her viewpoint was forged in absolute, unswerving, doctrinaire Irish Catholicism. Mine was a stubborn, rebellious, inchoate English bloody-mindedness, a refusal to be told what to do by a behavioural system that seemed to have nothing to do with me. Somewhere between Rome and Ireland, it seemed, a list of rules had been invented specifically to condemn a lot of things that, to my English eyes, seemed perfectly all right. Words like 'impure' and 'immodest' were applied to the way people dressed, or spoke or behaved together. Mini skirts, the bikini-ed lovelies in *Photoplay* magazine that illustrated the new James Bond film, see-through blouses, tight trousers . . . the lot.

People kissing on television came in for a lot of stick. Any screen kiss that lasted more than, say, five seconds would pitch the living room into a fever of muttering. 'Turn off that awful stuff,' Mother would say, and (if it extended beyond ten seconds) 'John will you turn over' – on a rising note of hysteria, as if the TV lovers might, at any moment, start removing their clothing. My father would be less urgent about it. 'Such rubbish,' he would murmur, though not all that disapprovingly. '*Suuuuch* rubbish . . .' There was a sweet languor about his disapproval to which I felt instinctively drawn. At such moments I felt like switching the bloody set off just to avoid the mortification of watching any more with my parents present.

I cringe to think of the family evening in which I watched *Langrishe Go Down*, a television film of Aidan Higgins's wonderful, hyper-realist novel about three sisters living in a mouldering Big House in County Kildare, their spinsterly hearts set a-flutter by the presence in the gate-lodge of a German student, played by Jeremy Irons. Not only were my parents watching but so were the family's top echelon of visiting religious, in the form of Father John and Sister Rosalie, my father's elder brother and sister. They all settled down in front of the TV, expecting a nostalgic Irish drama about the old days, and the funny habits of stranded Protestant toffs. For a while they nodded happily at the details: the street-lamps, the wheezing bus from Dublin to the outskirts of town, the ancient wind-up gramophone playing Count John McCormack singing 'Passing By' to an empty drawing room. A scene of drunken revelry featuring Harold Pinter (who wrote the script) as a nasty Dublin chancer elicited no more than a few tuts at the language. Having read the book, I knew there was a scene of seduction coming, and I prayed, perhaps the only time I my life I ever prayed for such a thing, that it would be done with a modicum of restraint.

It wasn't. Once Judi Dench, as the flightiest of the sisters, had decided that the German youth was her last chance of sexual bliss, Hell shortly followed. In the lamplight of the Langrishe drawing room, she bared her breasts to the young student, then scooped up some cream from the supper they had shared and anointed her nipples with it.

I was sitting nearest to the television. A hot flush stole over my face. I could not turn to look at how my mother, father, uncle and aunt were taking it, for fear they might all have turned to pillars of salt. I had, I think, urged them to watch this 'fascinating,' 'evocative' piece of Irish culture, and now I sweated for them as if I had personally dragged them into a porn cinema in Soho.

I knew there'd be trouble, but it seemed to be a long time in coming. My parents must have been stunned into silence by this eruption of smut – whereas, in fact, they were merely waiting for the seniors to make the first complaint. As Ms Dench moved wobblingly towards Mr Irons's manly frame, the tension in the room grew to bursting point. Finally Father John rumbled, 'This is awful boring stuff' and the floodgates opened.

'Turn it off, John' my mother exploded. 'How can you watch such awful things?'

'Is the news on the other side?' asked my father with airy but transparent guile (it was unlikely, being about 11.15 p.m.).

I turned to protest, such was the burden I carried of being the one who'd recommended they watch in the first place. 'For God's sake,' I said. 'It's just a love scene. It'll be all right in a second.'

'Turn over,' my mother almost shrieked at me. 'Or do you *like* that kind of . . .' I looked at Sister Rosalie on the sofa. With fantastic aplomb, she had seen what was coming, had somehow extracted a copy of the *People's Friend* from her reticule, had buried herself in its innocent pages, and now raised her head from it in mild enquiry, as if she hadn't been watching the thing at all. But the family evening was all but ruined and I slunk off to the study to stew in my shame.

Billy, in Keith Waterhouse's *Billy Liar*, constantly fantasies about having a different set of parents. In one incarnation, his mother is of the 'modern, London kind' who, when her errant son returns home from a night on the tiles, merely glances up from her game of solitaire and groans, 'Oh God, how dreary. Billy's pissed again.' In the same spirit, I fantasised about having modern, London parents. They would be cool and amoral. He would wear jeans and a moustache and sit in an orange-bomb sixties chair, smoking Gauloises inscrutably. She would drink dry martinis and interrupt her reading of Sartre to say, 'I think we'll have the Raphaels round on Saturday. I'm dying to know how he got on in Beverly Hills.' Both would have greeted the cream-on-the-nipples scene with ironic laughter ('Well, well, what a trouper Judi turned out to be') and say to me, 'Time you got yourself a nice girlfriend, darling.'

They wouldn't know much about pop music, of course, being old, but they'd know the people involved. George Martin would call in from masterminding the Beatles's *Sergeant Pepper* sessions, accept a glass of champagne, chat with my father about drugs ('they're probably fine with hash,' Dad would counsel George, 'but I'd tell them to go easy on the acid, if you want the thing finished on time') and ask my mother about names. 'It's a song Paul's written about a lonely spinster

113

called Madge Rigby,' George Martin would say, 'but the name doesn't fit the tune.' My mother would sip her Martini reflectively. 'Of course I don't *know* anyone like that,' she'd say, 'But perhaps Eleanor has a better cadence . . .' At all events, she would never have torn a poster of John Lennon from the wall of my room and screwed it up because she disapproved of everything he stood for, as my real mother once did.

She wanted everything for me, but everything on her terms. She wanted me to be successful, but it was far more important that I was decent, truthful and God-fearing. Above all she wanted me to be Catholic. She took any evidence of moral backsliding as an affront against the Church of Rome, and fought every instance of rebellion like a personal crusade. Curiously, she didn't want me to turn out especially Irish. When I embarked on a phase, at fifteen, of listening to classical music, and tried to talk to her about Mozart and Richard Strauss, she would say, tenderly, 'I'm glad you like . . . *nice* things, John.'

Symphonies and tone poems had never been part of her education or her enthusiasms, but she knew they represented the world of Lady Hambledon and Lord David Cecil, of chafing dishes and claw-footed baths and dinner-table port, and were part of a larger, aristocratic sensibility of which she, rather cluelessly, approved.

In a way, their very un-Irishness was a proof that I might be on the right track. My father, by contrast, had no time for this élitist British malarkey. If I put Beethoven's Sixth Symphony on the gramophone as lunch was being served on a Sunday, he would swat the air with his hands and say, 'Don't be playin' that awful heavy stuff', and would substitute an album of Irish laments by Father Sidney McEwan ('a gay but simple man', the sleeve notes ingenuously promised).

Neither had any firm notion of what I might do, or even what might be appropriate for the son of two medically-disposed Irish emigrants in the odd new world of sixties Battersea. Farming was never going to be an option. Medicine was clearly out, since my father had warned me off it. The rigours of law seemed hardly the thing for a scatterbrain such as I. Accountancy would be a problem, given my startling record of innumeracy in school reports. Perhaps business? Later, when I was starting out as a freelance journalist, my mother took me to one side. 'Look,' she said, 'all this writing is all very well, but could you not get a real job? One where you start off at the

bottom, in some department and, you know – work your way up?'
Just as Dickens never shook off the notion that the essential meaning
of 'work' was to be a meticulous manager who organises a sea of
disarrayed material into workable categories, my mother's notions of
decent employment were stuck in her Irish past. The men either
stayed on the farm or entered the professions, if there was room for
another medical or legal sinecure in small-town Sligo. At a pinch they
became businessmen. The women became nurses or secretaries, or
headed for the nearest city or for Dublin, and joined a bank or an
insurance office and stayed there until they were married. To try for
anything else was just asking for trouble.

So I headed towards my teenage years as a puzzle both to my
parents and to myself – confusedly pubertal, easily embarrassed by
displays of Celtic waywardness and British superiority, cowed by the
ever-present priests but with a small streak of London defiance growing
inside. Familiarity with Irish Catholics was breeding a terrible scepticism. I was becoming a fully paid-up member of the tribe, without
actually buying any of its beliefs and traditions. It was an uncomfortable
place to be. I was like an outsider at a square dance, one who knows
all the moves through constant repetition, but dreads being asked to
join in.

VII

MARTYRS AND MATRIARCHS

I didn't much warm to the idea of Ireland in my young days. It came to me in the form of people who crowded out the house, chattering in strange turns of phrase, or in songs or odd words my parents used, or as food or newspapers, or as names, some of them wildly romantic (like 'Lissadell'), some resembling names from children's books (like 'Bunratty'); but I was always a passive observer, or recipient of Irish images. When I actually started visiting the place, it was without much excitement, more with a neutral expectation that a holiday there would be an extension of those Sunday trips to Aunt Mary's dingy lair by the Thames, with the varnished occasional tables, the old Penguin thrillers and the smell of mould and wee.

We visited Ireland a lot when I was small. Between the ages of five and twelve, I travelled much more extensively in Ireland than I ever did in England. Going there was a day's drive across England, through the little Welsh towns of Pembrokeshire en route to the ferry at Fishguard and enduring the churning swell of the crossing: three hours spent sitting with a packet of crisps in a Guinness-soaked lounge, full of ashtrays and bellowing returning exiles, standing four-square in groups like cattle, their broken-veined faces contorted with laughter, their eyes creased with cigarette fumes. They were even louder and more overbearing than the crowd in my mother's kitchen, my father's dinner-party circle. I didn't like their presence. They didn't notice mine.

The ferry would dock at Rosslare in County Wexford, my father would ease our Renault Dauphine past the clanking rusted chains of the ferry doors and we'd move off into the rainy countryside. We drove through Wexford, New Ross – where John F. Kennedy's family had started out, as my parents reminded me every time we went near the town, both before and after he was shot – then a tiny side-road to Carrick-on-Suir and a long drag through Clonmel, Cahill and Tipperary and onward around the nasty environs of Limerick in search of the road through Shannon to the first sighting of the dry-stone walls that meant you were in Galway.

My father drove with a cheerful heart, commenting on the quantity of sheep in the meadows, the modest sweep of the Galty Mountains, the lack of traffic, the 'fine weather' – a term he'd apply with equal enthusiasm to a brief and blinding shaft of sunlight or a refreshing mist of rain – and the picturesque ancients by the roadside. Occasionally we would stop to ask some local pedestrian the way and would spend the next ten minutes like the worst kind of patronising English tourists, as my mother laughed at the quaintness of whichever old man had been selected to answer her piercingly English enquiries.

'Did you hear that?' she'd ask us. 'He said: "the road to Clonmel ye want? 'Tis dead straight for ye. I'll show ye here on me schtickeen."' And sure, wasn't his stick as crooked as a hunchback!'

Madelyn and I in the back of the car would laugh along with her. Dear, oh dear, the stupidity of these wild, indigenous Celts. And the old fellow who said, 'You see that horse beyond, at the edge of the stone wall? Turn left at that horse now and ye cant go wrong' when – hilariously – by the time we'd reached the wall, the horse was half a mile away! Or the old woman in the gen-u-ine shawl who said (we must have been approaching Galway): 'Have youse any Irish? I have very little of the English.' Amazing! In this day and age, my mother would marvel, the ignorance of the old dears around these parts who hadn't had the benefit of a proper education.

Mother was, of course, co-opting her children in a private conspiracy. She had left Ireland to make herself different, to become another person several rungs up the social tree from the family she'd left behind. She was a changed girl, hardly an Englishwoman exactly, but a new-wave Anglicised Irish socialite, alive to the sophistications of the post-war metropolitan world that had passed the west of Ireland by.

She had hung out with the nobs, rubbed shoulders with the quality, listened to their brittle chat at dinner tables where real footmen had tilted ancestral silver soup tureens towards her (albeit at the below-the-salt end of the company), and she had lifted the same silver ladle as Lord this and Lady that and had transferred her own quantity of seasoned aristocratic consommé or vichyssoise into her own bone-china bowl; from that world, with its pristine napery and formulaic small-talk, there was, for her, no going back.

Every turn of her head as she surveyed the unfolding Irish country-side, every flare of her nostrils as we motored through another godfor-saken little one-donkey town in Waterford or Clare, spoke volumes about her relief to have got out. Returning, for my mother, was at once an ordeal, an embarrassment and a sentimental journey – but the sentimental part of it was mitigated by the fact of what she'd become: a homecoming queen, a refugee made good, an English tourist. She glanced at the dismal fields of her childhood with the air of a duchess running her finger along the sideboard of a provincial parlour, and inspecting it for dust.

My father, by contrast, clearly loved being back. Shortly after we disembarked from the ferry, you could hear him inhale and exhale over the steering wheel, with the exaggerated relish of a convalescent at an open window, as if the wondrous air of Ireland were some kind of bracing ozonal tonic after the enervating fug of London. Yes there was a freshness in the air which lifted the spirits, especially once you'd established that, beyond the ferry port, the whole country was like one gigantic field, in which a few roads had evolved down the years into little villages. But the villages themselves seemed (remember, I was a London kid who grew up only one bridge away from Chelsea) dingy, mediocre little places, with boring, old-fashioned clothes shops, white net curtains in all the houses, pitiful chipped statues of the Virgin Mary beside the till in the grocery stores, and pubs which bore names like O'Hagan's or Toner's instead of those noble and mysterious London pub names like The Marquis of Granby or The Dog and Blanket.

We would stop in one of the pubs for lunch – my father would spend five minutes persuading my mother it was the 'lounge bar' of a 'hotel', not just a horrible pub – and, through the gloom and the bars of motey sunlight, would be served mushroom soup and coarse ham sandwiches, which fought a doomed sensory skirmish with the smells of Bass and Jeyes Fluid coming from the public bar and the kitchen. There was always a television on in the background, with a football or hurling game in progress and Michael O'Hehir's urgent commentary of high cries. There was precisely nothing about it to attract a child, or, anyway, me.

My responses to the places we visited were limited in the extreme. Given my present-day sensitivities to all things Irish, I weep for the callowness of my reaction. Wexford, for all its beauty and its martial history, became fixed in my mind as the Sweetshop Place. It was where, aged seven, I plunged my hand into a vast jar of sweets as part of a competition. Find the blue one, the label said, and win a prize. I unwrapped the sticky paper and looked at the lump of chewy stuff in my hand. It was a brilliant blue, the blue of victory. 'Good man, yerself,' said the sweetshop owner. 'There's the lucky winner. Have ya a tip for Leopardstown as well?' I didn't know what he meant, but I'd never won anything before, and my heart swelled with triumph. The prize was a plastic aeroplane, launched by a long rubber band on a stick. It wasn't exactly a trophy but to me – short, nervous and far from home – it was a wonderful thing. Whatever kind of bliss we had on that holiday (and I remember lots of fun and games and other children, happily befriended), nothing could eclipse that moment of blue glory. Shocking – but I was only seven.

Likewise, when our holidays moved further afield, and the ferry trip my father chose became the shorter and more sensible crossing from Liverpool to Dublin, all I remember when we explored the town of Drogheda was 'the Head'. Drogheda, in County Meath on the eastern seaboard, is a town most famous for having been sacked, and its inhabitants brutally massacred, by Oliver Cromwell's troops on 2 September, 1649. Its most famous son, Oliver Plunkett, became the Catholic Bishop of Armagh in 1670 but was falsely accused of masterminding the Popish plot eight years later. He was shipped over to London for a fake trial, then hanged, drawn and quartered, and his remains thrown to scavenging dogs. Some enterprising fan retrieved his head and bore it back to Ireland where I discovered it, in all its grisly glory, in a Drogheda church.

Try to imagine what it was like to walk slowly up that aisle; the head was the first dead human thing I'd ever seen. The Blessed Oliver Plunkett, his head inside a celebratory glass-fronted little box, the face as still as if carved in margarine, the eyes closed, the whole exhibit redolent of an unguessable, 300-year-old horror. On family holidays to Lake Como in Italy I had routinely experienced Catholic iconography at its most grotesque, in the shrines of Bellaggio and Menaggio – bleeding-eyed crucifixions, arrow-dartboarded St Sebastians, wall-painted miracles involving the Virgin Mary floating above potential drowners or near-suicides. But the shock of encountering their spooky and blood-drenched forms was nothing compared to the frisson of seeing Saint Oliver's posthumous, decapitated, thin-lipped and true-life human agony on the altar steps in front of you. The fact that he'd been murdered and had his intestines torn out virtually on my family doorstep back in London left me with a sudden shudder of guilt for the antics of the Horrible English that was to be repeated a dozen times in the next few years as I learned more about Irish history.

Once we hit Galway, a whole round of family visits ensued. We wouldn't stay with relations – something to do with my mother's dislike of the Galway crew – but would fan out from a convenient hotel, and take in Athenry, Monivea, Belclare, Tuam and a dozen other bits of Galway where offshoots of the Walsh tribe were lurking.

We'd call on Uncle Walter and Aunt Agnes at my father's family home of Ballybacka. Walter was one of his older brothers, a large and powerful man with a delicate quality about him and the face of a noble Amerindian warrior, like Sitting Bull. Behind his steel spectacles his eyes were watchful and critical. He spoke little, and did so in a low growl, an epic rumble that made everything he said sound like something from Holy Writ.

A down-to-earth gentleman farmer who mucked out his stables and tossed hayricks along with the labourers, Walter was also a cultured and well-read man, the two sides combining in my favourite memory of him. We'd just arrived in the yard at Ballybacka one summer's day. My mother extended her thirty-denier-stockinged legs from the passenger seat, looking for a clean patch on the muddy ground where she could place her immaculate shoes. From the outhouse came the shambling figure of Walter in a string vest and some dilapidated old trousers, upon which he wiped his hands. Judging by the reverberative noise within, it was clear he had just left off milking the cows.

'Hello, Anne,' he growled, offering her his reeking hand. 'I'm sorry you've caught us a little *déshabillé . . .*' *Dayz-a beel.* It was one of the most stylish things I had ever heard a human being say.

Agnes, his wife, was a bit of a handful. She would coo over

Madelyn and me, and stroke my angelic head. Then, after a glass of Tio Pepe, she'd come over all skittish. She would dash about the house in a social frenzy, calling in on us children every so often to ask, 'Would ye eat an apple?', before haring off again, reappearing ten minutes later to ask, 'Did ye get yer apple?' And perhaps twenty minutes after that, 'Did ye enjoy yer apple?'

I got the impression that she and my mother didn't much care for each other. Their exchanges were too polite, their conversation too brittle. My mother was wary of being in the Walsh family headquarters, with the brother who'd got all the family land, while Agnes was wary of my mother's metropolitan condescension. You could sense them prowling around each other, trying to sniff out the other's secrets. You could see my mother looking around the room, the way some ladies do, not actually saying anything about her sister-in-law's taste, decor, colour sense or cleaning regimen, but somehow implying a whole roster of criticisms.

We'd leave Ballybacka amid a shower of kisses and waves and a last prospect of dismal, muddy fields amid the rain. We never stuck around. My mother would never have stood for it. We'd call in on Aunt Peggy, one of Dad's younger sisters, and her husband Packy Moran, who ran a pub in Monivea, a tiny Galway village arrayed on two sides of a patch of grass as wide as a Paris boulevard. It was a place unique in my experience, for having a village green that was bigger than the village itself; later on, when Ireland was reinventing itself as a haven for tourists, I saw Monivea described in a brochures as 'boasting one of the widest streets in Europe'.

Moran's, was and is, a friendly little boozer where everybody drank in the public section and nobody, except fastidious Irish matrons, ever went near the chilly 'Lounge' section. It catered entirely for locals and was old-fashioned enough to sell freshly caught herrings on the bar. They lay in a fishy pile on a single dinner plate, their dead eyes shining like people who can't get to sleep but are loth to relinquish their recumbent posture. The uppermost one was gaffed by a little sign bearing their price – 2/6 each.

One day (I must have been about ten) I was leaning on the bar, watching the television, when a man came in and stood about six yards to my right, ordered a pint and said: '. . . and I'll take a couple of herrin's, Missus.'

'Help yourself,' said Aunt Peggy, busy with the till.

The man sorted through the silvery plateful and my attention wandered back to the television – until that is, I felt a clammy sensation on the back on my hand where it rested on the bar. I looked down. A predatory fish was trying, apparently, to nibble my fingers. I jumped back startled. The man whose fiddly endeavours had sent the herring slithering down the bar to attack me, raised a finger in the air and said: 'Sorry there.'

When not being attacked by local sealife, we'd gather in the back kitchen under the twin pictures of the well-known Irish saints: Pope John XXIII and President Kennedy. Little plastic figurines of the Virgin Mary stood on the TV and the aroma of washed clothes warmly pervaded the place with a domestic fug. Peggy would make tea for my mother and Packy would ferry drinks for my father from the bar where he presided.

He was a good egg, with thick spectacles, an efflorescent nose, and the air of a man endlessly on the point of amusement without actually telling jokes. He and my father talked politics and sport, and said: 'Oh, that's a good one' all the time, like people in a William Trevor novel, while Peggy gossiped with my mother about relations. Aunt Peggy had a way of saying: 'well now, anything new or strange?', which I later realised was a formulation you might have heard one or two hundred years before – asking returning travellers for news from the outside world. It implied 'if you can't bring an update on people we know, at least tell us something weird or peculiar, of battles or dragons or men with two heads and twenty mistresses from you sophisticated voyaging *beyond*.'

Moran's was fun. The guilty thrill of being backstage in a pub combined with the warmth and security of the little kitchen, the fruitcake, the fugitive whiff of bolting fish, the paraphernalia of statues and pictures and embroidered cushions and religiosity – the absolute essence of small town sixties Ireland.

We visited a house where my father's cousin lived. It was called Lydican, and was presided over by a spectacular matriarch called Missus Pat. She was a frightening figure for a child. She seemed a hundred years old, dressed in black widow's weeds and confined to a chair before the grate – not an ordinary armchair but a serious raised-up throne on a dais. Anyone who came to the house had to be brought to see her, for she was a creature of great inquisitiveness. She would inspect visitors, especially total strangers, at close quarters, touch them, feel their limbs and deliver judgement upon them. Once she wound a bony arm around my sister's thirteen-year-old waist and delivered her report: 'Arrah,' she said in her cracked and eldritch voice, 'a fine fat girleen.' Madelyn was thrilled, naturally.

Several of the old men my father went visiting were also called Pat. They seemed after a while, indistinguishable. They wore flat caps and grey tweed jackets and gumboots, and fluffy grey wires grew on their red-marbled cheeks like lichen or samphire. One kept bees and showed me his hive, lifting out the great honeycomb like a prize sculpture. Another took me round the front of the house and pointed to a tree filled with jackdaws: 'I've seen four o'them fellers lift the wire mesh guard off a chimney-pot, so they could build their nests in the warr-um,' he told me. 'I swear to God, they've got surveyors and engineers among them, and builders and carpenters, and doctors and midwives too . . .'

We visited more cousins, Maisie and Teresa, and sibling spinsters who hobbled about with tea and slices of cake, in hushed rooms with circular chenille doilies on occasional tables, and a loud, ploddingly heavy ticking of grandfather clocks. 'Now show some respect,' Dad would say, 'she's a fantastic woman.'

We would go walkabout in the streets of Galway, where my father would often start, like a deer who has seen the sidling leopard, and would abruptly jump on an ageing man in a mackintosh, yelling: 'James McNamara! Put it there!'

They would have some manly chat for a few minutes, and Dad's old friend would say: 'So this is one of yours Martin – a fine little fellow' and extract five shillings from his pocket. It occurred to me, at the age of ten, that nobody in England ever thought of doing that, of giving you a cash reward just because you were a fine little fellow. Would you get less if you were spotty or pigeon-toed?

Once or twice we'd meet an old girlfriend of my father's. One was a voluptuous, barmaidish lady called Nora who had merry eyes and a theatrical manner.

'Just the two kids is it Martin?' she asked saucily. 'I have six. Sure you'd have been better off with me all along, wouldn'tcha?' My father blushed with pleasure.

★

We never stayed in Galway, we just kept moving on, like a royal progress. In my head Ireland became a place of endless transit, without a real home in which to ground ourselves – like the larger life my parents were living, uncertainly gravitating between one country and another. We stayed in hotels with okay-Catholic names like the Sacre Coeur, where my parents made friends with the owners and promised to come back every year. There were genteel dinner-dances, for which my mother dressed up in rustling gold silk and my father prowled around the bar in a tuxedo, furiously smoking and looking like Humphrey Bogart in search of a casino.

We traversed the country. I got to know the town of Moate, a flatly-named place whose single distinction was that it lay exactly midway between Dublin and Galway and was, consequently, where most families, packed into their Vauxhalls and Rovers, chose to break their journey for a snack.

I found more and more triumphantly unprepossessing towns. One in a place called Feakle (did they have a newspaper called *The Feakle Matter*?), Madelyn and I were left stranded in a youth club bar while our parents went off visiting friends, and a row broke out. Some local boys, who had been denied access to the bar-billiards table by a slim youth from out of town, decided to gang up on him.

'Where're ye from?' they demanded.

'Mayo,' he said.

'Where in Mayo?'

'Ballyhaunis.'

The locals looked to their leader to deliver the killer blow. 'Hah!' he said, a thick-set gobshite in a V-necked sweater and greasy red hair, 'Balhaunis? *That* place.' He looked at his cronies.

'You know where he means lads?' They shook their heads. 'Ballyhaunis is only known fer one thing. And that's fer bein' the *arsehole* of the *worruld*.' His cronies shook with laughter. That was telling him. But the out-of-towner was unfazed:

'Nobody's who's been round Ireland could ever think that,' he said with deadly certainty. 'Not if they'd ever spent ten minutes in *this* kip.'

The redhead's eyes boiled. Rhetoric deserted him. 'Why you . . .' he said, like John Wayne in a saloon bar. A small unconvincing fight ensued, with a lot of pushing but not much punching.

Small town Irish civic pride didn't lend itself to anything as interesting as a punch-up, at least not with another small town Irishman. They knew they were in this together: that feeling of hopeless provincialism and ambiguous dreams of leaving – or dreams, at least, of ever getting out with a high and positive heart. Like millions of Irish men and women, they knew they couldn't stay here, where jobs were scarce and getting scarcer. They knew that life had to be grasped elsewhere; but they also knew their destiny was out of their hands, that they were for export. Wherever they ended up – London, New York, Toronto, Sydney – it would be because of financial need rather than existential choice.

How hard it must have seemed, at a time when English and American people were discovering the Kerouacian road, and the trail to Samarkand, the well-heeled dream of Elsewhere, to find that exile was a necessity not a hippie whim.

There was more fun to be had in West Cork, where we holidayed when I was twelve. The fishing village of Schull is on the southwestern promontory of Ireland, the final Cornwall-ish bit of country that extends its long exploratory fingers into the Atlantic. Despite its off-puttingly gothic name, it turned out to be an amazingly pretty place, its harbour crammed with yachts, its townsfolk as confident and sleek as any self-respecting yachting community in Chichester or Portsmouth.

Madelyn and I, left to our own devices, entered the life-saving course for young teens down by the harbour. She discovered a twenty-year-old lifeguard called Aidan, whose blond curls and blue eyes drove her into frenzies of teenage rapture. The fact that he was also training for the priesthood gave him, in addition, a *noli-me-tangere* charm. We hovered around the harbour like impatient seagulls.

I befriended a boy called Taig, and we hung out together, kicking tin cans down the street and talking about spies on television. I was a huge fan of *The Man From Uncle*, starring Robert Vaughan as Napoleon Solo and the flaxen-haired David McCallum, the girls' favourite, as Ilya Kuriakin. I loved it. It was the best thing in the world. Taig disoblingingly opined that, though the *Uncle* show was okay for, say, eejit twelve-year-olds, the only really good spy programme was *I Spy*, a similar buddy-espionage series with Robert Cup and Bill Cosby.

I'd never heard of it. It hadn't reached British TV yet.

'Oh it's marvellous,' he said. 'It's great. The two guys are meant to be international tennis players but they're working for American

Intelligence, and they were in Japan, and China and Hong Kong and them places, and always fighting off nasty villains. The dialogue was the key, the cross-talk between the two leads, 'twas marvellous. I'm surprised, now, a fella like you from London hasn't come across it.'

I grated my teeth with fury. It sounded wonderful. On our walks to the harbour Taig proceeded to evince a total recall of the finest conversational drolleries between Culp and Cosby, at which I laughed; myself, I couldn't remember a single amusing thing that Napoleon Solo had ever said to Ilya Kuriakin.

But I liked Taig. He was the same age as me, and considerably tougher, and had urchin freckles and a cow-lick of black hair over one eye. We climbed over rock pools together, and ate fish and chips out of greaseproof paper. We met up with local girls, two sisters called Brid and Celia. A photograph from that summer shows the four of us sitting on a bed. Taig is sitting beside Celia, looking like Bryan Ferry, cool and sussed at twelve. I have Brid's arm round my neck, and I am mugging for the camera, in a get-me-outa-here pose, as though in some *Carry On* movie.

How could I compete? I couldn't start watching *I Spy*. I was no good with girls. I could hardly brag about the wonders of the South Circular Road to a boy who lived in a fishing-village paradise in the roar of the Atlantic. I could bring up the Beatles and the Stones as part of my birthright, but he seemed to know more about their lives than I did ('that Brian Jones, he takes drugs. An' he was married and left his wife and kid. And he's only any good on the harmonica anyway . . .')

So, I started to talk like him. I started to say 'eejit' and 'fecker' and 'Is that right?' – not so obviously that it might seem like a parody, I just fed them into the conversation. Climbing on the rocks, taking a rowing boat with Taig around the headland, I started to sound like an Irish boy. I went back to saying 'cant' rather than 'carnt'. Taig didn't seem to notice. At any rate he made no comment, but I detected a chill in the air between us. The holiday came to an end. As my parents were packing, and Madelyn was trying to nail the flaxen seminarian for a last, desperate tryst, I went up the road to Taig's house to say goodbye. Halfway there, he appeared with half a dozen teenagers, his gang of buddies.

'Howya,' I said to him 'D'ja think there'll be any dacent fishin' to be had off the pier?'

There was an awful silence. One of the teenagers sniggered.

'You still here?' Taig said coldly. 'I thought you'd be gone by now.'

'Me Dad is after–' I faltered, '–is after packin' up the car.' Disastrously my new accent failed me at the last moment. I said 'caaahr' to rhyme with 'Tsar'. The sniggering boy burst out laughing. Clearly, Taig had told them about the English boy who was trying to talk like a Mick.

I felt like crying. Taig simply turned on his heel and walked off. The others went with him, up the hill, leaving me desolate. After a few yards, one of the gang turned round, looked at my stranded form, halfway up the hill. 'Go on home,' he shouted, 'y'English bastard.' Hearing it, the sniggerer turned. He picked up a small stone and flung it. It whizzed by my head. The others laughed, and searched on the ground for more missiles. A dozen pebbles came flying through the air. Two of them bounced off my chest. I turned round and ran down to the town, turned right, then left, and found the street where my parents were packing to leave.

'Where have you been John?' asked my father. 'Saying goodbye to the lads? I'll bet you won't forget this trip in a hurry.'

In the back of the Renault, tears pricked my eyes. I tried to forget my brief career as a Cork mudlark. I tried to stifle the fact that I'd been run out of town just for being insufficiently convincing. But then, my impersonation of an Englishman hadn't been much good either. That was always the way in Ireland for me, between five and twelve: puzzlement, alien voices, blue bubble gum, decapitated martyrs, hotels, weird or silent relatives; and always, always, moving on to somewhere else.

VIII

UP WENT NELSON

By the age of thirteen, I had Ireland sussed. As a geographical place, it was next-door-land but was, frankly, about as interesting as the neighbours in Battersea Rise. Sure, you'd see them parking their cars and re-pointing their walls every year, and coming and going listlessly, but you had no relationship with them. Certainly you'd never dream of visiting them, let alone think of going to live with them.

Ireland was an odd, muddy, indistinct place, full of fields without definition, shop-windows that offered nothing of the slightest interest, elderly relatives in vests and milking gear, broken-down old men who kept bees and talked very slowly, old women in the street with no make-up or sense of direction, dozy little towns where everybody stayed indoors all the time and you were expected to drink soup for your lunch, dingy holiday hotels where nobody ever noticed you, radios that played plinkety-plonk fiddle music on a folkloric tape loop, mild green hills and sweet valleys with funny names, televisions which had a chap reading the news in what appeared to be Russian. Everyone wore tweedy clothes, everyone seemed slightly cross, everything appeared to be broken, from the cars by the roadside to the crumbling wallpaper in your aunt's kitchen. A stay-home, constipated, unadventurous spirit prevailed wherever you went, in Wexford, Galway, Clare, Sligo. There were cows and horses and pigs and sheep to be seen but they didn't correspond to the tidy farmyard retreats where the kids in

English storybooks routinely went on their holidays. It was not an attractive picture. You were, on the whole, quite relieved to get back to London after one of our family excursions to this blank and dismal retreat.

Back in Swinging London, I would leaf through the Irish newspapers and magazines that my parents were sent by relations, as I looked for clues as to what Ireland might be about. There were few signs of hip goings-on, of youthfulness, of up-to-dateness. In the *Connaught Tribune*, the local paper of the West, Hollywood and rock 'n' roll seemed not to have established any foothold. The local dances featured special appearances by a bunch called Big Tom and the Mainliners, a promisingly druggy name, although it turned out to refer to simple railroad folk. The Gallowglass Ceilidh Band, whose records were propped up beside our gramophone for years, were still going, not wholly supplanted in trendiness by the cool new arrivals, such as Johnny McAvoy and Brendan Shine and a wild combo called The Cowboys, all kitted out in Stetsons and revolvers and yee-hah fringed jackets. The cinema at Ballinasloe showed double-bills of old Bogart movies in black and white. It all seemed hopelessly provincial.

One Irish magazine was *Our Boys*. It was aimed at youths of my age, and carried manly stories of derring-do on the football and hurling pitch, with a section of schoolboy jokes and puzzles. It was not a patch on *Valiant* and *Hotspur* and *Eagle*. Another was *Dublin Opinion*, a kind of Irish *Punch*, full of grown-up jokes about people called De Valera and Lemass, and lots of cartoons featuring animals and desert islands.

Another journal, called *Ireland's Own*, was similarly full of incisive little features about Irish politics – satirically intentioned but baffling to an English kid and featured words to extremely old Irish songs, as a kind of party aid. One page in particular intrigued me each month. It featured a woodcut that seemed to belong to a different era. It was a celebration of the peasant spirit, the 'old ways', and showed, for example, a heavy countrywoman lifting her skirts above a flounce of massive petticoats, as she got stuck into a dance at a country fair. It would be captioned with some brisk rubric like 'At the Hop' or 'A Hoolie in the Kitchen', and you couldn't tell if its intention was satirical or celebratory. I was just about alive to irony and sarcasm. I could tell the difference between an illustration and a cartoon. You could tell whether a depiction was meant to make you laugh or not.

I would look at these monochrome pages and be baffled. Should you be laughing at this gross Irish matron lifting her skirt, her face twisted in gargoylish rapture, or were you looking at something like an oil painting – like the Dutch peasants we were taken to see in the National Gallery – and encouraged to admire it? I hadn't a clue.

At the time, I was playing piano pieces. One of them was a tiny *jeu d'esprit* by Bela Bartok called 'Peasant Dance'. The piece was easy to play but unattractive, full of plonking discords. Boink-bink, boink-bink, boink-a-bink. 'It's supposed to sound odd at the start,' said my music teacher, 'because it's meant to represent a discordant peasant orchestra, all rhythm and no subtlety. Try to imagine lumbering rustics in their work clothes, trying to show off on the dance-floor without quite knowing the steps.'

Next time I came for a lesson, I brought the illustration from *Ireland's Own*. 'Like this woman?' I asked.

'Exactly,' she replied. 'Full of stamping and glory.'

Aha! So the point of the illustration was to glory in this fat lady's not knowing *how* to dance but *trying* to dance anyway. It seemed an odd thing to be celebrating. It was a far cry from my mother's favourite magazine, *The Lady*, a thin and glossy English production containing lots of pictures of Princess Margaret, advice about bedding plants, articles headed 'Do You Know About This Tea?' and small-ads for 'Ladies' Companions', 'Home Helps' and 'Paying Guests'.

By now I was going to dances for the first time, at the parish hall in Wimbledon where the abject losers among us still wore their school blazers and gazed at the Convent girls in their short pink dresses with daring holes cut around the armpits and midriff. Flowery shirts began to appear at the local department store, and I longed to own them all. But when I bought one and secreted it home, I looked terrible, a pale weed dressed up as a begonia bed.

One day, something different arrived in the youth-fashions department of Arding & Hobbs, our local store. It was a gold lamé shirt. It sparkled when you tilted it this way and that. It was a deep, burnt, sexy gold colour and must, I thought, confer instant attractiveness on anyone who bought it. I asked my mother if she would do so.

'John,' she said, when I'd dragged her into Arding & Hobbs to see it. 'What can you be thinking of? Never, never, in a thousand years, will you ever wear such a shirt.' She seemed shocked. I was baffled. What on earth could be wrong with it?

'But Mum . . .' I said.

'I don't want to hear another word,' she said. 'I don't want you dressing like those . . . those *awful people*.'

It became a talking-point among my mother's lady friends who sat in the kitchen discussing my wayward taste in clothes. They took sides:

'D'you like them kipper tie yokes, John? I think they're desperate. They're just for the likes of yer man on the radio, what's his name, Tony Blackbird . . .'

'Do you like the see-through blouses, Anne?' Mother's friend Rosemary would enquire, saucily. 'Wouldja wear one o'them things yourself? You'd have patients flockin' to the door and half o'them wouldn't be patients at all.'

'And the mini-skirts are a great invention so they are,' Mrs Regan would say. 'Did you see Monica from Lavender Gardens walkin' around in a little mini that'd hardly . . . hardly keep the flies off her, and her blue with the cold?'

Sooner or later they would return to me and my supposed passion for trendy clothes. Rosemary would wind my mother up about 'the lurex shirt' I coveted, insisting that every English fashion magazine was crammed with pictures of gold lamé chemises, as if it were the cornerstone of every young person's wardrobe.

'Sure, poor Seaneen, he's only wantin' to look like one of them fellers in the Rolling Stones,' she said once. 'Lookit John, tell me how much it costs, and I'll buy it for you myself.'

My mother hit the roof.

'You will do no such thing,' she said in a fury. 'Don't encourage the children to defy their mother.' Rosemary shrank back in her chair as if my mother's fangs had raked her cheek. 'I am not having my son dressing up like those . . . awful people.'

Jesus. Who *were* these guys? Pop stars? (These were the days before they mutated into 'rock stars'). What did she have against pop stars? She didn't like John Lennon, because he was rude to figures of authority (and she didn't care for that reedy Liverpool delivery either). She didn't like Mick Jagger because of his raw-liver lips and his slouchy posture; if she'd met him in the street, she'd have told him to stand up straight and take his hands out of his pockets. She didn't like Donovan because she thought he was bonkers (she'd heard the 'Electrical banana' line on 'Mellow Yellow'); she was also suspicious of the marital circumstances of whoever was 'rising' in the 'morning' on his song 'Colours' ('In the mornin'/ That's the time/ That's the time/ When Ah bin loved'). Mother treated pop music as a frightful cacophony, several miles removed from the songs she grew up listening to, but also as a kind of coded subversion. Embedded in the lyrics, she knew, were terrible secrets, immoral suggestions, casual allusions to impure activity, encouragements to the young to wear tiny skirts and tight hipsters (and lamé shirts), do lots of kissing, play with themselves, go to parties and behave, under cover of darkness, in shocking ways beyond the chilly rules of the catechism. She listened with horror to the chorus of 'Let's Spend the Night Together' and practically fainted when she heard The Troggs singing 'Wild Thing.' She looked at Dusty Springfield's pitch-dusted black eyes and at Sandie Shaw's bare feet and knew something was going badly wrong with young people in this country. Was this what she meant by 'those awful people'?

It was only when I bought a leather forage cap, in emulation of Dylan (and Lennon) that she suddenly came out with it. 'Take that thing off,' she said severely. 'I'm not having you turning into one of those will-do-can-do people down the road. You're better than that. You come from a nice family. Those people are worthless. Why do you want to be one of them?'

I could see she was genuinely upset. 'Why do I want to be like one of who?' I asked, baffled.

'One of them will-do-can-do people down the road.' Her eyes filled with tears. 'Because I didn't bring you up, and drive you to school year after year for you to turn into . . . into . . .'

The penny dropped. The local market traders down our way had been putting on the style. They'd taken to wearing winkle-picker shoes and Dylan caps and growing their hair over their collars and looking cool. Soon they'd be turning up for work, at the greengrocer's stall or the wet-fish shop, in Afghan waistcoats and yellow loon pants. And as they served my mother, as she asked for two pounds of carrots, they said 'Will do, love' and 'Can do, my darlin'', until she'd started to squirm. The ignorance of some people, she'd have said to herself, and the familiarity. Did they not know they were talking to the doctor's wife, who once sat at a walnut dining table with the finest quality people in the land? And somewhere, in her horror about the people one had to deal with, day by day, in this un-aristocratic dive called Battersea, a small suspicion had crept into her imagination and lodged there like a virus: the thought that I, her son, the skinny English gentleman she was trying to 'rear', was secretly evolving into one of the Northcote Road desperadoes. Despite all her hand-rearing, her organisational energy, her search for good schools and her moral example, I was going to turn into an English yob, a hirsute, round-shouldered, coarsely-spoken good-for-nothing. Any minute now, I'd start calling her 'Doll' and my father 'Squire' and hawking globules of phlegm into the gutter.

I tried to reassure her, but I was secretly pleased. For I was a wild revolutionary outlaw. I performed shocking acts of civil disobedience, like walking up the stairs at Clapham Common tube station when the sign at the top clearly stated, 'other side up'. (Sadly, there was nobody around to see.) I adopted the look and swagger and pose of a rebel, only occasionally frustrated by my mother's counter-revolutionary tactics. I tried to grow my hair over the collar of my school blazer, and was sent off to the barber's on Lavender Hill on a Friday morning, to have it pruned to convict proportions. I tried to coax some rudimentary bumfluff on my cheek into sideburns, but it was a doomed enterprise. I tried to smoke my father's Guards cigarettes (disgusting), his pipe and Holland House tobacco (too fiddly) and his Henri Wintermans cigars (too pungent). I concealed stolen cigarettes in ingenious hiding places (two of them down the hollow legs of a plastic Airfix model of Napoleon), smoked them on the train from school to Clapham Junction, craftily applied a breath-renewing potion called Gold Spot to my tongue (it tasted like earwax) and went home, where my mother immediately, and angrily demanded: 'Have you been smoking?'

The only small rebellion I actually won concerned the picture in my bedroom. I wasn't allowed to decorate my own room to suit myself; it remained a huge, gloomy spare room at the top of the house, with a great walnut wardrobe, a bookcase and two beds. Expressions of personal taste weren't allowed. The wallpaper was classy, striped fleur-de-lys stuff that wasn't put up just so that I could Blu-Tack pictures of girls onto it. Mostly I said nothing. But one day Mother put a framed picture of the Sacred Heart on the wall, with Christ walking along a foggy pathway extending his flayed heart for all to see, and I complained loudly. Mother gave me one of her sad-but-understanding, Madonna-of-All-Sorrows looks, to indicate that even the best and most virtuous mothers have sometimes to carry the burden of their Godless children. Two days later, I took down the frame, removed the picture and substituted a colour print of the Rokeby Venus by Velasquez. As rebellion goes, it was a masterstroke. In theory, my mother should have found a thousand objections (taste, virtue, morality, religious belief) to my replacing the image of the Redeemer with a picture of a large naked female bottom. But this was incontro-vertibly art. She knew that the wanton hussy lying there so languor-ously, studying her naked chest and her vain little face in a mirror held by a cherub, was, despite all signs to the contrary, fine art. It was the kind of thing Lord David Cecil and his friends would have gone into raptures about. He probably had the original in one of his drawing rooms. She couldn't criticise it without opening herself to accusations of being provincial, a foolish chit of a girl, with no clue about the sophisticated world out there. The Rokeby Venus went up on my wall and stayed up in her glory, long after I'd got sick of the sight of her.

Oh, I was a mad one, all right. I was desperate to be cool. And at the time, nothing in the world seemed less cool than Ireland. The ladies chattering in mother's kitchen were part of a hopelessly ancient and out-of-date world for whom my generation had no respect, just as we were rapidly going off the church and its irritable priests. We were starting to live for clothes and pop music and X-films. I was still too young at thirteen to actually get to see these movies, but their very existence, the spikiness of that four-pronged 'X', the hint of unutterable wickedness that leaked out of posters and trailers and newspapers made me swoon with sinful rapture.

On Saturday evenings, my family used to go to St Mary's Church, a handsomely Gothic monstrosity near Clapham Common, in order to attend the Novena, a glum half-hour parade of prayers and sermons which, if you attended it nine times in a row, qualified you for special blessings or a couple of weeks off your sentence in Purgatory. The only real interest I took in going near the place was the road where my father parked the car. There was a big movie poster site on the corner. It changed every week, but seemed to specialise in shockers. *Maniac* was illustrated by a pair of huge staring eyes and the legend: 'Don't go alone – take a brave, nerveless friend with you!' *The Damned* showed a lot of radioactive children gazing out of a prison somewhere that looked like Dorset. Even they (poor mites) were evidence of a far more entrancing world than the gloomy church service we were about to go in to, with its ranks of lonesome, tubercular, badly-dressed oddballs listlessly singing the *Ave Maria*.

And what were Madelyn and I doing there on a Saturday night anyway? The whole sixties world was shouting for us to join in, to pile in and be groovy. There were names in the arty press like Antonioni and Mary Quant, allusions to pubic hair and contraception. This was 1966. England won the World Cup and the nation fell in love with a toothless curiosity called Nobby Stiles. Something called satire turned up on television on Saturday nights, in which a chap called John Bird pretended to be the prime minister and puffed a pipe in a parodic way. My parents watched it all, filled with nostalgia for the days before Young People started running the country. Once my mother was making conversation with Madelyn's clever friend Catherine. The conversation turned to TV shows.

'And Val Doonican is always wonderful, isn't he?' gushed Mamma. 'Don't you just love Val, Catherine?'

'I certainly do, Mrs Walsh,' said Catherine. 'In fact I'm such a fan that I'm going to knit him a jumper with his initials on the front.'

'Oh, that would be love . . .' said my mother.

Bliss it was in that dawn to be young and groovy. London, by the reckoning of no less an arbiter than *Time* magazine, was the swingingest city in the world. But Ireland figured in none of it.

But there was, amazingly, one area where Ireland got a foothold on my attention. In the spring of that year, in an event hardly mentioned in the English papers, the IRA blew up Lord Nelson. Not, obviously, the column in Trafalgar Square, London, but Nelson's Pillar in O'Connell Street in the heart of Dublin. It was a bizarre colonial insult that the great British seadog should still be standing on a memorial plinth in the centre of the Irish capital over forty years after Ireland had gained her independence. But, beyond a few passing insults (in *Ulysses*, Stephen Dedalus tells a story about a Dublin lady leaning over the wired-off platform at the top of the pillar, spitting plum-stones onto the people below, uncomfortably aware of the 'one-handed adulterer' looming above her in his imperialist glory) it had escaped injury. Early in March, the top half of the pillar was blown up and Nelson had landed in bits all over Dublin 1. Nobody was hurt, so professionally contained and discreet was the blast. But when Dublin Corporation came to remove the stump that remained, they shattered every window for half a mile around. The Dublin crowd loved it.

Ireland's Own and *Dublin Opinion* treated the monstrous outrage of a bomb as a colossal, guilty jape. The IRA enjoyed a brief period of being thought splendid fellows. Across the sea in London my father beamed with pleasure.

1966 was, by an accident of birth, his special year. He had turned fifty in January. The year of his birth, 1916, was one of the most significant in Irish history – it was the year of the Easter Rising when a handful of Irish intellectuals, poets and believers in 'blood sacrifice' occupied the General Post Office in O'Connell Street and issued a proclamation on behalf of the 'Provisional Government of the Irish Republic'. The British Army, distracted from the larger war in Europe, moved in and crushed the Rising in a week. 450 people were killed, 2600-odd were injured and, barely a month later, the British government passed ninety death sentences, commuted most of them but still summarily executed fourteen of the rebellion's leaders.

My father was never a hotly political Irishman. If anyone had wanted it in writing he would have written 'Nationalist' rather than 'Republican'. As an Anglicised, middle-class Battersea doctor, he was ardently Conservative; even when confronted by the spectacle of such frightfully English leaders as Sir Alec Douglas-Home and Edward Heath, he could not bear the prospect of voting for a Labour government. He had evidently been warned off the doctrine of socialism as a young man, seeing it as a charter of equality that favoured the indigent, the drunk and the work-shy (undoubtedly Great-Uncle Martin's view). But at the anniversary of the Irish Revolution, his heart swelled for the old IRA. He turned into a Fenian 'rebel dog' (the one my mother had once impersonated in an amateur play). He told Madelyn and me about the Rising, about Michael Collins and Padraig Pearse and Connolly and MacBride and De Valera. He got Madelyn to recite Pearse's Gaelic poem '*Mise Eire*' (I am Ireland/ I am older than the Old Woman of Beare . . .) at her school assembly. He dug out a poem by Louis MacNeice called 'Dublin', which seemed to foreshadow, in 1939, the events of 1966:

> *Grey brick upon brick,*
> *Declamatory bronze*
> *On sombre pedestals –*
> *O'Connell, Gratton, Moore –*
> *And the brewery tugs and the swans*

On the balustraded stream
And the bare bones of a fanlight
Over a hungry door
And the air soft on the cheek
And porter running from taps
With a head of yellow cream
And Nelson on his pillar
Watching his world collapse.

I'd never known the old man so fired up about Ireland. Because I still desultorily collected stamps, he sent off for a complete set of the Irish Rising commemoratives: the *Oifig an Phoist* (or Post Office) had done the revolution proud, bringing out handsome portraits of the fourteen dead freedom fighters. I carried them proudly around with me in my wallet and sneaked a look at them now and again. They didn't look like revolutionaries, more like schoolmasters – stern and beaky coves with spectacles and pince-nez, all except Pearse who was handsome and clean-cut and looked a bit like a curate, or one of the silly-ass suitors that might call on Lord Emsworth's pretty nieces in the novels of P. G. Wodehouse.

With admirable speed, the tiny Irish recording industry brought out two songs to commemorate the O'Connell street blast. One was by The Dubliners. It began with Ronnie Drew's marvellous rasp:

Pewer oul' Admiral Nelson is no longer in the air –
Toora-loora-loora-loora-loo.
On the eight day of March, in Dublin city fair –
Toora-loora-loora-loora-loo.

And ended:

. . . Old Nelson took a powther an' he flew –
Tell the Dublin Corporation, it's a service to the nation,
So poor old Admiral Nelson, toora-loo.

Once we knew what it was all about, we howled with laughter. There was a second version called 'Up Went Nelson', a more manic song which began with a spectacular explosion. The lyrics were written as though by the bombers' fan club:

Early one morning in the year of '66,
A band of Irish laddies were knockin' up some tricks.
The corporation thought that Nelson overstayed a mite,
So we helped him on his way with some sticks o'gelignite.

Madelyn and I played it again and again, opening the windows of the living room so the initial explosion would disturb the traffic going by outside on the South Circular Road. Dad beamed with delight and said: 'Don't play it too loud, or the police will be round here looking for suspects.'

It was heady stuff. In the year of the Beatles' ground-breaking 'Revolver' album and the Beach Boys' seminal classic 'Pet Sounds', when these defining sounds of the sixties' pop revolution were being played on every clued-up Londoner's tinny hi-fi, when everything was changing in advertising agencies and TV drama departments, and the first boutiques were appearing, and the whole idea of 'revolution' was yet to be marketed as a Zeitgeisty fashion statement, when the Summer of Love was a year away, when the year of student revolutions and global upheaval from Prague to Ohio State University, and the fiery rhetoric of Tariq Ali and Daniel Cohn-Bendit, and the Stones singing 'Street Fighting Man' were still two years off, this was a small, localised rebellion that my sister and I took passionately to our hearts. It was our own. It was our Rising, our Rebellion. Nobody we knew at school had anything to feel half so passionate about. Like deracinated Cubans, we revelled in our proxy insurrection. We cheered the bombers, God forgive us; we saluted the detonation of an imperialist monument in a city that we barely knew. We hurrah-ed and cheered the seeing-off of the ghastly British yoke. We watched Dad's face become a radiant, cherry-cheeked glow of national pride, and egged him on to tell us more about the Rising. We learned about the Black and Tans, the nasty, paramilitary wide-boys ('the dregs of English prisons' my father confided, 'released on the understanding that they'd keep the Irish seditionaries quiet, no matter how they did it'), and the iniquities they had inflicted on innocent Irish folk. I read about Patrick Pearse. He had an English father and an Irish mother, but I could hardly claim him as an in-betweenie like myself, since he spent most of his time trying to set up an educational system that was almost entirely Gaelic-Irish. He had a refreshingly brutal approach to the business of politics. Half poetic, half pragmatic, he wrote in 1913:

We must accustom ourselves to the thought of arms, to the sight of arms, to the use of arms. We may make mistakes in the beginning and shoot the wrong people; but bloodshed is a cleansing and sanctifying thing, and the nation that regards it as a horror has lost its manhood. There are many things more horrible than bloodshed; and slavery is one of them.

Around London, radical chic was getting under way: the image of Che Guevara was going up on posters, headbands, the awnings of hairdressers. It was an emblem of young revolution, made cool for the new generation of preening sixties narcissists. But I had a different revolution in my head, a different hero in Pearse, a struggle that was local in that it involved my grandparents and a time that was mystically connected to my father. Dad was, genuinely, a child of the revolution, born just before the flames. It meant something to me in a way no historic revolution could.

It didn't last, of course. By the end of the year, the Rising anniversary was a memory. My father had stopped talking about the Civil War and the Black and Tans, while Pearse's sanguine imagery about the 'Red Rose Tree' that blooms above the grave had loosened its grip on my imagination. He was, clearly, nuts: a poet trying to be a soldier and dying as a result.

The sixties London world closed over my head like a wave. I returned to pop music and to coaxing sideburns where none existed. I sneaked into my first X-rated film, *Dracula Has Risen From The Grave*, boasted about it at school, and discovered that most of my class had moved on to Swedish movies of teenage seduction. I bought the gold lamé shirt for 36/6, wore it to a parish hall dance and none of my friends would speak to me or stand anywhere near me. 'You look like a victim of the *Torrey Canyon*' commented my father, alluding to the famous oil slick disaster of the day. And of Irish matters, not a word was said. I was a groovy little Englishman in a glam shirt, a Simon Dee hairstyle and a Dave Dee Dozy Beaky Mick and Tich brain.

IX

THE ROAD TO GRAIG

It's odd to think that everything changed between me and Ireland because of a boy at school called Mark and a historical novelist called Jean Plaidy. They have only peripheral roles in this story, but as catalysts of events they were absolutely crucial. All Miss Plaidy did was to awaken in her readers a sudden interest in family history. And all Mark did was break my sister's heart.

Madelyn was sixteen and studying for her A-levels at the convent school in Wimbledon. Mark was sixteen too and in the year above me at Wimbledon College, geographically just one street away from the convent but sexually, a whole planetary system apart. Despite the best attempts by debaters, film-goers and the like to set up inter-school societies with regular after-school meetings and informal, ad hoc discussions afterwards with perhaps just a few bottles of Corona Cherryade in case anyone got terribly thirsty (or tongue-tied), there was no formal structure of meetings between the institutions. But like so many aspiring Romeos and Juliets, the College boys and Convent girls sometimes managed to circumvent the parents, nuns, priests and moral guardians, and would get it together in the cinema on Wimbledon Broadway every Saturday afternoon.

With Mark and Madelyn, it was more than that. It was young rapture. It was hot romance, the kind that involves whole days spent together, and long passionate walks on Surrey hillsides. He bought her a ring – not an engagement ring you understand, just a ring – and he met my parents and the Fitzpatricks across the Common. It was my pretty sister's first Big Love.

And I thought he was a bit of a star as well. He was a sporting hero at school and, being a year ahead of me, was unimaginably grown up. So when Mark promptly dumped Madelyn it was a tough break for all concerned.

She was desolate. Nothing in logic or literature, in the annals of betrayal or male fuckwittage, could absolve or explain his behaviour. Fleets of counsellors working round the clock, had any been available then, would hardly have begun to heal my sister's fractured heart. Her schoolwork suffered. She stayed in bed all the time. Her relationship with her mother, never in much danger of being confused with a millpond, deteriorated sharply. She was abandoned, bruised, damaged and in danger of failing her exams. What could be done?

My father stepped in. He was fairly clueless, I suspect, about the emotional needs of British teenage girls circa 1968, but he knew she needed some kind of psychic convalescence, far away from London, school and faithless boyfriends. Did she fancy going to Ireland?

She did, provided just the two of them went. She didn't want a hectoring mother around, telling where she had gone wrong and stealing her tragic limelight. She and Dad resolved that, as soon as she could get a week off school, they would go to Galway together. She wasn't, perhaps, expecting much. She had been several times before, met the uncles and aunts, seen the crumbling relics and evil smelling cowsheds, the flat fields and dry-stone walls and the hopelessly old-fashioned shops. But this meant more to her than a holiday; it was a hard-won freedom from everything she found oppressive about England. To take a week off school (the doctor's note from my father assured the headmistress that Madelyn was suffering from 'nervous exhaustion') to go on an all expenses paid jolly with her indulgent Papa in tow, a portly, fiftyish courtier to her impulsive queen, was a triumph of teenage manipulation.

There was one other consideration – her compulsive reading of the historical fiction of Jean Plaidy. Miss Plaidy had given her a taste for dynasties, for clans and royal intermarriages and wicked cousins and illegitimate offspring; all of these were represented by the vertical, horizontal and (rather shocking) dotted lines of the family tree. She had been making a family tree of her own in her bedroom. One evening by the fire in the sitting room, she went through it. There we were, Madelyn and John, down at the bottom, and our parents Martin and Anne, and their parents, Pat and Bridie and Henry and Margaret, and Anne's sisters Catherine and Bridie and Margaret, all in America, and Auntie Sister and John, the brother who died of TB; Martin's siblings, Walter and Father John, and Cecilia (who'd become Sister Rosalie and frightened me half to death on the stairs at four because of her bat-wing headdress), and Nora and Peggy . . . 'and don't forget Paddy,' said my father.

'But who,' asked Madelyn, 'is Paddy?'

Dad furrowed his brow. 'My youngest brother. You know Paddy. Paddy at Graig Abbey. You've met him.'

'No I haven't. I know all the others. I remember every *detail* about the Irish relations. Why have I never met Paddy?'

'Oh, that's right,' my father conceded. 'You'd have been about three when you saw him last.' My mother, reading the paper on the other side of the fire, stirred a little.

'But why not since?' Madelyn demanded. 'Why did we never visit him when we visited all the others? Is he so awful? Did you have a row or something?'

My father did not respond. 'Has he got any family?' Madelyn persisted, anxious to move onto the next line of the family tree.

'Paddy has six children,' said my father, quietly. 'And his wife's called Dolly.'

'*Six children!*' said Madelyn. 'Jesus. Are they old or young?'

'The youngest would be about your age.'

'And you've never said a word about them in – what? – *thirteen years?*'

My father was silent. Around my mother another, quite distinct silence seemed to glow.

'Well we'll go and see them *now*, shall we?' asked, or rather declared Madelyn. 'Just so I can tell them who I am?'

'Oh,' said my father, 'I suppose we might look in . . .'

At the bottom of this, of course, lay a row. It dated back to 1955: a classic Irish family row, compounded of short tempers, long memories and seething implacability. My parents had visited my uncle and aunt and their children, bearing Madelyn and me in the family Renault.

Everything was fine as Mother and Aunt Dolly sat outside in the sunshine on a rug, taking tea and admiring Madelyn's innocent curls and my enchanting dimples. My father took off in the car with Paddy to put a few quid on a horse. By the time they got back in the late afternoon everything was ruined for years.

The cause of the row was a man called Major Bowes Daly, a local huntsman, Master of the Galway Blazers for a record twelve seasons between 1928 and 1948, and a legendary figure. He had married a Mrs Trundle and, my mother maintained, treated her badly.

'Not at all,' said Dolly, 'he was a delightful man.'

'From what I hear,' said Mother firmly 'he was horrible to her.'

'Impossible,' snapped Dolly, 'you've been listening to the wrong people.'

'I have it on the highest authority,' said Mother.

'Anybody with an ounce of sense or judgement would know Bowes Daly is an admirable fellow,' said Dolly, 'though evidently you don't know anybody like that.'

'If you admire a man like that,' said Mother, 'there must be something badly wrong with you . . .'

And so it went on. When the men returned, Mother and Dolly were no longer speaking. Dolly was inside the house. Mother had remained outside with us children on the rug, refusing to come in, even though the cold evening was closing in. My father gathered up his stricken family and drove us away. That was the last Mother or Madelyn or I saw of them. Dad, it later appeared, had kept in touch with Paddy on the quiet, learned the news from Athenry, even bunged the older children a few quid when they were at university. But he hadn't ever mentioned them at home in Battersea. Because of a ridiculous difference of opinion about an Anglo-Irish huntsman, they'd remained a family secret.

Until now. Madelyn wrote to her newly discovered uncle at Graig Abbey and asked if she could come to visit. He wrote back by return of post, saying they'd be thrilled to see her. She and Dad were gone a week and when they came back, Madelyn was all smiles and was even civil to my mother in a newly *de haut en bas* fashion, as if recently admitted to some sorority from which mothers were barred. My father looked pleased with himself too, as if he'd won a prize and was entitled to smirk. But if they were asked how it went — if my mother asked, or if I asked in my mother's presence — they would act dumb. 'Oh lovely time,' they said, '*lovely*. The weather was great, thanks, and yeah, we saw a few of the relations, same as ever, and had a pretty relaxing time of it.' My mother was deeply suspicious but stopped asking after a while. But Madelyn explained all to me the first night home:

'John, you have *got* to come to Ireland with me soon. You have to meet the Graig Abbey lot. It's this fantastic big grey house outside Athenry, with acres of land and these huge rooms and an enormous wolfhound, and there's Aunt Dolly who sings and smokes like mad, and Caroline and Louise who play harps, and John, who's got this droopy moustache and plays the guitar, and Cecily who . . .'

It was a selling proposition. I got an hour of thumbnail sketches, with ancillary notes and digressions and rapt descriptions and much laughter. It was the first sign that my sister, until then as much a Londoner as Twiggy, had been overwhelmed by Ireland.

From that day to the day she went to live in Galway for good, she seemed never to have doubts. After growing up in Battersea for sixteen years, not knowing the neighbours, never playing in the street, having no sense of community beyond the throng of Irish exiles in the kitchen, she knew what she wanted – to be a part of a larger social organism, with roots, with history, with tradition, with the long, slow gestation period that makes a family into something dynastic. I felt no such need. But I wanted to see what all the fuss was about, to check out this extraordinary eruption of family into our lives so late into the day. So I went to see for myself.

We turned right off the main road, which stretched out towards to the horizon between two vast fields, a long, hundred-mile dead-straight Roman track, bisecting the bleak flatland. There were trees on the right, great high sycamores that might just hide some human habitation amid all this dismaying flat rusticity. Two hundred yards further, we passed a single house, set back from the road, that bore some minimal indication (an ice-cream sign?) that it might be a shop. Then, all at once, we came upon a pair of iron gates, set into two stone pillars that looked as if they'd been there for centuries. One of the gates was open. The other wasn't. 'So,' my father said, 'they're half-expecting us . . .' I got out and opened the left-hand one that creaked arthritically, got back in, and we drove through. Inside was a low stone bungalow, ruined, desolate, Wordsworthianly abandoned.

'There we are, John' said Madelyn. 'Whatcha think of Graig, then?'

'This is it?' I was crestfallen, but strove to conceal it. 'I thought it'd be *much* bigger.'

My father sniggered. 'Ah now,' he said, 'you'd be surprised how roomy it is, once you're inside.'

'Like the Tardis in *Doctor Who*,' said Madelyn.

'But this can't be the place,' I said crossly, 'How can they all be living in there? You said there was this staircase . . .'

I gazed at this ignorant little shack before us, willing it to be bigger, grander, more substantial. Madelyn and my father burst out laughing. It was, you see, the gate lodge. We drove on over a little bridge, beneath which water vibrated in the sunlight. Where were we going? Piebald cattle began to appear on the left. Huge trees lifted their mushroomy bulk in the faint wind. The air seemed to thicken in anticipation. The car was suddenly heavier, sweeping us like a weighty chariot towards some ceremonial shrine. I stopped looking from right to left and, with a sudden understanding, looked forward, past my father's bulky shoulder.

Up ahead, discreetly announcing itself a quarter-mile off, stood a grey mansion, quietly rearing out of the bleak countryside. I took in ivy-covered walls, a noble doorway, some kind of outhouse, a grass-covered mound like a sunken church. It was a little overwhelming: 'Don't go so fast,' I said to my father, silently, 'I can't handle all this at once.' We swept on.

The Rover swung round a semicircular drive and parked. From inside the house came the noise of barking, and, as we emerged from the car, the door was pulled open. A man I'd never met before, a man with a more weatherbeaten version of my father's face, stood in the doorway.

'Ah, Madeleen,' he said beaming. She hugged him proprietarily. 'And this,' she said, 'is your nephew, John, at last.' He seemed to shake with pleasure; the delight of having an old family feud suddenly patched up in a new generation.

'Well John,' he said, sticking out his hand, 'you're as welcome as the flowers in May.' We shook hands. My father, who'd been hanging back by the car to witness this significant moment, ushered us into an echoing hallway, where a picture of an African lion hung over the lintel, and everything we said reverberated. Beyond lay a cavernous, dark, flag-stoned passage. On either side, vast, embassy-sized state rooms with their doors ajar. I saw the lazy marmalade glow of a turf fire throwing shadows on the wall, and the moth-flickering light of candles in dark spaces. I felt as if I'd walked out of the dreary neutral rain into a burst of nineteenth-century splendour.

Within, all was rush and hospitality. The drawing room was the biggest reception room I'd ever been in, a room too large for ordinary furnishings. The mile-wide carpet didn't reach the skirting-boards. A long leather sofa seemed ludicrously small, as if left by the far wall as an afterthought of the removals men and forgotten by the owners. A banqueting table, as from some celebratory Valhalla, was pushed to one side, to enable visitors to walk about in front of the giant fireplace, crammed with blazing logs and a hecatomb of turf bricks. Toby jugs stood on the mantelpiece. Books filled the lonely space between the fireplace and the door.

By the fire sat Aunt Dolly. I'd heard all about her flamboyance, her idiosyncrasies, her style, her conversational mannerisms: she was a small, doll-like woman, rouged and broken-veined and smiling with a professional, Rank-charm-school smile that suggested an English sophisticate from the thirties, well used to greeting people she cared nothing about, although she just might make an exception in your case.

'*Soooooo*, this is John,' she cooed, and gave a thrilling laugh. 'And how's your dear mother?'

As I was negotiating this familial minefield, the cousins came in to greet the arrivals. One was Caroline, a stately eighteen-year-old with sweeping chestnut hair, high cheekbones and a soulful expression, like that on the face of Lady Lavery, whose image then adorned Irish pound notes. Louise, the baby of the six cousins, a year younger than Caroline, had jet-black hair and a tiny lipsticked mouth, like her mother, whom she addressed as 'Dolly'. She seemed to give the orders around here. Cecily was a feline piece of work with a wide and dangerous smile that showed a lot of teeth, between which a lit ciga-rette was clenched. 'How's the goin', cousin?' she said to me shortly. I was reminded of the lion in the hallway picture. Cecily, evidently, was not a girl between whose jaws it could ever be wise to introduce one's trusting head. The girls made a great fuss of my father and Madelyn, and left me standing, an unknown quantity yet awhile, as I tried to take in the details of the enormous, draughty room. Abruptly, Uncle Paddy arrived with a tray of tea-things. He had, it seemed, absented himself from the general convivium to go and make a colossal fry-up – rashers, sausage, eggs, tomato, black pudding – just in case anyone was hungry after their epic two-mile journey from Athenry.

I made my way to the kitchen. It was a walk I was to repeat approximately a million times in the next few years, until that short-pitched tramp from the drawing room, down the echoing flags and round the corner to the kitchen door, now falls on my memory like a song. It was where, in years to come, I'd always find Aunt Dolly, immovably parked in the armchair by the ancient Rayburn, holding court while fruitcakes were sliced, tea mashed, songs hummed, lemons sliced for gin-and-tonics, and the floating population of Graig Abbey cats gathered round the little square window, their hungry eyes opaquely reflecting the gleam of the cooker, the copper pans, the Waterford crystal glasses, the flash of Cecily's Zippo lighter. They crowded to the window like spectators, a puzzled but appreciative audience.

Inside the drawing room, I stood in teenage disarray, shy and uncertain where I was supposed to fit in, my hands sunk into my English sports jacket. I felt like the kid in L. P. Hartley's *The Go-Between*. I was horribly overdressed in the Galway countryside. I was an English fish out of water, welcomed and fussed over, but utterly mystified and mysterious to my own flesh and blood. They had no idea what to do with me. I had no idea what to do with, or to, them. I had no gossip, no news, no act, no performance, no ballast of *stuff* against which they could react. I was sixteen, self-conscious, suspicious, hopelessly suburban and becalmed in Englishness.

Literature came to my aid. Louise was doing her leaving certificate (the equivalent of English A-levels), at the Presentation Convent, and we talked about T. S. Eliot and Blake and *Macbeth*, wherever our respective scholarly schedules overlapped. I had discovered Louis MacNeice's poetry and could talk with teenage sophistication about its cocktail-bar urban music; she was passionate about Patrick Kavanagh, the essence of self-taught Irish rural energy, a truculent culchie who had re-created himself as the poet of Dublin's leafy canal-side quietude and wisdom. We got on fine as I strove to impress her, trotting out half-remembered paragraphs of school essays under the guise of drawing room chat, noting, with whinnies of internal panic, the sharp intelligence of her dark eyes.

I thought: I don't know any girls in London like this. In fact, I don't know anyone at all, back home, with whom I could have a conversation like this, so seriously, unpretentiously, engaged with the pleasure of literary texts. I found myself trying different ways of standing before her – hands on hips, hands in pockets, arm on mantelpiece, finger in ear, hand holding elbow, ruminative index finger caressing right-hand sideburn in what I hoped was a gesture of poetic intensity – as I melted before her ferocious, interrogative gaze. God, I thought, those eyes.

Uncle Paddy, assiduous as a rumpled six-foot sheepdog, appeared by my side. 'John,' he said, 'do you take a drink yet?' Why yes, I had actually been recently introduced to the joys of drinking pints of light-and-bitter in pubs on Wimbledon Common over the summer – mostly followed, hours later, by the Whirling Pit effect as I tried to sleep it off in my bedroom, knowing it would shortly be followed by the Dash To The Bathroom at 3 a.m. – so, 'yes indeed,' I said, 'a beer would be fine.'

He handed me a bottle of Harp and moved on. Suddenly I had a prop with which to cover any awkward gestural moments. But I was still only a pathetically inept actor in this fantastic stage set, where my sister was telling Dolly and Caroline some girlish news about the way foul London men treat sophisticated women like herself, and my father was making Cecily laugh with gross stories from the London surgery. They were so at home here, so miraculously plugged into this alien scene, so *earthed* into this sweet-smelling party atmosphere.

Two or three lagers later, the evening shifted on one of those invisible fulcrums, and everything was transformed as in a pantomime. From somewhere in the vast peat-fire-blazing drawing room, two harps had appeared. Caroline and Louise, fresh from a season performing, in plunging décolletage costumes, at Beleek Castle in Mayo (a paler cousin of the medieval tourist extravaganzas at Bunratty), sat down without undue ceremony, tuned up and began to play.

Their fingers moved along the coloured wires like spectacular, sensate, arachnid feelers, combing and plucking and gathering the notes into their girlish, cotton-fronted hearts. They played a gorgeous sailing song called 'The Queen of Connemara', and a tragic ballad called 'The Woods of Gurthnamona', and 'Plaisir d'Amour', and a dozen others, with the businesslike precision of teenagers who know there is a job to be done well or badly, and they'd chosen to do it well. They weren't dealing in romance, merely playing instruments, irritated by the occasional false note or dubious harmony or wayward string, which they would correct, severely, with a ratcheting device, as prosaically as plumbers tightening up a loose faucet.

It all fell on my teenage heart with a swoony rapture. I'd never heard live harp music before, and the thrilling glissando of its elongated chords, the cool, thumb-plucked rhythm that drove towards the chorus: 'Oh she's neat, Oh she's sweet/ She's a beauty, ev'ry line/ The Queen of Connemara is . . . [hanging pause, one, two, three heartbeats] . . . that *bound*ing bark of mine.' The more professional, the more sensible my new cousins became in their performance, the more agitated I grew.

Was this, I wondered, really mine, all this stuff? Could I lay some kind of claim to it? Could I pretend that this harp-reverberating, turf-glowing rapture was anything to do with me, in my nasty sports jacket and my embarrassment? Would it be okay to take it inside myself, to become part of it, to sign up with this family, this Irish throng, this unknown pot of gold beneath the family tree? Could I be part of the song rather than just the audience?

These speculations dissolved with the arrival of Cousin Marjorie. It was like the entrance of Sheridan's Irish diva, Lady Teazle, in *The School for Scandal*. I gazed at the eldest daughter of Paddy's sensational brood with astonishment. Imagine Hayley Mills in her early twenties, with nervously dancing eyes, a way of standing before you holding her hands so they seemed about to embrace you but always moved away, a trick of the head that meant she was always tossing her hair back, as if to scrutinise what exactly you were up to – Marjorie was, even against the stiff competition of her sisters, a dreamboat. She must have been eight or ten years older than me, and I fell instantly and totally in love with her. We were introduced. 'Well John,' she said, 'about time you came to see us' – but I was so foolishly drunk by then, I remember only making some pathetic lowing sound, like a bullock caught in a steel trap. She danced her flirtatious, mignonne way around my father, evading the insinuating hoop of his right arm, and stood by the fireplace, coolly surveying the room and its newest, gob-smacked, English occupant. The evening became, in my memory, a constant quadrille of movement, with my father and sister, the four girls and their parents and me, all talking in ever-changing knots of family bonding about our relatives, about school, London, Irish politics, poetry, nuns, the local hunt, the places where the cousins would soon be headed – Canada, Switzerland, Paris – the foreign students who had camped out at Graig, the ruined Abbey which was now a grassy hump outside the dining room windows.

I visited the washroom arrangements upstairs. In the lavatory the walk from the door to the cistern was longer than a cricket pitch. In the bathroom, the tap handles were enormous brass shamrocks a century old, and orange bog-water cascaded from their wide lips. The house smelt of ancient wood, nicotine and sweet burning turf. Coming downstairs, the conversation from the eight-strong family beyond the drawing room door was a boisterous and exciting thrum. I felt like the kid who had hung out for too long on the stairs in his dressing-gown, eavesdropping on the sounds of adult conviviality, but invited to enter the mysteries at last.

I didn't meet the male cousins until later. They were Maurice, a hugely tall, genial and omnicompetent handyman, the eldest of Paddy's children, the first to get a job, the one you'd look to in a crisis. He was an argumentative rationalist, for whom everything in the world was either right or wrong. If it was wrong but he was too polite to say so, he'd say it was 'middling'. Once I showed him a short story I'd written, at seventeen, about a man who discovers that the dry leaves all over Clapham Common have been miraculously changed into pound notes and he had until daybreak to gather them all up, a brilliant Borgesian conceit . . . He said he thought it was *middling*, and I knew I was sunk. But he was away in Dublin, that first summer, studying for a law degree, and I didn't get to run around with him as I did with the others.

Especially with John Louis, thus named to distinguish him from me, John Henry. He and I got together over drink and girls. He was twenty-four when we met, I was sixteen, but he let me hang out with him as if we were students together. He was a piratical figure, with a Zapata moustache, a black leather jacket and a lock of fine black hair flopping over one eye. His voice was soft with a slightly feminine courtliness about it, though it was clear from all other evidence that he was as tough as nails. We'd drink pints at the Jersey Bar in Athenry, surrounded by ancient farmers all dressed in nondescript suits and flat caps, and talk about music and women, although my experience of the latter was then still stuck in the theoretical stage. He described his love-rat adventures with fantastic insouciance rather than sexual braggadocio. I learned about the Casanovan goings-on in this nurses' home, at that party, in the street behind this ballroom, under a tree in that field. He wasn't a braggart; he always sounded slightly amazed by what women would let you do to them, given half a chance. I tried to keep up, with my own minor-league, virginal tales of furtive unhookings in cinemas and outside discos at Wimbledon parish hall. But it was clear I had a long way to catch up.

After the Jersey Bar, we'd weave uncertainly to Mrs Duddy's terraced house in Athenry's main street. It was not, as you may be thinking, some place of ill-repute, but the house where the drinking classes went for late-night chips. Mrs Duddy was a thin-faced, rather severe-looking woman, who knocked up French fries in her kitchen and sold them, wrapped in newspaper, to the pissed desperadoes around her front door. She stood no nonsense from anyone. She would gossip with John Louis in the freezing night as we shook salt over the fat wodges of potato that scalded our hands under the lamp-light. She liked to enquire about what the family was getting up to, but it was obviously a matter of some disapproval that the majority of her customers were a little *moggleyore*. She seemed never to have made the connection between the 11 p.m. arrival of her clientele and the six-pint reason for their sudden need for snacks.

I remember trying to charm her with some footling gallantry about her pretty daughters, who would crowd the hallway with their friends to see what class of gentlemen callers the night had brought out. She listened to me in silence, then turned to John Louis: 'You'd better look after this feller,' she observed shortly, 'because them lads from Turloughmore are in town and I'd hate to see what they'd do to the likes of him.' Clearly she had me down as an effete young English twit, asking for trouble by talking too much in that ridiculous accent. I felt like Oscar Wilde, hunted by the philistines. But I was glad to get home, all the same, before the myrmidons of Turloughmore found me out with their boots, their sarcasm and their long teeth.

★

That summer was the start of a wholesale love affair with Ireland, with Galway and with Graig Abbey and its occupants. After that initial meeting, I went back every summer: I crashed out around the house in a sleeping bag, walked through the fields and woods, was chased by inquisitive cows, blasted away with rifle and shotgun at the crows in the trees, watched the Galway Blazers hunt go by, encountered my first fox, which turned its triangular mask over its hunched shoulder and glared right through me, as if to say, 'Yeah? You wanna make something of it?'

On quiet afternoons, I would take Uncle Paddy's bicycle and pedal a mile or two to Carratubber Lake. No road sign announced it; no local map featured it; only Paddy seemed to know its name. It was a great wide boggy puddle in the middle of nowhere; around it wading birds stalked and dipped and inspected whatever pondlife darted and breathed unsuspectingly in its shallows. I would park the bicycle and stand for an hour, watching skeins of geese arrowing overhead. The sky seemed immense, just like the Paul Henry paintings of which my mother was so fond: landscapes in which little roads and cottages and signs of humanity were dwarfed by the turbulent greys, pinks and purples of the clouds. These visionary excursions were the nearest I'd ever got to meditation in a life usually surrounded by chatter and far too many people. The place was lonely, deserted, beyond the reach of property developers or civic landscapers – and, because nobody ever came there, it was mine. The sky would turn to herringbone one day, to a mile-high tumbled pillow of cloud the next, through which a single bright ray would stretch down to the land like a finger of light from Heaven. It was a struggle, for a quavering atheist such as I'd become, not to be infused with religious feelings for whatever God-like figure lurked overhead.

Then I'd cycle home to Graig, clatter down the echoing flagstones to the kitchen, to take tea and cake with Aunt Dolly. Dolly was a bewitching hybrid of Englishness and Irishness: born in Ireland, she'd grown up for a period in Kent, and maintained an accent compounded of scornful debutante Home Counties and posh Galway. She would, with the same alacrity, discourse about the Norman clan of De Burgos, from which the Browns, her father's family, sprang; and about the less elevated clan of Athenry locals, by whom she was greatly amused. She'd tell me about the woman who'd been swinging on a vocational door-hinge for years, entering and leaving convents as if through a revolving door; she'd talk about the adventures of Baba and Tess and Nell and Kate until you felt you were in an Edna O'Brien novel, and she'd always know the whereabouts of lost members of Athenry families in England or America.

And she'd ask about me about Oxford and ask who exactly was this Simone de Beauvoir that her daughters were so keen on reading. In her fondness for family tress, in her affectation of being *thrilled* by things, in her voice and manner, she was terribly English: at parties she would sing English novelty songs of the thirties like 'I'm One of the Nuts From Barcelona', and 'Abdul Abulbul Amir'. To please my father, she'd sing 'Will Ye No' Come Back Again', the Scottish lament for Bonnie Charlie that became his favourite non-Irish song. (And mine. Dolly was the only person who knew all the words, and the third verse, about English bribes and loyalty, and how 'Silver canna buy the heart/ That beats alone for thine and thee,' became a sentimental attachment for me when he died). She often seemed like a pre-war flapper, stranded out of her period in the flat fields of west Ireland, wondering however she had ended up there. But in the way she gesticulated, and smoked, and sat with her feet up on the Rayburn cooker, holding court through the afternoon, she couldn't have been anything but Irish.

The stuff about the De Burgos gave me a taste for finding out about the Walshes. Suddenly I shared my sister's interest in family history. I never knew my grandparents. All four of them died before I was born. I had no sense of that family continuity you get from seeing your parents' parents getting older, and watching the relationship between them develop. My mother and father hardly ever spoke about their parents, thus ensuring that, in my head, the old guard became even more distant and separate from me, inhabiting a foreign realm, almost a different century. They were consigned to a far-off unvisitable region. Until I found Graig Abbey, Ireland seemed to exist in the historical past; Galway and Curry were ancient burial grounds to me, and little more. Graig offered a mainline link to the past that was neither sentimental nor foreign. It was right there in front of you.

Of course my grandparents *were* from a different century. Great Uncle Martin, the family superstar, was born in 1848 – truly dreadful timing, as far as time and place were concerned, for the Irish famine was at its height. He was one of nine children – seven sons and two daughters – born to a head schoolmaster called Walter Walsh from Boherleahan, Co. Tipperary, who came to Galway and settled in the house called Lydican in the 1830s. The sons were a remarkable bunch. Martin, Tom, Henry, Michael, Pat, Dan and James. The girls were remembered only by their husbands' names – Corfield and Hannon.

Great Uncle Martin, the eldest, made a fortune out of land acquisitions, retired at thirty-six, hoping to spend the second half of his Biblical span in serene retirement and found his retirement stretching to two-thirds of his life. He died at ninety-six. He played the stock market and did well out of his shareholdings. He bought the family estate of Ballybacka and its adjoining property of Tubbernaveen, and settled his brothers there. He bought two pubs in Galway, on two of the corners on Eyre Square, the city's central plain, and installed his brothers Michael and Tom Walsh behind the bar. It was a matter of some pride that the Walsh family occupied such significant coigns of vantage in the centre of town – although the brothers became deadly rivals and they would regularly meet for a punch-up in the middle of the square.

Dan had a vocation and was groomed for the priesthood. Then one day the horse he was riding bolted, and, in the flurry of equine limbs, Dan broke his right hand. It was never quite right again, twisted slightly out of alignment with his arm – but it was enough to guarantee that he could never be a priest. The church fathers agreed: he could never give out Holy Communion with a hand like that.

Henry, my grandfather, was very devout. He used to go off to Mass in the family sidecar, and said the Rosary three times a day. He was addicted to the Stations of the Cross, and would patrol the circuit of Christ's torture and death with passionate empathy. Once he burned his hand on a sulphurous match. When the burn came up an angry red, he said: 'The Lord will heal it.' The Lord didn't; it became infected; he very nearly lost it. (Hands are a constant *motif* in my family's history.) Even in Catholic Ireland, his was an unusual level of devotion. Not everyone was impressed. Great Uncle Martin would come stamping into Ballybacka looking for his brother at harvesting time and, on learning that Henry was upstairs saying his prayers, would shout, 'Jaysus. He should've been a priest instead of gettin' married.'

Henry, I learned with some pride, had been fixed up with the last arranged marriage in Galway. He had decided, at fifty, that having acquired land, wealth and social status, it was time he did something about producing an heir for all the land that had come his way. He'd found a matchmaker, once a flourishing profession in Ireland, and initiated a search for a suitable bride among the passed-over, late-twenties women who lived within a twenty-mile radius of Athenry. They had behaved, the landowner and his professional Pandarus, with the etiquette of an earlier generation: you make an appointment, you arrive together at a house, bearing a bottle of whiskey and pull up a chair with the girl's father. You talk terms, dowries, farm prospects, cattle futures. You drink the whiskey. And after a couple of hours, if all was well, the prospective bride would appear, to be complimented and considered from all angles, like a mare at a market fair. Then you'd either strike a deal or go home to try a few more houses on the morrow.

The only surviving photograph of Martin and Henry show the two brothers smiling together beside a tree one sunny afternoon. Both are wearing hats, waistcoats and wing collars and look as if they have just returned from a fair. Henry is a little uncoordinated, his jacket buttoned at the top, his features dominated by a pronounced nose, inherited by several Walsh menfolk and, incidentally, by my sister. Martin is more obviously the country gent, a slender, puckish fellow with a wide cravat, a stick and a white, pointy beard.

The more I learned about this ascetic entrepreneur, Martin, the more remarkable he seemed. He checked the time on a solid gold hunter watch that he carried in a fob pocket; but he worried about being assaulted by footpads so, instead of training a gold chain across the waistcoat front, he tied a length of hairy string to the watch and sported that across his middle, to confuse would-be muggers into thinking he was poor.

Martin would upbraid his livestock as if they were human; if there was a ewe which refused to suckle its lamb, he would harangue it – 'Arrah, what kind of unnatural mother are you?' – and smack it across the face until it learnt some manners. With his own workmen he was more subtly cruel. At the big post-harvest supper every summer, when the dining-table at Ballybacka creaked under the weight of stew, bacon and cabbage, potatoes and turnips, he would announce to the labourers: 'Now lads! The man who eats the most vegetables can have the most meat,' and chuckle to himself as the hungry harvesters laid into the spuds and turnips until they were too full even to think of approaching the steaming plates of mutton. A teetotaller all his life, he was laid up with pneumonia at ninety-two. The family doctor examined him, said his circulation was low, and recommended a nip of brandy with his hot milk at night-time.

'No, doctor,' he said, 'I've never touched the stuff. I wouldn't want to start now.'

'But Mortcheen,' said the doctor, reasonably. 'You're an old man. You need to keep the circulation going. Wouldn't you try a little drop of brandy, just to perk it up?'

'Ah no, doctor,' Martin replied. 'I'd be afraid I'd get fond of it.'

And that was that. He never married, died in 1944, aged ninety-six, and left a small, triumphal poem behind to explain his modus vivendi:

Wine and women I did refuse,
And late suppers I never used.
My hands and feet I kept from the cold —
That's why I lived so long, to be so old.

He was a great patriarch, if you can so describe a man with no wife or children. His nephew, Uncle Paddy, never touched a drink either, but was a keen gambler, like Paddy's son John Louis. I chased these family genes with rapt absorption. They made sense of your life; they connected you with history.

Back in London after this golden summer, I met Cousin Michelle, a tall, glamorous and slightly terrifying suburban socialite. She was the daughter of Aunt Dolly's sister Peggy who had left the family embrace in 1946 to live in Nottingham with her Irish husband Tom Rohan from Taiquin. She was now a fully assimilated London-Irish woman living in East Sheen, married to a charming Yorkshire businessman called Richard. Michelle and I looked at each other, established in precisely ten seconds that we were cut from the same Hiberno-English cloth, and became firm friends. Through her I began to see that the best response to having our exotic relations was to accept it as a gift, use it when it was appropriate, feed off the vivid family anecdotage as you pleased and never let it stand in the way of your development as a wholly paid-up British citizen.

I appreciated her breezy, clear-eyed familiarity with her Irish connections, but I couldn't share it. I was too much the recent convert, the Hiberno-zealot, the craven sycophant of all things Galway.

Michelle had had the childhood I'd missed because of the family row between my mother and Aunt Dolly. She'd been visiting Graig Abbey since she was born, had spent much of her infancy there and had grown up with the cousins. She had memories of the place that were pure magic realism.

Once, when sleeping in an upstairs bedroom, she'd been awakened by a drop of liquid falling on her face. One drop, then another and another. She'd sleepily turned her head aside, only to feel more drops landing on her upper lip. Instead of springing out of bed and looking for a tin can to catch the leak, she'd remained languorously supine, as the droplets had gathered into a tiny flood and strayed over her lip and into her mouth. Her tongue had licked the creeping fluid and . . .

She sat up. Jesus, what *was* this? It was honey. The sweetest, most concentrated honey in Ireland had leaked down from the ceiling as she awakened. Up in the eaves, a nest of bees had been working away for months at the honeycombs, until their labours had spilled through the brickwork and into the room. It was a perfectly rational explanation, but I was entranced to hear of it. You just didn't get genuine ambrosia dripping from the ceiling anywhere in England.

My love affair with Graig Abbey was, in hindsight, about old things. The texture of life there, from the grand piano and the pictures of solitary monks and nuns on the wall to the immemorial turf fires in the grate, were all connections with a past that was suddenly far more real to me than anything in London, just as the Irish songs from my young days locked you into the past, and the words my parents spoke to me came from a hundred years before.

Unfamiliar too was the constant sense of moving between community and solitude. You could walk across a dozen fields by yourself, read a book against a tree, and brood romantically on the empty landscape and, a couple of hours later, be pitched into a whirl of socialising. Things were always moving at that extraordinary house. Nobody ever seemed to spend an evening in front of the television. Nobody in Graig ever went to bed early. No one ever said: 'I'm tired. Shall we call it a night?' There was always harp music, and relays of ham sandwiches provided by cousin Caroline, and beer bottles pressed into your hand by Uncle Paddy, and urgent conversations on the stairs, like plotting courtiers in some Elizabethan masque. There were always the lights of a car arriving at 10 p.m., seen through the windows ('Who's this coming now?') with the excitement of a Jane Austen family readying themselves to greet an intruding neighbour, with a very Jane-ite mixture of speculation and sarcasm.

If you were lucky it would be Martin O'Grady, deputy headmaster of the local school, a dynamic priest from Kinvarra; he was miles removed from the kind of cleric you'd meet in London. He was a muscular, busy, passionate, polyglot, hard-riding and heroic man, with thick black spectacles and an air of bursting-at-the-seams enthusiasm for life. Dark wiry hair sprouted wolfishly from his dog-collar. His sleepy-lidded brown eyes and lazy manner reminded me of Robert Mitchum: he had a Hollywood charisma about him. He was very Italian, Romanesque in looks, Da Vinci-like in the sweep of his interests and thoroughly Renaissance in the way he'd argue about the meaning of a word or the best way to urge on a thoroughly slathered mare to jump across a dangerously toppling dry-stone wall. But he was Irish in the way he'd stand among the men clutching a whiskey glass, nodding conspiratorially.

He never slept. He would ride all day at a Galway hunt, call for hot brandies in the Craughwell bar beside where the hounds were kennelled, attend a wake in Kilcolgan, stay up till three talking to the widow, then drive all night to marry two family friends in Wicklow at 10 a.m. He never sang, to my knowledge, but he got everybody else to do so, with huge engulfing cries of 'Mighty!' and (if somebody began a song on too tentative a note) 'Don't be afraid of it!' He was extraordinary, like Yeats's friend Major Robert Gregory ('Soldier, scholar, horseman he/ As 'twere all life's epiphany'), and I longed to get his attention.

O'Grady was a guest at the longest party I ever attended – the fifteen-hour wedding reception after the wedding of Paddy's eldest daughter, Marjorie. Since my first encounter with her, she had taught in Dublin, emigrated to Canada, changed her mind ('I didn't see a blade of grass in three months,' she explained), moved back to Dublin, visited London, headed for Dublin again, met a merchant naval officer called Denny Kessler – an Anglo-Irish Protestant, to my mother's alarm – and agreed to marry him.

At Graig, everyone pitched into a frenzy of activity, repairing, rewiring, reglazing, sawing, decorating, hoovering, silver-polishing, buffing, re-puffing, re-ticking, re-upholstering. Half-a-dozen back rooms, closed from lack of use, were opened up and spring-cleaned. Daylight filtered in where no daylight had been seen in thirty years. The old house hummed, like a dowager duchess being given an electronic massage. I spent a day and a half polishing each individual terracotta tile in the back kitchen, only to have Maurice come in and dump a hundredweight of soggy mud-stemmed flowers all over the floor. The front of the house was turned into a gravel arena in case some cars might need parking.

And when the day came, cars crammed the whole front lawn. That long January wedding day remains in my head as a series of gorgeous images: the darkening sky on our way back from the church at 4.30p.m., lit by flaming torches of hay-and-pitch, held aloft on forks by local workmen, an honour salute to the bride; my aunts Peggy and Nora, dressed respectively in poster-paint blue and red, parked in the doorway of one room so they could see everything that was happening in the other room across the hall; the first time I'd seen a turkey in aspic, upon which miraculous curlicues of tomato skin had been wound into red roses; the woman to whom, during lunch, I patiently explained my views on the State of Modern Ireland for ten minutes, before she turned to her friend on the next chair and said, cutting across my fascinating socio-political analysis, 'Hasn't he the beautiful speakin' voice?'; the trio of Christian Brothers who worked the rooms together like Groucho, Chico and Harpo; the moment just before Marjorie and her husband drove away, when one of her aunts wondered aloud if she should go and explain to the bride what indignities lay in store; the sexy organist, Martina, whom I wooed with drunken urgency at 3 a.m., proposed marriage to at 4 a.m., and quite possibly discussed children, mortgages and pensions schemes with at 5 a.m.

I wanted to stay there forever. I wanted to move into Athenry, set up home, ride to hounds, have parties, write books, see my cousins all the time and issue long-range invitations to friends in England to come and stay in my idyll.

Back in Oxford, cycling over the cobbles or sitting in the echoing silence of the Radcliffe Camera, I sometimes dreamt myself back again to the Graig drawing room on the night before the wedding. The house was crammed with family and putative in-laws, and all the bedrooms were filled with visitors, so I volunteered to sleep by the fire. Of all my memories this was the happiest – lying in a sleeping-bag, reading *Tristram Shandy* in the dying glow of the turf bricks, as shadows flung themselves about the wall, and spiders abseiled onto the window ledges, and I lay with a martial cloak around me, the smell of turf and hot whiskey in my nostrils, drowsing before the Celtic hearth, lost to England, drenched in Irishness at last.

X

HUNTING THE SPOOKS

There wasn't a lot to do in Athenry in the seventies. A wild evening might consist of drinking pints in the Jersey Bar, a few games of bar billiards in the Western Hotel, a sighting of the town beauty known only as 'Thighs', as she wandered laughing through the streets with her girlish cronies; and a final slug of Jameson's in Hanberry's Hotel. There, under the gimlet eye of Miss Hanberry – a tiny, etiolated spinster in a bun, about as near to the classic image of a pub landlady as, say, Edith Sitwell – we'd encounter Uncle Walter.

He always stood at the same spot, at the turn of the bar, a stolid figure who never removed his overcoat, and whose wary eyes, in that great Indian-chief face, were made harder to fathom by his Himmleresque steel-framed spectacles. I'd often find him drinking with two mates: Willie Higgins, who ran the local garage, and Father Joe Fitzsimons, a genial, self-mocking priest who, should you happen to call him 'Father', would whip off his Catholic dog-collar and half-circle it around the bottom of his Guinness bottle, silently implying that he was now off-duty. None of them was a voluble conversationalist or natural showman, and silences would fall like snow over the five of us. They were epic silences. Huge civilisations could rise and crumble and vast herds of wildebeest crossed imaginary plains, as we waited for Walter to rumble his next oracular utterance. My first reaction to this was embarrassment, as I searched for something to say to break a conversational hiatus that seemed likely to go on for ever, until we were all covered in cobwebs and mildew. But after a while I started to accept it as part of the rhythm and flow of Athenry sociability. Learning the importance of shutting up in the company of the tribal elders, until something emerged that was worth listening to – that was a lesson worth discovering.

Another lesson you learnt was the power of facts. Irish bar room conversations depended on an exchange of information, rather than merely opinions. If you could bring anything, however meagre, to bear on a discussion by reciting a statistic or reporting a statement of warlike intent from some European politician, it would be the signal for much nodding and head shaking.

Walter and his friends were in the great tradition of Irish democratic seriousness, patiently absorbing the news of far-off wars and passing slow judgement on it all as if they, rather than the politicians or the media, were the arbiters of what was important.

I invited my Oxford friend Robert to check out the Athenry scene. In Hanberry's Hotel, the troika of Walter, Willie and Father Joe were ranged in the same places at the bar like a Greek chorus, unchanging through time and cyclical tragedies. Father Joe's dog-collar sat by his bottle like a white pet snake. I introduced Robert to the elders. They were wondering about Uganda and Idi Amin, and why all the Asians were being expelled, and the nature of the British Immigration Act. Who would be entitled to a passport? And where was Uganda anyway?

'Let me show you,' said Robert, pushing next to Uncle Walter with what seemed to me insanely presumptuous familiarity. He pointed to a spillage of beer on the bar. 'Okay, here's Africa,' – he drew a rudimentary continent with an index finger – 'and here's Uganda, and the other countries with Commonwealth status are here and here . . .'

A minute later, Robert went to the gents. There was a silence as Walter digested the brisk, geo-political history lesson he'd just received from this Englishman. He sucked his teeth, judiciously. 'Awful nice feller, that friend of yours,' he growled.

We crazed Bohemians had to make our own fun. One night, when I was still only sixteen, it was decided we'd go on a spook-hunt to a ruined castle. John Louis and I, Madelyn and her Athenry beau, Liam, arranged to meet up with a dozen local tearaways and drive off together looking for ghosts. The castle was seven miles away and had been disused, to the point of ruin, for years.

We had flashlights and a guitar, several bottles of cider and huge party-cans of Smithwicks to keep us going. It was an unsettling little excursion: real ghosts, real dread, a sense that things could go badly wrong in the dangerous darkness. The castle was reputed to be rotting away. The floorboards wouldn't sustain your weight. At any moment you might be pitched through soggy timbers into the ancestral dungeons, or worse, down through one whole storey and through the antique damask canopy of a disintegrating four-poster bed where a now-skeletal Miss Havisham, in her crumbling nightie, would hold you fast in her horrid embrace and lower her grinning-skull teeth to your panic-stricken, silently screaming mouth.

Then again, probably not. This was, John Louis assured me, going to be about as frightening as a game of postman's knock, with all that implied in the likelihood of getting off with the girls. 'Mark my words,' he told me, 'you'll score tonight.' Not with Bernadette, obviously, since she had the boyfriend with her, or with Julia because she was definitely John's for the taking; but, he said kindly, I might try my luck with the young one, Grace.

Grace was a scornful fourteen-year-old tomboy in a jumper and jeans and by no means a sexual pushover, as far as I could see. But I ventured out into the chilly night, glowingly aware that I'd never done anything like this before, out past midnight in the countryside, burgling a vast, deserted stately home under a bright, betraying moon, wondering about girls.

I can't recall whose cars brought our little party to the castle grounds; I remember only the trek along the path, strewn with pine-cones, between two long files of looming trees towards a moonlit flat horizon with no sign of a castle, no sense of battlements or keep or moated drawbridge. It was a Samuel Palmer landscape with that sense of enormous things softly hidden in the folds of the rising fields. John Louis, beside me, kept up a stream of nonsensical chat. 'The only road t'fight fascism,' he announced over and over, 'is t'smash it right in t'ugly face,' a political bromide he'd recently picked up from some English trade union tract. He was a rhetorical magpie, testing out quotations and lyrics as if seeing whether they fitted his voice. All you could do in return was answer with quotations of your own. I chose Bob Dylan: 'I've stepped in the middle of seven sad forests,' I intoned, walking through the eighth of them, 'I bin out in front of a dozen dead oceans. I bin ten thousand miles in the mouth of a graveyard. But I ain't seen anything like *this* before.'

John Louis cocked an eye at me.

'Did you ever learn to play the gee-tar?' he asked.

'No,' I said. 'Piano lessons drove me mad enough.'

'Time you did,' he said, 'I'll teach you.'

We'd suddenly left the pine track and were heading over barbed-wire fences into mud and unfriendly terrain. Up ahead Madelyn and the local hero, Liam, strode purposefully on. The middle group of local kids, including the teenage babes who were the targets of John Louis's wolfish interest and my shy virginal dreams, picked their way through the sucky loam with girlish shrieks and lost shoes. Beyond a brace of immense poplar trees, a huge wall stood before us. It was all of four storeys high and spectacularly unwelcoming. We all instinctively crowded together.

'Over there,' said Liam, the spook-hunt veteran, 'there's a door.'

'Liam,' said Madelyn in her bored-but-might-just-be-scared voice. '*Why* are we doing this?'.

'It'll be great,' he whispered. 'Great gas. You'll see.'

There was indeed a door, off its hinges and leaning drunkenly. We yanked it aside. Then a nasty boot room, with a white, ancient sink, and a narrow corridor smelling of dank mildew – the smell of the air-raid shelter at the bottom of our garden in Battersea, I noticed, with a thrill of connection between home and Galway. We passed through in worried silence. One of the girls bumped into me and said, 'Oh, sorry,' but it wasn't a moment to take advantage of. Someone lit a candle, then another and another, and we looked around.

'Jeepers!' said one of the young ones with feeling. We'd stumbled into a kitchen, one that had once been the cuisinal epicentre of a thriving, Anglo-Irish Big House. It was the size of a school dormitory, with a black roasting-hearth like a church altar on one side, and a sink with two slatted wooden draining-boards on the other. Where there used to be a wooden table for chopping onions and cabbage, where some Galway matrons once sat plucking the feathers from a Christmas goose in a snow-dome shower of feathers, there was nothing but a gigantic hole in the floorboards. 'Take care now lads,' said Liam, 'or you'll fall through the floor and never be seen again.' We edged around the chasm in the floor, as gingerly as explorers navigating around a volcano lip, awkwardly carrying our candles, spilling wax on fingers. A litre bottle of cider clunked to the floor and rolled towards the rotting timbers. John Louis trapped it with his foot, a footballer's instinct. We filed past a complicated arrangement of looming doorways and found the hallway. Liam pushed open a pair of double doors.

'A-ha!' he said. '*Here* we are.'

You'd think he'd been popping in and out of the castle for years, though he was clearly just guessing his way around. But somehow we'd found the drawing room in its ancient glory. It was disappointingly unmajestic – there was a solid old table, presumably too large for the last owners to have taken with them, but no Tintoretto-painted ceiling, no vast mahogany sideboard, no four-seater horsehair sofa. What had I been expecting? Something along the lines of the National Trust mansions to which my mother had dragged us, in her occasional bouts of nostalgia for the old style?

One by one, our candlelit procession turned from their fearful scrutiny of the windows – and saw a magic line of other lights approaching us, like a fairy funeral heading our way.

'Jesus Mary and Joseph!' said Grace. For ten long seconds our eyes bulged in our heads as we regarded our own reflections in the biggest, widest mirror I'd ever seen. 'Ah for God's sake,' said John Louis. 'Will'ya cop on and don't be scaring yourselves. Put the stuff on the table and give us a drink in the name of Jaysus.'

And there we stayed, in this spectacular old drawing room, glad to have found somewhere to stop wandering. The party began. Seven cans of Harp were punctured and upended. Frothy beer spilled out across the old table. John and Liam broke out their guitars and tuned up, and in the moonlit interior we arrayed ourselves like languid squatters, talking and piss-taking our fears away, exploring with mounting boldness the limits of the room, the cobwebbed windows through which the moony light shone behind the trees.

John and Liam played their repertoire of country and western songs: 'North to Alaska', about Big Sam who left Seattle in the year of '92, but who mysteriously seemed, two verses later, to have also left it in the year of '91, in order to fit the rhyme scheme. 'Go *north* [*falsetto*] to Alaska/ Go north, the rush is on,' the boys sang, and by the end we all joined in, as unbothered as if we were in a lounge bar, back in Athenry.

We drank the beer from little paper cups, and I held the hand of Julia, the pretty redhead, as she fussed herself in and out of her dainty shoes. She had hardly looked at me before, but every so often her eyes flickered into mine with a quick, appraising interest that was, surely, nothing more than checking out the newcomer in town.

Others sang slightly elderly American folk songs, with faltering teenage bravado: 'The Banks of the Ohio', 'The Battle of New Orleans' which Lonnie Donegan had been singing ten years before. I just about recognised them. Why did nobody want to sing 'Ruby Tuesday' or 'Get Offa Ma Cloud' by the Stones? Hendrix was clearly a tall order for a two-man folkie combo, but could nobody play anything by the Beatles? The nearest the singers got to contemporary music was 'Sloop John B' by the Beach Boys, already an antique in 1969. It hardly mattered. I'd never been to a teenage party at which live singing had been a feature. I'd only known the curious mixture of embarrassment and elation at my parents' singing-round-the-table dinner evenings back in Battersea. How weird to find it was what you routinely did on Galway spook-hunts.

As the drink took hold the singing dwindled and we turned to ghost stories. The candles melted away into darkness and were replenished with new ones; their lambent flames became the backdrop of chilly tales – stories from the famine years.

Lisa, one of the local girls, told a story that freezes my blood to this day: visiting a friend in Donegal, she'd learned that the girl's mother used to sit in a high chair by the living room window, not too close to the fire because she wanted to read her book without falling asleep. A year after they'd bought the house, she still had not rationalised away the odd little rustling noises that seemed to come from beyond the curtained glass. She'd drawn back the thick, fustian drapes that hung from the brass rail to keep out the night chill, but there was nothing there to explain the tiny susurrations that crept into her consciousness as she read determinedly on, through the pages of Trollope's Irish novels and the colonial works of Somerville and Ross. Then, one evening, the rustling noise changed into something far worse. It became a tiny whisper.

'Oh please,' it said. 'Oh *pleeeeease*.'

It was the voice of a young child just beyond the windowpane.

The mother froze in her Parker-Knoll armchair. 'What?' she asked the little ghost through the curtain, the glass and the dark night air: 'What is it you want?' There was a silence.

'Oh *pleeeeeease*' said the voice, never explaining its racked and pitiful requirements.

She looked down at her book, Trollope's *The Macdermots of Ballycloran*, published in 1847, at the height of the famine. It seemed to swim before her eyes. There was no going back to it now, such was the urgency of the tiny, elfin voice just beside her head. Anybody, Lisa pointed out, would have been driven mad by it. Her friend's mother, however, was made of sterner material. She simply could not have ghosts invading her peace in this new home where she was to live out her declining days.

'Child, child,' she said. 'Do not frighten me. Whatever ails you, and whatever you want, I cannot give it to you now.' Whereupon the little voice melted away, a small re-echoing 'pleease' withdrawing away into the unimaginable darkness.

The mother talked with the local people, and learned there had been a terrible tragedy in 1847: a family of six children, the father dead, the mother reduced to grubbing for herbs and dandelions, had come up to the Big House on the Donegal strand and begged for food. Receiving none, she had joined hands with her children and walked into the Atlantic, singing together, until they had all drowned, rather than face a slower and nastier demise, twined together in their pathetic hovel, chewing firewood until they all starved to death.

It was a desperate tale. No amount of revisionist history could shake it from my mind. That night, we sat by the single candle flame and shivered. Julia squeezed my hand. I tried to lighten the proceedings by telling a couple of modern English urban myths, the sort of charming tales that were popular at school just then: a couple are stranded on Dartmoor; their car is out of petrol; he goes to find a garage, she stays behind; he's gone for ages, she starts to worry and finally hears a thumping on the roof; gets terrified; finally climbs out to discover a madman whacking her boyfriend's dismembered head on the silver metalwork . . . But the mood of the company was fatally darkened. And then, just as Madelyn was suggesting another song, there was a noise outside the window of the room we sat in.

It was a low moaning, the kind you might mistake for the wind, or a cow in pain. After a minute it resolved into an unmistakably human voice, an awful keening sound – *nnnnneeeeaaaaahhhh* – that was precisely the last thing any of us wanted to hear. I looked at the senior boys. Liam's face was stretched and bug-eyed in the light of the single candle. One of the girls started to cry, noisily. John Louis, my hero, my only hope, was saying, 'What the *fuck* . . . ?' Something had gone badly wrong with the evening. Something evil had eclipsed our trick-or-treating revels. Something nasty had crept after us, on our foolish trek through the footpaths of the pine woods, had coursed up to the windows of this dismal, Gothic ruin and was now about to steal in and enfold us all in a funeral-cloth of dank and seedy night.

Then, thank God, somebody rattled a chain. Somebody was going: 'Heh-heh-heh' and making rather too-obvious ghost noises. 'Bastards!' said John Louis, leaping from his wooden bench and making for the door. 'I'll kill the little fucker!' shouted Liam, running out after him.

I looked at Madelyn. 'It's bloody Padraig trying to scare us,' she yelled. 'Liam's brother. He's followed us all the way out here on his bloody bicycle.' Galvanised by relief, the other boys hurled themselves out into the hallway, made suddenly vivid by the hunter's moon, and ran after the ghosts who were fleeing away in the darkness. I tried to follow but I must have been drunk, for I fell down some steps and lay there awhile, puzzled by the shouts, the long cold grass that tickled my nose, as the firmament whirled above my head.

I don't know how long I lay there. I may even have slept for some moments, on the chilly grass of the Ascendancy grounds. But I gradually realised that an enormous eye was regarding me with horrible fascination. The kaleidoscopic sky suddenly seemed less important than this incurious but baleful gaze. It was a donkey, one that had presumably made its home in the castle grounds, cropping the heathery weeds that had overrun the once-manicured lawns.

We looked at each other for a while, as I wondered if it was real, not just some additional prop supplied by Liam's amusing brother. Eventually I got myself back inside, my jacket drenched with early dew. There was a party can of beer to welcome me, and singing had broken out again in celebration of having routed the intruders. The night had turned on that invisible lever nights turn on when you're young and fantastically drunk, and it's after 4 a.m. Energised by terror, the chase, the bravado, the nap on the greensward and the fact that whole cans of Harp and Bass and Smithwicks remained, I became recklessly talkative. I slid an arm around Julia, who had become more beautiful in the candle-glow and the lightening dawn, and at some point we began to kiss.

It was only the second or third time I had kissed a girl, and I felt an amateur's tremor that I wasn't doing it right. There had been Jane back in Wimbledon, with her ironing-board chest and the fusty smell of her sensible blue school jumper as we snogged hungrily in the Odeon cinema during the boring, look-here-Professor-what-exactly-is-going-on bits of *Dracula Has Risen from the Grave*; and Celia, a tall and fumingly irritable blonde I'd got off with in the garden at a party in Raynes Park. But they had been difficult, rites-of-passage claspings without much enjoyment on either side.

This was different. This was the middle of the night in a castle on the west coast of Ireland, far from home, caught up in smells of mildew, beer, grass, fags and Julia's perfume, a combination of earthiness and sophistication.

Julia put her arms around my neck, as if stretching after a long sleep, and tilted her lovely face so our noses slid by each other and our lips met in a bleary ecstasy. The others in the room didn't seem to be registering this spectacular turn of events. It felt, suddenly, as if getting off with girls was almost a normal thing to be doing. London had been full of the protocols of convent school and Jesuit college, where sex was fraught with disapproval: the severe, rosary-belted nuns, the memory of my mother's suspicious face in everything I did, the priests warning you about 'Nature's warning signal' as they cutely described the male erection. It was utterly liberating to sink into Julia's sixteen-year-old arms and forget everything else. We drew apart, talked about school and America and kissed some more; I ran my hands under her black pullover. 'Go on outa that,' she said. 'Somebody'll see.'

Later, we went out onto the terrace. It was a hundred yards long, the kind of thing I'd only seen at Hampton Court or on late-night Sunday vintage-car television dramas. We strolled together — it was the only thing you could do, stroll — and Julia took my arm like a Regency consort (La, my Lord, why dost thou bring me out onto yonder concrete strand? You will not use me rudely, I hope?). We walked on and the dawn revealed what the night had kept hidden: the long sweep of grounds from the castle down to the woods. It was brutally landscaped, as though by an Irish Capability Brown, and fell away before us in a seamless vista. I could instantly summon up a whole false memory of the castle in its heyday, the terrace filled with post-prandial English squireens in their hunting jackets and frock coats, taking the air with cigars and talk of horses and shouts of laughter, gazing down the long defile of manicured grass, past the peacocks and flamingos or a few grazing pheasants that had been spared the local shoot for their plumage of blue and iridescent green, down to the horizon where there must surely be a lake crammed with enormous, tiger-sided goldfish.

Centuries of English conquest were summed up in that moment: I felt a creepy colonist's instinct for how right it would have seemed to take over this wild landscape, to make a rich man's home of it and possess it all, its hundreds of acres, its deer and fish and birdlife, to construct a Lord-of-Tartary estate out of respect for its wild splendour and, frankly, sod the peasants who inconveniently lived on the land without owning any of it.

I wanted to have been there in a previous life, the owner, the resident magistrate, the rotten-borough English Parliamentarian who left his Galway estates, grudgingly, thrice a year for key debates at Westminster – but (I drunkenly imagined), a kinder version, a nice guy, the sort who, on his return from England, would be helped off his horse by an ancient serving man with the words: 'Ye're welcome home, sor. There's bin a colour of sadness in the air since you left . . .'

'I'm cold,' said Julia. 'Rub my back.' I did and we dallied awhile until someone called us back inside. Somebody was singing 'The West's Awake', terribly slowly. The drink had taken its toll. A couple I'd never got to meet were wrapped together on the floor, oblivious of the tired company. John Louis was sitting on the table swigging the last cider bottle. It was time to go home. The darkness had melted away like the candle flames, leaving us bereft, starkly awakened by the strip-light of reality. Instead of a cool platoon of explorers, we looked like a little gang of scrawny intruders: drunk, shagged-out and longing for bed.

John Louis and I went to dances at the Seapoint Ballroom in Salthill, the Brighton-beach end of Galway, where they still did things the old way. A showband, driven by accordions, guitars and drums, would sway through fifties waltzes and American country music and, after every three songs, the MC would announce: 'That's all fer now; yer next dance please.' Depending on the level of mutual heat generated by your limpid footwork and sparkling conversation, your partner could either exit gracefully or decide to stick around for more, provided you said 'Will you stay on?' in a sufficiently cool and unwheedling tone.

Most of the time, the girls disappeared, off to the right-hand wall where, for some reason, they stood arrayed along the edge of the dance-floor like a resting army. There'd be a moment's breather or two as they retrieved their handbags and exchanged disgusted reports about their recent conquests, then – I looked on in amazement as all the men herded across the floor in a desperate, Gadarene rush, grabbed the girls' hands and elbows, stuck sweating red faces towards the lipsticked *moues* of the available women, and all but yelled at them: 'Willya dance? C'm*o*n.'

Amazingly, the girls usually complied. Unable to compete in this flesh-market free-for-all, I waited until the first wave of dance invitations had found their targets and the couples had hit the floor. Then I went in. Cringing with embarrassment, un-suave to a Woody Allen degree and dressed in a sports jacket bought by my mother, I was a shockingly resistible sight.

'Would you, um . . .' I began, beside a cross-looking beauty whose arms, in a short-sleeved blouse, were Aertexed with goose pimples. She stared across the pullulating dancers, like the French lieutenant's woman contemplating her absconded lover. Had she not heard me? I leaned towards her, inhaling a fruity whiff of Aqua Manda.

'I wondered if by any chance . . .' She continued to look away, a tragic visionary at eighteen. In desperation I poked her left arm. 'Would . . .' Finally, her eyes blazed at me.

'No I would *not*, thank you *very* much.' I heard my mother's voice in my head, saying: 'Really, the *i*gnorance of some people.'

I'd made a shocking gaffe. For this glammed-up would-be Belle of the Seapoint to have been passed over in the last raucous wave of sexual advances was bad enough. For her to have to endure seeing her companions, Maura and Sinead and Geraldine and Philomena, all securing partners and now being brazenly romanced to the strains of 'Memories Are Made Of This' was bad enough. But to be then approached by some pipsqueak in a blazer and a funny accent, as if she was some kind of booby-prize when all the best prizes had gone – it was worst than insulting.

Later I danced with Deirdre from County Mayo, who was down on holidays with 'a fierce crowd'. She was clearly looking, I just knew, for love with a smooth-talking Englishman. She said she liked the Rolling Stones. She thought Mick Jagger was 'a gas ticket'. She laughed at my sardonic views of the show band. I was in with a chance at last. I held her hand, twirled her round and attempted a rudimentary Charleston to amuse her during 'Anything Goes' – a perhaps surprising choice to find in a dancehall anywhere in the world in 1968. After three dances, I asked if she'd like to 'stay on'. It sounded oddly lubricious, as if I were asking her to stay the night. She laughed a bit more, but with an odd cracked quality, like glass shattering. A huge ploughboy figure in thick corduroys appeared beside her, perspiring freely. He jerked his thumb. It was hardly an invitation, more an order. She looked at him, then at me, then at him again. No contest. She disappeared into the throng, eyes shining with pleasure.

I stood becalmed once more amid the hurtling bodies, thinking, Christ, what is *wrong* with me? I had only one comfort. Irish dances were different from London hops. They carried a tang of desperation. Unlike London, where the girls danced with their friends, and with guys from the next school in a temporary social accommodation with lust, here they were after something more permanent. Unless they were planning to move to Dublin, or London or Boston or Sydney, here were the male partners – the line-up of beaux, the identification parade of talent – from which they would sooner or later have to choose a husband. These girls were, even at their tender age, in the business of making life choices. And it wasn't a pretty sight.

By my third visit to the Seapoint, I'd had it with Irish dancehalls. They were smoky, violent, chauvinistic places with too much naked testosterone in the air and, worst of all, nobody seemed to fancy the likes of me. But I had cracked the protocol. Urgency was important. You had to ask for a dance with a busy, distracted air, as if you had to be at an important meeting very soon, and couldn't hang about. Second, a girl would be more likely to 'stay on' if you offered to buy her a drink – and if she said, 'I'll have a mineral,' it generally meant red lemonade, the Irish equivalent of Tizer. (My friend Rob from Plymouth, who I later took on holiday to Galway, listened to a teenage babe ask for this odd choice of refreshment, thought for a moment and said, 'What did you have in mind? Lime?') Third was the use of compliments: rather than ask where she was from, what she did (they were always nurses or they worked in a bank or insurance office) or whether she'd ever been to England, you remarked in wondering tones on the loveliness of their shoes, their earrings, their perfume or their startling resemblance to Julie Christie (if blonde) or Sandie Shaw (if brunette). One did not dance with redheads, despite Stephen Dedalus's insistence in *Ulysses* that 'redheaded women buck like goats'. Thus you learned what you'd never learn at English dances: the *lingua franca* of the international seducer.

Not that it got me very far. 'The ride' (as John Louis called it) was still a couple of years off. But I did meet Mary Ann from Loughrea at the last-ever dance I went to. She was about my age, coltish and sweet and indefinably *on* for something. She stuck around for nine or ten dances, she accepted a lemonade and she stayed talking with me between dances without coercion. Emboldened by her loyalty, I tried to kiss her in the middle of a ghastly up-tempo version of 'Eleanor Rigby.' 'Don't,' she said. 'You mustn't. My husband might be watching.'

Her *husband?* I looked on her creamy, milkmaid complexion – what was she? sixteen? seventeen? – as she glanced at the upper gallery of the dancehall, where parents and elderly guardians sipped milk stouts and hot whiskeys. 'You can't be married,' I said, pleadingly, 'You're far too young.'

'Indeed I am,' she said, 'but we don't get on too well.' Visions filled my head of an irate husband coming after me, mid-waltz, with raised fists, or some metallic piece of bullock-castrating equipment. Things between us cooled a little after this revelation, and we went back to dancing like cousins. But at the end, when I said, 'I expect you'll be joining your husband now,' she replied, 'Oh, I think he's gone on ahead. You could always walk me home.'

Mystified, I walked her through the backstreets of Salthill. The moon was overwhelmed with bright, vivid clouds. You could hear the soft wash of the Atlantic creaming over the groynes of the nearby strand. We held hands and she asked me about London and jobs there, about which I knew absolutely nothing. I assured her I could find her a position in a King's Road boutique anytime she liked. We reached a clearing in front of a large municipal building, where she waved her hand at a solitary, lonesome bench. 'This is me,' she said. It took a minute to realise that, far from being her home, this was the last possible snog location before reaching the hostel (nurses? students?

orphans?) where she probably shared a dormitory with twenty other girls. So we sat on the bench at midnight, and talked some more and kissed each other with a frantic awkwardness, as her eyes darted here and there, looking for someone who might betray her. Then without a word she was letting herself in through some metal gates and, without a wave, was gone.

With amazing luck I ran into John Louis, who had been dropping some more productive *inamorata* off at a hostel around the corner, and we trudged home together. Girls, we decided in our men-of-the-world fashion. They tell you such lies, don't they? We walked along in our leather jackets like local bravos, talking about life, thumbing lifts, scoring a last bottle of beer at Graig Abbey. I didn't need to affect an Irish accent. John Louis never felt the need to explain or apologise for his English companion to the drivers who picked us up. I was no longer in no-man's-land. I had a home in the West to retreat to, a big house that was more Irish than Anglo-Irish, a town whose secrets I'd started to penetrate.

I learned to play the guitar; John Louis taught me the chords of D, A and G major, taught me to strum and led me through the words to 'The Times They Are A-Changin'. It took ages. My performance jerked along in fits and starts, but after two weeks I seemed to improve. He taught me a ghastly farrago of leprechauns and mysticism called 'Uncle Nobby's Steamboat', and a lachrymose cowboy ballad called 'El Paso' complete with a cantina, a flashing-eyed maiden and a lot of gunsmoke. The chord of D major began to grate on everyone's nerves, so I moved to C major, with its impossibly painful shift into F. I suddenly realised that James Taylor's 'Sweet Baby James' was in C, and Joni Mitchell's 'The Circle Game' and Donovan's 'Catch the Wind', and that, if you did something amazingly clever with the little finger of your left hand, you could produce a gorgeous-sounding halfway-chord, an interrupted cadence that ached to reach its dominant chord. I was away.

John Louis was far too cool to play old Irish 'come-all-ye's' and rebel songs and 'Come Back To Erin' laments. He played country and western instead, looking for inspiration to America, rather than to Ireland or England. I did the same. I would as soon sing Beatles songs in Galway as I would have sung 'Greensleeves', or 'Sweet Lass of Richmond Hill'. So bit by bit, I brought the new wave of American singer-songwriters into the repertoire of Graig sing-songs. I discovered Leonard Cohen. I became a slavish fan of the seen-it-all Canadian visionary with the four-note vocal range. I discovered that 'Suzanne', his most famous song, started in E major, but that most of his other ones began in A, and learned them all. In six months, I'd become an eight-chord musician, minor ones included, and introduced the thunder-struck Irish west to the bittersweet dirge of 'Lady Midnight' and 'Bird on a Wire'.

The Graig cousins were glad, they said, to have a respite from John Louis's spaghetti westerns and Yukon adventures. He and I began to play duets, he with an infinitely delicate touch, I with a lot of crashing discords and moments when I missed the soundboard completely and raked my thigh with a plectrum. We sang 'Brand New Key' in funny voices, and 'So Long Marianne' with lots of high wailing, and I, rather flashily, memorised all the words to 'A Hard Rain's Gonna Fall' and always affected to be overcome by emotion at the end of the ten minutes it took to sing.

When a New Zealand family called the Barys moved in to Attymon House, a nearby mansion that used to be the local priest's house, the two families sealed their friendship with drinks and the accompaniment of two guitars playing Paul Simon's 'Me and Julio Down by the Schoolyard'. Both daughters, Stephanie and Sarah, were beautiful, arty and sophisticated. John Louis and I gazed at them and said 'Whatcha think of yours then, cousin?' in our professional-gigolo way. John married Stephanie a couple of years later. Sadly, I couldn't persuade Sarah to forsake her natural good taste and try her luck with me.

Music liberated me. With my inspiring cousin I became an act: the Two Johns, impromptu performers and terrible show-offs, available to enliven your party, wedding, hoolie or wake. No Irish or English stuff, just the best folk songs around. We'd play up a storm. We'd sing in harmony. We knew all the words. We'd break your heart. Without him, I could still make a fist of playing the guitar and singing. I could amaze the Irish relations by singing things they knew, singing their culture back at them. Or I could try and bring them, as it were, news from abroad. In the kitchen where Aunt Peggy used to say, 'Anything new or strange?' I played 'American Pie' for Uncle Walter and Aunt Agnes and, though it clearly meant absolutely nothing to them, they liked the sound and the energy and the newness of it, as if it were a tale of dragons from across the water. I was the singer who mediated between the modern world and the ancient homeland. *Mirabile dictu*, I had a role at last in Ireland, and a temporary home.

XI

THE COURT OF THE HIGH KINGS

It was about the time I was heading for university, that my father first started pining seriously for Ireland. He was fifty-six, he'd been in London for twenty-five years, locked into a community of exiles without ever forging much of a relationship with the English host population. As his retirement loomed, it struck him that he could either end his days sitting on the other side of the coal-effect fire from my mother, bored to death in London in a living room on the South Circular Road, or he could finish up smack in the Walsh heartland; perhaps in the middle of Galway, like his great-uncles, but perhaps in a new landscape, with a few acres of land on which to raise pigs or bantam hens, seeing a score of ageing cronies from Galway student days, a flourishing brood of nephews and nieces and cousins with whom to share all the news.

I'm sure he built my mother into his plans, though as an unwilling partner, in this rediscovered fascination for his homeland. For she had no interest in returning to Ireland. Most of her relations had deserted Sligo for the suburbs of Boston, and she would no more think of retracing her steps to the lonesome hills of Curry than they would give up the joys of Massachusetts.

He had to go back. So he started planning his triumphant return. Being the man he was, he couldn't just announce his intentions to half a dozen estate agents in Connaught and wait to see what rolled in. His instincts were towards complication, the careful weighing-up of pros and cons, balancing probabilities and having long directionless conversations with his London-Irish mates about the future politico-economic prospects of the Republic. You'd think he was an industrial company planning to utilise some tax-free zoning benefit rather than a sentimental fiftysomething Irishman with a sentimental hunger for his homeland.

He took to visiting Ireland by himself on reconnaissance missions, taking the car one day and vanishing off 500 miles away. In Galway, he would drop in on Graig Abbey, and on his sister-in-law Teresa, and on Sweeney the lawyer and, by a inscrutable network of introductions, he would learn that just the house he was looking for was about to go on sale over in Kilcolgan or Tuam or Salthill. Endlessly convinced that he was about to be taken for a sucker by smooth-talking estate agents in side-partings, Dad took advice about houses from everybody except those most capable of giving it, and he bought – as though 'on approval' – a succession of odd and grotesquely inappropriate dwellings for his horrified wife to inspect (and reject).

One was a draughty, stucco-fronted nightmare with metal-framed windows and a front door that opened onto the Silverstone-like main drag from Tuam to Galway. Another, in the centre of Galway studentland, had a charming view from the kitchen window of the largest and most depressing cemetery in the city. Some of the stone angels' heads had been lopped off by local vandals; the ones that remained had had their noses painted blue. In order to sell that house, he had to accept, in part-exchange, a plot of land near Bearna, on the edge of Connemara, on which not even he could seriously imagine building anything. He kept up this punishing schedule of acquisition and disposal for two years, dropping me little notes in the post from obscure bits of Galway and The Burren, which I would read in the porter's lodge of my Oxford college, wondering if my father had completely lost the plot at last.

'I've done it!' one note announced in his tiny, electrocardiogram scrawl. 'I've found the dream home. It's in Tipperary, or maybe it's Clare, I'm not sure, but it used to be a guest house and it's got a beautiful view over the Shannon. A place called Killaloe. Don't tell your mother. I'm just signing the deeds today, yr affec. father, Dad.'

I was nineteen, in my first year at Exeter College, reading English. Madelyn was at Leeds, studying History and Politics. I'd met some of her friends on weekend visits. She had popped into Oxford to see how I was getting along, and marvelled at the gang of effete poseurs and exquisites I had fallen in with (it was 1972, the eye of the glam-rock storm, when hefty footballing chemists and tremulous modern linguists alike were painting blue-glitter varnish on their nails and pretending to be bisexual for about a week). As it gradually dawned on my sister and me that our father had somehow bought himself a huge house with a dozen bedrooms, four bathrooms, outhouses and a garden beside the Shannon river, we began to hatch a plan to move in there for the summer, co-opt our friends, meld them into a dynamic Leeds-Oxford partnership, and tart the place up.

Every time either of us got drunk at our respective universities, or sentimental, or began talking about holidays, the invitations would start to fly from our lips. Come to Ireland, dear boy. My father has this house in Clare, or possibly Tipperary. Just pop over. Take the ferry, it costs nothing. The nearest station is called Birdhill and you may have to walk a mile or so, then ask. Yes of course Gail (my girlfriend) will be coming. And Justin, and Will and . . . oh lots of people you know. At the other end of the M1, Madelyn was inviting her mates along with the same airy largesse.

It was the summer of 1973, a beautiful July. We went over to see about the house and ended up staying for six weeks. Twenty-six people turned up. It was an invasion of young British student life into a small town that used to be the capital of Ireland, and a symbolic testing-ground where English and Irish would be pestled together into a gorgeous, new Anglo-Irish hybrid.

Killaloe is one of the most beautiful towns you'll ever see. It's about a mile south of Lough Derg, where the Shannon river abruptly widens into a sparkling lake, and yachts and sleek holiday boats cling to the narrow waterway on the lake shore. It's got a thirteenth-century cathedral, St Flannan's, and a stone bridge with thirteen arches and a plaque commemorating the shooting of four IRA Volunteers by Black & Tans in 1920. But none of these things mattered to us. We went to Killaloe as English groovers, as hippie students looking for fun.

I got there alone, a few days after Madelyn and her friend Kate. I had my instructions off pat. Ferry to Dublin, train to Birdhill, then walk. Bring sleeping bag and bed linen and kitchen utensils, especially can-opener and corkscrew. Plus chemist requirements: lots of guest soap, flannels, shampoo, Anadin, diarrhoea pills, Rennies, spot cream. And money, bring lots of money because there's very little here and we'll be starting from scratch.

On the train to Killaloe there was a young black guy – a student at Trinity College, I assumed. Black people were a rarity in Ireland then, like a flamingo or a sun-dried tomato. Coincidentally the student alighted at Birdhill, and I was able to watch the reaction of the local kids to seeing a genuine black person in the flesh for probably the first time in their lives. As he ambled through the tiny village, and headed off down the hill, five or six youngsters followed him in a silent group. They didn't mimic his walk, or call him names, just followed him, entranced, stopping when he stopped to lay down his heavy suitcase, starting again when he resumed. If he noticed his audience, he gave no sign. There was, I think no racial hostility about their interest in him. They were just fascinated to see something they'd otherwise seen only on the television. They followed him on the off-chance he might do something funny, like breakdancing.

The bridge came into view, and the wide, calm Shannon river. It was a lovely sight. The little town sat in a bowl of hills – the Arra hills of Tipperary and the Slieve Bernagh mountains of Clare – looking impossibly pleased with itself, its streets rising up a hefty incline, over-seen by the modest battlements of St Flannan's church. Unlike Galway, the countryside was hilly and dotted with woods, its nearest fields divided into neat little green patches, its outlying meadows extending away into the dark shadow of an almost-mountain. The white walls of the houses shone in the sunlight as I walked across the bridge. The yachts at their moorings looked like so many expensive cups hung up in a dresser. Goodness, I thought, this is, like, *home*?

The house my father had bought was the biggest in Killaloe and twice as tall as anything else in the neighbourhood. I could recognise it from photographs, though they failed to evoke its great bulk as it loomed impressively over me as I toiled up the hill. The door featured a curly motif of two wrought-iron birds on a bough. Behind it, a glass pad swung back to reveal my sister's face. She and her friend Kate ushered me in like two fussy old-lady companions who'd lived there for decades; wipe your feet, they said, don't put your suitcase down there, someone'll trip over it.

The hallway was gloomy, but the front room was sensational. A huge antique mirror, silvered and mottled with age and neglect, occu-pied the whole of one wall, while a half-size billiard table was fitted snugly against the windows, taking up far too much space. Great wooden shutters lurked behind high skinny doors. It felt like a room that had seen some action. Upstairs, a dozen vast rooms echoed with emptiness. One was a bathroom, although it was the same size as the master boudoir: the floor was carpeted and the bath was in the middle of the carpet, its metal claw-feet crouching into the shagpile.

Through the dog-dark hall I found the kitchen, where a green Aga stove stood like an ancestral furnace, its round hot-plates as black and worn as old cannonballs. A clothes-drying apparatus on a pulley hung complicatedly over our heads. A long trestle table turned the place into a potential mead hall. Awestruck, I moved outside into a cobbled yard with a stable and outhouse. I stood in the doorways and gazed into their cavernous, sick-smelling interiors.

The sharp cry of a lapwing led me down through the garden. It stretched to a dry-stone wall a hundred yards distant. A twisted tree rose out of the grass in a gnarly spiral. I walked towards the ivied wall, wondering what might be on the other side. And as I approached it, the river Shannon reared up and spread itself out in all its glory. The wall looked over the river at its most beautiful part, where it curves round a headland and vanishes up towards Lough Derg. It was, someone told me later, where the European water-skiing champion-ships were held a few years back, and they'd never got round to removing the ski-jump ramp that stuck out of the water like a dorsal fin.

There was one more surprise in the garden. He was called Philip, and he stood nervously in among the trees, like an inept burglar, clenching and unclenching his fists. He was about seventeen, I reckoned, and had not seen a proper meal or a change of clothes for at least a week.

'Hi,' I said,

'Hi,' he replied.

'We're looking around this house because we're the new owners. My father bought it and we're here for the summer,' I explained.

There was no reply.

'So why are *you* looking round the house? I'm afraid we've com-pleted the contracts. . .'

' 'Tisn't like I'm trespassing,' he said, 'I've left home.'

'You're from the town?'

He nodded. 'I just told them, I'm going off, and so I did.'

'And where exactly are you going?.'

'I've a friend in Spiddal, says he'll find me work.'

'Jolly good,' I said. 'So when are you off to Spiddal?'

'I cannot go yet,' he said. 'I'm – I'm waitin' for somethin'.'

I looked around the garden, and at him and his clothes.

'Let me guess. Rain?'

'No, somethin' comin' in the post. I hafta wait for it.'

'Before you can go to Spiddal?'

'Yeh.'

'Does it occur to you that you'd be better off at your house, where the post will actually get delivered, than in the garden of a completely different house, where it won't?' I asked, crushingly.

''Tis comin' to the Post Office down the road. I go in an' check every morning.'

'Hang on,' said Madelyn, 'Does this mean you've been living here, after leaving home and having to wait for your mysterious package?'

The boy looked more guilty than ever. 'Just a few days.'

'How did you get in? The doors are all locked and bolted.'

'In the garden. Just a few days in the garden.'

'But what did you live on?'

The boy gestured at the twisty, serpentining tree. 'Apples.'

'Jesus wept,' said Madelyn. 'We'd better get you some food fast.'

She put her hand on the arm of his denim jacket. 'Come inside. I'm Madelyn and he's John.'

'Philip's the name,' he said weakly.

As we steered him into the house, I puzzled over his predicament. Philip had run away from home, but couldn't get further than the end of town because he was waiting for a package that would arrive in the GPO, rather than his parents' house, bringing some – what? Money? A job offer? News from abroad?

I talked to Madelyn and Kate about it in private. 'It's oddly literary, isn't it, Philip's in-between state? He can't quite leave home and can't quite get anywhere else. Until the money arrives, he's just waiting, having nothing of his own, dressed in rags, living on apples, out under the elements. It's a very Beckettian situation. Although there are shades of Pinter's *Caretaker*, waiting for his papers to come from Sidcup, and of course Billy Bunter's postal order . . .'

'John,' said Kate. 'Will you wise up? There's only one reason why he would be getting a package sent to the Post Office. It isn't a package of money. Philip is waiting for a *stash*.'

Exploring the kitchen, Mad and Kate had discovered there were no knives or spoons or forks, no plates, no utensils of any kind. Apart from the corkscrew I'd brought with me, we were on Planet Primitive. What should we do? Buy a canteen of cutlery and a twenty-six-piece dinner service? Together we tried to make a list of essentials to buy that day: bread, washing powder, beer, lightbulbs, fuses, milk, lavatory paper, bleach, Anadin, fruit, eggs, screwdrivers, bacon, string . . . God, the multiplicity of all the things we hadn't got. In the end we gave up, went down the hill and into the first pub we found.

It was called Hayes's Select Bar and lay at the bottom of Church Street. The owner was a burly, shambling, white-haired, mulberry-nosed gent in his seventies, who looked like a retired boxer. He was Matty Hayes and was, he explained, the former mayor of the town. Anything you need doing, he said, mention my name and it'll be done. Madelyn and Kate took in his grog-blossomed cheeks and the air of disappointment that hung over his 'select bar', and thought, yeah, right. But after an hour of his company, his patient questioning about the degrees of Irishness that had brought them to this spot, their families and boyfriends and the subjects they were studying, the girls stopped caring about Matty's *bona fides*. After two hours they were big friends.

One of the customers who walked into Matty's bar that first night was Ger Cochrane, a handsome, serious, accountant in his late twenties, who was to be our *entrée* into Killaloe society, our chorus-leader and friend, our route to acceptance. Madelyn and Kate invited him back to the house, poured him drinks, made him coffee. He stayed for hours. The next night, he introduced his friend, Charlie O'Connor, a plump and conspiratorial fellow with slicked-down hair and a boisterous laugh. Through some invisible local network, people heard that we lacked a few vital things. Mrs Kelly next door, the mother of ten children, gave us some plates. Mrs Whelan from the VG stores came up with a score of knives and forks. Sacks of carrots and potatoes appeared, unasked-for, from the grocers, apparently on tick. And as if in response, the English people began to arrive.

Everyone my persuasive sister knew at Leeds University seemed to pitch up at the front door, with its wrought-iron birds and its glass partition: Andy, who always wore shades and Jeff, with his Robert Plant curls and Christ complex, and Ken, a bearded bear in NHS spectacles, and Mike and Janet, he a noisy roustabout with a car, she a volcanic sexpot with a wardrobe of T-shirts featuring roaring lions on the front; and my two Oxford Williams, one a gypsyish figure in T-shirt, bell-bottoms and neckerchief, the other an uncoordinated member of the Northern gentry in a striped black blazer, Angie my sister's half-Irish friend, and Daniella, a beautiful patchouli-scented Oxford philosophy undergraduate, on whose amazingly supple and bendy nineteen-year-old body I longed to pounce. They all appeared at the door in the same two days, without much ceremony, dumping their rucksacks in whichever room you randomly picked for them, saying 'Hi, man' and 'What's for lunch?' as if we were meeting in a students' union bar, rather than in a grand eighteenth-century mansion on the Shannon's green banks. Madelyn and I had planned on accommodating about five friends per week, their arrivals carefully timed to avoid overcrowding. Soon there were twenty-six people crowded into the house.

After a week, we had to sell off bits of the furniture, to buy more beds and mattresses. Madelyn went into Nenagh, the nearest town, and bought a job lot from the auctioneer. He beamed at Madelyn's elegant form, asked if she was enjoying her holiday and where she was staying.

'Oh Killaloe is so lovely this time of year,' he said, 'and the people so friendly.' His face clouded over. 'Have you been disturbed by the hippies at all?'

'Which hippies?' asked Madelyn.

'Have you not come across them? I hear there's a big crowd of them from England that's moved into one of the old houses that's been sold. Squatters, that class of thing. They do not a *stroke* of work. They have big parties there all the time, and no one can get up in the morning.'

'I hate to tell you this . . .' said Madelyn.

In fact Killaloe, on the whole, didn't mind this influx of young curiosities. Through Matty and Ger and Charlie and Philip, we heard what they thought of us: we were a commune, a religious sect, a travelling group of fringe-theatre actors, a sex cult, a sporting club, a crew of well-heeled international squatters. The short-lived but baffling rumour that we were a naturist colony could be traced to a single afternoon when Jeff, Ken and I were painting the outside window sills and the wrought-iron birds. It was a boiling day and we were stripped to the waist. Jeff had bare feet, too, as part of his modest self-identification with Jesus Christ. Somebody had worked out, with faultless logic, that we had put some clothes on, as a nod to public decency, rather than taken some off because it was hot.

We didn't quite know what we were doing there either. What were we expecting? Too young to have many social graces, Madelyn and I hadn't a clue what to do with the arriving squad of university acquaintances, once you'd got past the hugs in the hallway, and explained about the leaking boiler in the upstairs rooms. We were playing at being members of the Irish *haut-bourgeoisie*, temporary chatelaines of the house, the garden view, the high street, the smell of turfsmoke, the orchard, the stables. It was like having a huge toy, a do-it-yourself kit in being Irish, and we had to make up the rules as we went along.

Only the girls rose before noon. Breakfast was a simple but slow process. The Aga was a troublesome cooking device. It took a week to poach anything, a fortnight to stew anything, a month to roast anything. Madelyn and the sisterhood would place twenty eggs in a giant metal cauldron and go down the hill, buy the morning's bread in the VG before crossing the road to Matty's bar for Lucozade and a chat. An hour later, they'd wend a slow path back up the hill, pausing to talk to Catty from the Dispensary, to Mrs Kelly and the other neighbours. When they got home, the eggs would be done, their golden yolks flowing and succulent.

Afternoons were spent climbing the local hills, gazing at the Shannon, sunbathing in the grounds of the Lakeside Hotel, or reading with your back against the twisty tree. Everybody would eat at 7 p.m. and complain at their peril about the high incidence of mince, the ubiquity of potatoes. From eight till ten, we'd drink in Matty's small lounge. Grave young intellectuals from Oxford and Leeds found themselves taking bets with the neighbours about whether the pregnant Mrs Doyle, mother of six girls already, would manage to have a boy this time. At ten, Matty would shut the place (he disapproved of late nights) and we'd cross the bridge to Mills's Bar in Ballina. Tony Mills and his wife Bridie, a sweet-faced woman with the tiniest voice in the world, watched with interest as more and more English faces came daily through the door.

Mills's was a rather bare shebeen in 1973, in which the most eye-catching furnishings were the rows of bottles ranged on shelves behind a simple counter. Elderly advertisements for Guinness, and photographs of the local hurling team in their hours of triumph, were the only concessions to colour. There were no optics, no snugs, no food and, thankfully, no very strict adherence to licensing hours. We went there night after night like homing pigeons. After a while, the Killaloe burghers – like the local vet, a pipe-smoking anecdotalist – started drifting across the bridge to see how the hippie commune was getting along.

One evening I brought out my guitar, and strummed 'The Banks of the Ohio' to see how it went down. After that, we sang all the time. The locals sang Irish ballads, like 'Spancil Hill' and 'The Cliffs of Doneen' and 'Leaving Tipperary', a tragic wail of exile that turns into an accelerating gallop of optimism; we in turn sang Joni Mitchell and Dory Previn. I used to sing 'Twenty Mile Zone', about a traffic cop flagging down a screaming lady motorist. The Irish liked it, despite its Californian scream-therapy idiom, because they like tales of mad Americans. Kate sang 'Lemon-Haired Ladies', in which an ageing sexual tigress regretfully acknowledges that she will one day lose her young lover to the wiles of 'those lemon-haired ladies of twenty or so'. Mills's Bar hadn't a clue what it was about but 'Sing the one about the lemonade ladies,' they'd encourage Kate, as if Ms Previn had been warning her toyboy to steer clear of fizzy drinks. Ger Cochrane, who had the best voice of any of us, sang 'Dainty Davy', a slow heartbreaker about a girl pining for her renegade lover away at sea. Thumping chords like Pete Townshend, I learned to make a fist of 'Lord of the Dance', a bouncy piece of Christian allegory made popular by the Irish ex-nun Mary O'Hara; some of the Irish locals would even take each other waltzing across the spit-and fag-strewn floor of Mills's, halfway through.

The evenings grew formulaic, as the weeks went by and the same songs came round again. It gradually became a three-hour ritual, at which the most recent arrivals from England would gaze in astonishment. Most of them had never sung in any company outside rugby-club bath nights or a yearly 'Auld Lang Syne'. Here they were persuaded to take part, just as I, at four, was bullied into delivering 'Eileen' in my dressing-gown. If they joined in the chorus, they'd be slapped on the back. If one of them ventured a song the company hadn't heard before (a nervous Oxford classicist amazed himself by performing an intense version of Neil Young's 'Heart of Gold'), someone would buy them drinks.

Tony and Bridie didn't live in fear of the cops storming in and revoking their licence; Irish pub landlords have a relaxed relationship with the local crimefighters. But they were alarmed one evening, around midnight, when someone came in and said, 'The sergeant's outside! I just seen his car parked outside! Quiet everybody!' We waited for the awesome majesty of the law to come in. Five minutes went by. Another five. Someone checked the window. 'He's just sittin' there in the car,' they said. 'I wonder if he's all right?' We started to leave. We called out: 'Thanks for the private party, Tony,' and stepped out into the starry night. Tony later told me that whilst we were on the way home the sergeant came in. 'Just making sure everything's okay, Tony,' he said. 'I didn't want to break up the singing. Lovely tune, isn't it, that "Leaving Tipperary".'

By 1.15 a.m. every night, we were crossing the bridge for home, carrying take-out six-packs of Harp and Guinness and heading up the hill to the big house, for packet soup and chat and more drink. Charlie O'Connor would tell jokes punctuated by his bellowing laugh, Tommy Nolan, the local dude, would perfect his Warren Beattyish, crinkly-eyed glare and the random collection of British intruders would talk to the Irishmen about rock 'n' roll, the Heath government, the unions and the fortunes of Chelsea and Leeds United.

The English would politely enquire about 'the North' and Bloody Sunday and would receive the usual platitudinous response: quasi-religious sectarianism was to blame and that was that. Nobody in a middle-class place like Killaloe was radical enough to argue the Republican cause with a crowd of English students. But there was, I think, a gleam of satisfaction in Ger's and Charlie's eyes when they'd trained up the English blow-ins to sing the chorus of rebel songs in their 'posh' accents:

> Come out you Black and Tans, come out and fight me like a man;
> Tell your wife how you won medals down in Flanders.
> Tell her how the IRA made you run like hell away,
> From those green and lovely lanes of Killashandra.

Food became a problem. There was never enough. Nobody thought to draw up a roster of shopping and cooking. Those that could cook became too stoned, too tired and too overwhelmed by the demands of preparing meals for twenty-odd people; those that couldn't lived on pies and crisps from the VG market. One day Paddy Crowe, son of the house's original owner, arrived with eight pounds of pollock (a kind of prognathous cod), he had caught in the sea the day before, and tipped them into the kitchen sink. Kate volunteered to make some delicious pollock 'n' mash for supper. What could be simpler? You poach them for an hour on the recalcitrant Aga, boil a few spuds, nothing to it. Everyone went for a reviving afternoon walk to build up an appetite; they returned to find Kate in tears, slumped at the sink like a Victorian parlourmaid, her arms covered in fish guts, defeated by the effort of eviscerating and de-heading several dozen wall-eyed fish with Desperate Dan jaws. 'They kept making this awful *noise*,' she wailed.

I came to marvel at the resourcefulness of Paddy Crowe, whose father had sold us the house. He seemed to operate by different rules from the rest of the world. Once he bought six sheep at the local mart and brought them into our garden on the way home. He casually rolled a cigarette as the sheep cropped placidly away. I left my breakfast and went out to him.

'Paddy, erm, these animals . . .'

'Your father wanted the grass cut,' he said shortly. 'An' I have no mower.'

He also introduced a worrying, ghostly note into the amusements. It seems he was genuinely plugged into psychic powers. One evening he was walking home from the Lakeside with my sister when he heard someone calling his name from the Killaloe side of the Shannon. 'Who's there?' he called back. There was no reply, but a moment later it came again: 'Padd-eeee' borne on the warm night air. 'Who the hell is messing . . . ?' he called. The next morning, he told his mother. 'As sure as anything, now,' she said, 'there's a MacDonagh dead' – that is, on her side of the family. And there was. The news came at lunchtime. It was one of her cousins.

Romance broke out all over the town. All the Irish boys pined for Kate. It was her maternal streak, her huge bosom, her willingness to cook. Sometimes they'd make their move at the wrong time. One youth called Eamonn tried it on just as we were all leaving for the pub. He seized her arm and said, urgently: 'Kate – have you got a court?' – meaning a boyfriend.

'A coat?' said Kate. 'I don't think I need one. It's the middle of July for Heaven's sake.'

The Crowe brothers formed a *tendresse* for two of the Oxford girls. Andy got off with Jill, as everyone had predicted, but Alison refused to get off with Ken, who was just too large and bearlike. Nobody wanted to try their luck in the sack with Philip. Will Atkinson, something of a curiosity to the locals because of his velvet shoulder-bag, his liquorice-paper roll-ups and tremendously deep voice, tried his luck with Oxford surreptitiousness: he squired Daniella around, took her sunbathing at the Lakeside Hotel and romanced her on the lawn as she lay in her underthings. The Yorkshire contingent were more direct. One night as I was lingering in Danni's shared bedroom, Jeff, the one with the Christ complex, walked in with nothing on, his member waggling like a nasty parsnip as he looked her up and down in the bed. 'Jeff,' I said. 'What the hell . . . ?'

He held up a hand. 'Any time you're ready, Danni,' he said meaningfully, and walked out.

'Jesus,' said she. 'Who does he think he is? Mellors?'

For a small, unassuming kind of town, Killaloe had an air of grandeur about it. Maybe it was because of the wide bridge and the rearing cathedral, and the sleek waterway and the aristocratic hill-rise of the main street, but it felt as if richness and nobility were its natural condition. I bought a local guidebook and found that the town was once the home of Brian Boru, the High King of Ireland from 1002 to 1014; his palace was called Kincora and stood at the top of the town, eerily close to my father's new house where so many students snored and breakfasted and shagged the mornings away.

The story of Boru's demise stuck in my head and I told our house-guests how the great chieftain – perhaps the only genuinely regal Brian that ever lived – after years of fighting off the Vikings who had ruled Ireland for so long, called all the chiefs to his court in Killaloe and told them his problem. His son, Murrough, had mortally offended the King of Leinster. They had had words during a game of chess, some terrible implied insult had wafted across the chequer-board, over the carved innocent heads of knights and bishops, and Maolmordha, king of the eastern reaches, had become enraged. The game had ended abruptly, the king swore revenge for the insult (mad-deningly, nobody ever knew what it was that so upset him; it was a classic Irish row) and declared that he would enlist the help of the Vikings in teaching Boru's son a lesson in manners.

Back at the Kincora court, Boru went ballistic. He summoned all the fighting men of Munster (the south) and Connaught (the west) and told them their only chance to save their country from the Norsemen was imminent. The Battle of Clontarf ensued, the Vikings were sent packing, but Brian Boru was killed at his moment of victory. Back in Killaloe, the court poet Mac Liag wrote a tragic lament:

O where, Kincora! is Brian the Great?
And where is the beauty that once was thine?
Oh where are the princes and nobles that sate
At the feast in thy halls and drank the red wine?

Well I'll be damned, I thought. *Here* is the beauty that once was thine. 'Guess what, everybody,' I told them one morning. 'We're living next door to the ancient court of the High King of Ireland. The big meeting before the Battle of Clontarf was just up the hill from here.' A dozen pairs of eyes turned on me, blankly, before returning to their bowls of porridge and boiled eggs. 'Surely you've heard of it – the battle that finally saw off the Vikings, that let the Irish rule themselves. While the Normans were conquering England, in 1066, Ireland had already kicked out their invaders in 1014. It means we're next-door neighbours to the Irish Windsor Castle.'

Nobody, sadly, was impressed. History, whether English or Irish, came some way down the scale after Smithwicks Ale, black pudding, water-skiing and sex.

One evening, towards the end of the holiday, my father visited from London to see how his investment was progressing. He took in, without undue panic, the Himalayan pile of empty cans and bottles in the back yard, the pong of musty sleeping bags, the steady drip from the upstairs water tank, and the twee arrangements of fairy lights in the kitchen. The girls made a big fuss of him and greeted him like a sugar daddy who had bankrolled them in some undemanding career.

The Leeds boys said, 'Ow do, Mr Walsh?' and 'Nice place you got 'ere' and then forgot he existed. Madelyn and I assured him his new house was a kingdom, a palace, an unforgettable resort, although, of course, one or two minor adjustments might have to be made before Mother arrived to begin their blissful retirement together.

'D'you think she'd like it,' he asked eagerly. 'How could she *not*?' we replied. It was the only thing to say under the circumstances. We knew Mother could never live there, not in a million years. Anyone with the briefest acquaintance with my mother would know that. It was too large, too sprawling, too unconstrained for her controlling temperament. It was, with its ancient white sink, its kitchen press, the stable yard and the dim, sun-moted hallway, a sight too old-fashionedly *Irish*. We all knew it wasn't going to last. It would have to go the same way as the Tuam house, the Graveyard View, the Connemara Site. . .

As her arrival drew near, we drowned our sorrows in Hayes's Select Bar. Matty poured Dad a gin and orange and asked how he got the scar on his lip. Dad told him it was a hurling accident he'd got when he was captain of the Galway University Minors, and they were away. Matty talked about boxing; Dad rhapsodised about Jerry Quarry and how he'd damn near nailed the great Ali in 1973. Matty shifted the conversation to rugby, and Dad lectured him about the genius of the French and how the Irish team was never so good again as when Tony O'Reilly was playing. Matty bought him a triple gin and brought up the subject of chess. Oh absolutely, said my father, this Yank Bobby Fischer is all very well, a genius no doubt, but what about the brilliance of Alekhine in the days when the Russians were less obvious in their attack? They moved on to golf and Christy O'Connor and how he'd once given the Golden Bear, Jack Nicklaus, a run for his money. Fragments of their conversation, their absorbed interchanges about past battles won and lost in a dozen sports, drifted over to Madelyn and Kate and me as we talked about more immediate matters (like how to clean up a sudden flood in the kitchen before Mother's arrival). It registered that the ex-mayor of Killaloe and its most recent property owner were getting on just fine.

Dad told Matty he'd been watching a lot of snooker lately. It had become a trendy sport on English television, five hundred miles from the wasted afternoons in Galway where he'd learned to pot a stray red ball snuggled right up against the cushion, by angling the cue *this* way. 'Sure you never lose it, once you have the knack,' said Matty. 'And now you have the table old Misther Crowe left you, you can take it up again.' He paused for a sip of Guinness. 'As long as you have a decent cue, sure you'd be on top form again in no time.'

My father considered this. 'Have you a cue of your own?' he asked.

There was a silence. ''Tis upstairs somewhere. I might be able to dig it out agin,' said Matty.

'I'd say you used to be pretty handy at the table in the old days. Would that be right? The old 147 break a few times?'

'Ah now, when I was a young man, I could pull the odd stroke, right enough. I cleared the table a few times when I was lucky and not in drink.'

'Do you fancy a match up at the house one evening?' asked my father.

'I'm too old now,' said Matty. 'And too worn. And the old back is killin' me for all that bendin'.'

'But you just said you never lose it when you have the knack.'

'Yeah but Martin, when you get to my age. . .'

'Tuesday night,' said my father. 'How about it? I have to leave on the Wednesday, when Anne gets here, so we might as well make a night of it. Will you come? Sure you will, with your fancy cue from upstairs.'

'Ah no, no,' said Matty, emptying the last of the Cork Dry Gin into my father's glass in what, by eye alone, I estimated as a quintuple measure. 'I'm past all that malarkey.'

'We'll be expecting you,' said my father, clinking glasses. 'Don't let us down.'

Next morning, I watched the bleary departure of the Oxford Williams. The young kids from Crotty's and Rohan's came out to watch them lug their rucksacks down the hill for the last time. Good-bye to the under-the-counter poteen at the butcher's shop, the ad hoc chat with Charlie O'Connor's mum in the middle of the street, the infallible headache cure at the chemist, the flirtatious lady from the betting shop; goodbye to the cathedral that none of the pagan British invaders ever got round to visiting, to the bridge we crossed every night in an alcoholic daze, to Mills's Bar, home of fifty singing evenings. Goodbye to all that unexpected magic.

For those who remained, there was an epic cleaning shift, a final roster of bin liners and bottle clearing and hoovering. We looked at the flood that still formed puddles on the kitchen floor and knew it was all over. Mother was due to arrive in twenty-four hours. She would bring all the revels to an end. She would close us down.

In the grocery shop Madelyn told Ger that her father had challenged Matty to a snooker match at the house, and that he might like to pop in for a final carouse that evening. By 3 p.m., it was all over town. Matty Hayes was playing the table again, up against the doctor from London. We cleared out the bottle-strewn yard, polished the hallway until it shone, fumigated the living room, opened the upstairs windows to remove the lingering essence of student, and took the moulded tarpaulin off the billiard table. Underneath, the green baize was a little threadbare at the far pockets, but it still offered a fertile meadow of combat. The snooker balls were lustrous through inactivity – vivid heavy spheres suspended in a pool museum. We had located the cues, the spidery rest and even some pre-war chalk.

That evening, the end of Killaloe, we were subdued. There were only eight or ten of us left and the cleaning-up had broken a spell. Once the decadent miasma of party-going had dispersed, we were on our best behaviour, as we prepared for the matriarch's arrival. We had the umpteenth shepherd's pie, the millionth round of coffees, poured a few beers into glasses and drank them respectably. My father came round at about 7.30p.m. Nobody had seen Matty all day. He'd obviously forgotten about the snooker. He was too old, he had chickened out.

'What harm?' said my father. 'We'll have two drinks at Mills's to say goodbye, wait for him, and if he doesn't show up, we'll have a game with Charlie O'Connor and call it a night.'

At Mills's, Tony and Bridie gave us drinks on the house and wished us Godspeed. We were back home by 9 p.m., peering through the curtains for any sign of Matty. We rang his place but there was no answer. 'Oh fuck it, Dad,' I said, 'he's not coming. Rack them up and let's get on with it.'

Just as my father was chalking his cue and squinting down it at the white ball, there was a banging on the door. It was Philip. 'Come quick,' he said, 'there's a procession down below.'

We walked down the road, my father and sister and I. The moon had risen and the evening was still light. At the turn of Church Street there was a little crowd outside Hayes's Select Bar: Charlie and Ger, and Tommy, the dude with the Elvis sideburns, and the girls from the VG supermarket. As we drew near, Matty appeared through the door of the pub. He was dressed in a serious suit – the first one anyone had seen him in for years. His hair was brushed, and rather spiffily middle-parted. In his right hand was a long wooden box with a handle. It was the magic cue he'd dug out from the lumber of his long life. The gleam of battle was in his eye. He nodded briefly to my father, as combative as a boxer at the weigh-in, friendliness replaced by the formality of competition.

'Are we on?' he said.

'You bet,' said my father.

Together they started to climb the long hill. I went to the shop to buy some packs of Harp and a bottle of Jameson's, and found a dozen Killaloe citizens beside me, shoving a few more just-in-case supplies into brown paper bags. As we were leaving, the Ballina vet and the guy from the *Limerick Leader* came in with their wives.

'We heard that Matty's playing your old man on the table tonight. Is it true?'

'If you don't hurry up,' I said, 'it'll be all over by the time you get there.'

There were twenty of us around the table by the time it began. There was no wooden triangle to rack the balls, but in every other respect it was the most formal occasion the house had seen all summer. No one sang. Anybody caught humming an air was silenced with cries of: '*cuinis*' (silence) and 'best of order, please'.

Matty took the break, and sliced the corner red into the top right pocket. The cue ball rolled obediently within six inches of the black, which was slammed without a moment's hesitation into the top left pocket. The old man pitched into the attendant reds and sent them sprawling over the green table like a scattering crowd in a thunderstorm; but none found a home. 'Eight points to Mr Hayes,' said a voice. Philip, the local boy who'd lived on apples in the garden, went to find some paper to keep score.

My father chalked his cue thoughtfully. He potted a simple red in the middle pocket, tried to screw the pink into the far corner and watched as it juddered against the cushions and refused to go down. 'One to Doctor Welsh!' cried a voice annoyingly.

Matty's slicked-down hair was coming adrift and some elderly wisps hung over his forehead as he bent over the table. He whacked in a red ball from half the length of the table, turned his attention to the brown and watched it creep across the baize into the middle hole. A small cheer went up from the vet and the *Limerick Leader* journalist. The former mayor of Killaloe allowed himself a tiny smile. But he overreached himself two shots later, and watched, mortified, as the cue ball hopped up onto the metal hoop of the end pocket and crashed to the carpet. 'Four away!' said the voice. 'Hayes twelve, Welsh five.'

I watched my father as he struggled to regain the initiative. While Matty played like a young champion, full of angry, heavyweight shots that aimed to kill the coloured balls stone dead, Dad stroked his cue judiciously, gliding the white sphere towards its target with maddening calm, as if every pot was a matter of logic. The old man in the brown suit was in a hurry to reclaim his youth, his sense of angle and dynamism undimmed by the years. But, at fifty-six, the younger challenger was more diffident about his strokes, taking his time over the practice slides of the cue across the web between thumb and forefinger, before making the next stealthy connection with the white ball. As the town watched its crumpled tribal elder blaze away across the billiard table, I watched my father apply the wisdom of his years: don't be too hasty, cast no clout, don't *hop* the ball . . .

It lasted two hours. Matty won the first frame, 116–89 and Dad won the second with a weird run of luck. They paused for bottles of beer and talked about, of all things, hurling, and the glory years when Tipperary had won the All Ireland Trophy. Ham sandwiches on sliced white bread appeared from the kitchen. The women sat around in armchairs, sleepy but reluctant to leave. Tommy Nolan remarked on how Matty's soft-shoed circumnavigation of the table reminded him of Minnesota Fats in *The Hustler* (leaving my father, I suppose, in the Paul Newman role of the handsome, upstart intruder, which would have pleased him). And then at about 1.30 a.m. they played one last frame, to be king of the world.

Dad took the break but bungled it. Matty slaughtered three reds, one pink and one yellow, but left the black hanging over the top pocket. Dad took over, hammered in a red, then the black, then another red, the black again, brought the white ball down to the semicircular home-base; from there he cannoned reds, and the blue and the yellow, into their snug redoubts. Matty recovered with a tight assault on the far pockets, finishing off the reds, slamming in the black again and again in both corners.

An hour later, they were square, with only one red and the pink left. More ham sandwiches appeared. Even the least competitive guest could see this was a moment to be treasured, a Homeric hiatus. The two men eyed each other, prowled around the table like elderly tigers unwilling to admit extinction. For fifteen minutes, no ball went down. The pink and the black sashayed around the table like neurotic party guests, anxious to avoid the impertinent white ball.

At last, Dad drove the pink slowly into the side pocket, which it entered as though with a sigh. Six points to him; seven left on the table. The black lay poised tight against the cushion. But his cue ball barely touched it, left it with a kiss of regret and settled a foot away.

'Ah,' said Matty. 'Are you givin' it away?'

The crowd in the living room shrieked: 'Go on Matty!' 'Give it some stick!'

His pale blue eyes narrowed in concentration. He took his time and chalked the cue as if his life depended on it. He bent down, sighted the straight line of the white, the black, the hole.

'I'll never get this,' he said. 'Shall we call it a night?'

'No!' the crowd yelled.

Nobody wanted a draw – kind though it would have been to my father. A tribal instinct prevailed at the last moment. They preferred to see the 'blow-in' beaten fair and square.

Matty extended and stretched his arms. Up came his cue, a slender wooden spear against the old enemy. 'All right so,' he said. He bent his full length over the table, his arms across the greensward and let fly. The black ball shot off the white into the far pocket at an astound-ing angle and sank.

There was uproar. The old dog from Clare had beaten the London invader. In our living room, on the last night of this curious Anglo-Irish idyll, the local boy had won. Madelyn hugged Matty. Kate hugged my father. Ger Cochrane beamed. Charlie O'Connor embraced any available women. My father adopted his we-was-robbed face and consoled himself with a foaming beer.

'This night'll never come again,' my father used to say when party guests in London expressed a desire to go home at 2 a.m. For once he was right. This night would never come again.

XII

IN THE HEART OF THE HIBERNIAN METROPOLIS

A year after university my father said, 'I've a bit of money saved up from the child allowance. Why don't you go and do a postgraduate degree in Ireland, if you're so keen on the place, and I'll give you the money.'

It was a nice idea. With my modest Upper Second in English Literature I'd been considering an academic career. I needed a year-long course, nothing too challenging, to see if solitary research and I would ever be suited, and I needed one in Ireland.

A morning on the telephone established that there were two possibilities: Trinity College Dublin, a Protestant university where once it had been considered actually sinful for Catholic Irish parents to send their children, and University College Dublin. University College offered a masters degree in something called Anglo-Irish Studies taking in literature, history, politics, folklore, mythology, dialect, an intense one-year crash course in the soul of the Irish culture in English. It sounded perfect. It would be the first time I'd lived outside the British mainland.

But what did I know of Dublin? I'd travelled through it half a dozen times. A noble city in a different but familiar country where everyone spoke English as my parents spoke it. That western metropolis, a centre of ancient culture, a maze of backstreets full of the ghosts of mythologised figures – Behans, Kavanaghs, Flann O'Briens and a Nighttown of Molly Blooms, of girls eyeing you under streetlamps, dark goings-on in doorways, sudden claspings and fumblings 'darker than the swoon of sin'? Perhaps I was just a little too influenced by Joyce; but then I was passionately keen on Irish literature. In my new role as Honorary Irishman, I was outraged to think that the Irish contribution to the Western canon had been so casually expropriated by the old colonial enemy. Look, I used to rant to my Oxford buddies, if you want to see how much Ireland has contributed to English letters, try removing a few of its major players from the English Literature Premier League and see what a hole it makes: take away Swift and Burke and Sterne and Sheridan and Goldsmith, remove Wilde and Synge and O'Casey, Joyce and Beckett and Yeats and what are you left with? Does the twentieth century boast a finer poet than Yeats, a better prose writer than Joyce, a better playwright than Shaw? Look at the Irish Nobel laureates: there's Yeats and Shaw and Beckett. And the English can offer . . . ? Ah yes, Kipling (an embarrassment), Galsworthy (a total has-been) and Bertrand Russell and Winston Churchill, whose connection to literature, rather than to philosophy, history or rhetoric, has always been a little hard to fathom.

In Dublin I wanted to explore the see-saw of my dual heritage, to immerse myself in Irish writing, to try to connect up the imaginations of my favourite authors, to see how subversively they used the language of the oppressor. And finally, of course, I wanted to join in. I wanted to be not just a writer but an Irish writer. 'And of course,' said my father, realising something of this, 'you'll have a chance to check out your roots. You've been a fake Irishmen over here long enough. It's time you tried being a fake Englishman over there.'

I applied for a place on the course and, to my delight, got in. I said goodbye to London, to my family and university friends who were gradually drifting into the metropolis, caught the ferry and rented a flat on the north side of O'Connell Street. My cousin Maurice from Graig Abbey, now a solicitor living in a district Venetianly named Rialto, was appalled.

'North Great George's Street?' he shouted. 'Of all the places you could choose to live in Dublin, why there?'

'It seems okay,' I said, 'and it is very central.'

'So is the Liffey,' observed Maurice, 'but you wouldn't want to live in that either.'

'What have you got against it?'

'John. *John* . . .' Maurice performed a characteristic gesture of holding up his right hand before his face as if about to swat an enormous wasp. 'The place is a *kip*. You could get shot living up there. It's one street along from Gardiner Street, and the police won't walk up there except in twos. The place is full of gurriers who'll set fire to your car unless you pay them protection money.'

'But Maurice,' I pointed out, 'I don't have a car.'

'Mark my words,' he said. 'Terrible things will happen to you.'

Maurice's concern turned out to be unfounded. North Great George's Street *was* a kip, but no more so than any of the dives, crash pads, lock-ups and attics in which students the world over find themselves temporarily billeted.

The Dublin I found seemed a spectacular honeycomb of student dwellings and nurses' quarters, like the barracks of a visiting army. After a few weeks I'd worked out the housing rules. If you were Dublin-born, young and single, you tended to live gratis with your parents. If you were too rebellious or too grown-up to live at home, you shared a house in Rathmines with others, sleeping in a bedroom strewn with Cup-a-Soup packets, paper tissues, old newspapers and socks, pretending not to notice the student debris that was enveloping you. If you were from out of town, you found digs which you shared with a family. You just put up with whatever you could afford.

My new home was the tiny top-floor eyrie of a high Victorian townhouse, once, presumably, the sleeping quarters of the under-house parlourmaid. To reach it you had to climb a staircase so grand, so long and flowing, it was like the staircase down which Joan Fontaine disastrously glided in Hitchcock's *Rebecca*. The attic had been converted into a flat. There was a living room, which featured a cooker at one end and a chaise longue languorously parked at the other, a separate bathroom and a boudoir large enough to contain a bed but little else. Some days, sunlight would spill into the hallway from the skylight on the sloping roof.

On my first morning I was awakened by the sound of two gulls noisily fornicating overhead, their webbed and hooky feet slipping on the glass. I rubbed my eyes. Seagulls? But of course the Liffey was only about half a mile away and the Irish Sea not much further. I'd never lived anywhere like this – an airy garret with a mansion below and a pair of Yeatsian white birds directly above. I unpacked and plugged in the hi-fi, filched some bricks and planks from a neighbour-hood skip and built a rudimentary bookcase. I painted the bedroom a sexy Celtic Twilight blue and, at 11a.m., cooked my first breakfast of eggs, middle-bacon rashers and black pudding, studded with sinewy white fat pearls. I surveyed my new home. Sunlight, the strident clang of nearby scaffolding, the fiddle-and-*bodran* backed voice of Christy Moore on my record player, aromas of drying paint, bacon, patchouli incense (a small nod to my London life), seagulls . . . they all crowded rapturously into my senses. I lay on the chaise longue and closed my eyes. Me and Dublin, I thought, we're going to get along fine.

My immediate environs were bleak – Gardiner Street, as my cousin had warned, was full of wrecked cars, abandoned housing projects and holes in the road. But at least the worst thing that happened in the immediately vicinity – a volley of gunfire outside a discotheque in Parnell Square some weeks in the future – I only read about in the *Evening Herald*. I was still entranced to be there, and to be so close to the heart of the Hibernian metropolis (to borrow a headline from the 'Aeolus' chapter of *Ulysses*).

I walked all over the city in my first few weeks there, marvelling at how compact, youthful (two-thirds of the population were under twenty-five) and how breathtakingly bricky it was. I was amazed by it all. There seemed to be far more brick buildings than in London – oceans, tidal waves of brick coursing through the immensely wide thoroughfares. Leeson Street, Baggot Street, Merrion Square, Fitz-william Square – they seemed unfeasibly broad, exceedingly grand, the long Regency terraces spaced apart as though to deny any connection with their neighbours across the road. A walk down Leeson Street, through tracts of Irish boulevard, was a dismaying enterprise; you felt dwarfed and helpless, as though you'd never get to your destination. The city had been built on epic lines. The streets were like those built during a totalitarian regime: long, wide and straight so there'd be no shelter for fleeing dissidents and counter-revolutionaries once the shooting started.

But away from the posh end of town, and the bower-strewn walkways of Stephen's Green, where I strolled every day and fed the ducks, Dublin was a city of snugs, tiny saloon bars, a tight warren of shops and impromptu stalls. The longer streets seemed to change their name every hundred yards or so, as if embarrassed about giving themselves airs. The biggest surprise was Moore Street, tucked away like a secret halfway down O'Connell Street. Here lay a street market apparently unchanged from the 1950s, where the traders – mostly women – stood tough and indomitable in their pinafores, like figures straight from Millais or Breughal, with accents you could cut with a butter-knife.

'*Par*-snups, only ten pence!'

'Ta-*mah*tas, thorty pence a pow-und. 'Tis givin' it away I am'

'*Arrnges*, twenty-foi-ave pence. Willya go *on* . . .'

It took me back to Battersea and my mother doing her dainty Lady-of-the-Manor saunter among the market traders; but the men on their barrows in the Northcote Road seemed more like characters from a Terence Rattigan play compared to the amazons of Moore Street.

If you paused for a moment to window-shop at the butchers a couple streets away, you would be disconcerted to hear a voice coming over the shop's Tannoy, telling you, in a clever, oleaginous parody of Gay Byrne, where to look among all the meat on display: 'And, emm, we have some lovely chops in this morning, *lovely* lamb chops, not too small, plenty of meat on them for the family's tea. Or if you were thinkin' of goin' out this evening, and you'd need a bite to eat, just somethin' quick before goin' out, what could be nicer than the chump chop? Look at them, there, just in front of you and to the right . . .' You couldn't actually see who was doing this sales pitch, or if their patter was on a tape loop or was being individually tailored for each passing customer, but the effect was of being bullied. You felt it would be unwise not to direct your gaze where the voice told you. I never bought anything in the shop, for fear that I might hear the Tannoy announcing to the whole street that I'd made some terrible retail blunder. ('That fella there in the blue jacket, *look* at him, the eejit, he's just bought *one* spare rib, Jesus, spare *ribs*, the cheapest thing in the shop, he must be some class of student, if *that*'s all he's gointa live off for a week, the hoor . . .')

And who was Gay Byrne? He was unmissable, on the radio five mornings a week, and in glowing television colour every Friday on Ireland's popular talk-fest, *The Late Late Show*. Every morning you'd wake to his precise, insistent tones on RTE radio, where he combined two roles: that of eezee-listening DJ, flirting with the housewives and reading out the names of supermarkets where the best bargains in Daz or biscuits were to be found, and secondly, the more discreet and unannounced role of the nation's conscience. Under his compassionate probing, the radio phone-in became a national forum where the disaffected, the lovelorn and the socially disadvantaged compared notes about their state and complained about it to the rest of the country. Most of the audience was Irish housewives, but Byrne had a way of implying that their problems were the nation's problems. His radio programme received a letter one morning from a woman in the rural west, complaining that although her husband gave her an allowance every week for food, housekeeping and buying the children's clothes, he never actually spoke to her any more – that is, literally, he had not spoken a single word to her for years, except perhaps to mutter 'Happy Christmas'.

Should she expect more? Had she a right to complain? It was a tragic letter, a terrible confession from an intelligent, fluent and frustrated country wife, and it elicited a flood of replies from women with similarly bleak and silent marriages all over the country. It raised questions of what constituted being 'a good husband', of the unbreakable Catholic marriage, of the feminist rumblings that were being heard in the Republic in the mid-seventies and of how the Irish male was stuck in the behavioural patterns of an earlier generation. Heaven knows what could be done about the phenomenon, but it momentarily raised the consciousness of all concerned by admitting there was a problem at all.

Not for the first time, Gay Byrne gave the impression that he was presiding over a nation talking to itself, a three-million-strong audience who had suddenly become a discussion group, focused on a single subject and looking for a solution. It was fantastically un-British. I had heard disc jockeys sometimes air serious topics on British radio shows, but they would be subjects pre-chewed by the newspapers. They didn't deal with issues at (literally) the grass roots. The British population is just too huge for a single subject to hold the attention of the majority for more than a day, with the sole exceptions of the World Cup and the death of a famous Royal.

Lying in bed in my north Dublin student eyrie, I listened to the radio a lot. I liked the advertisements. The Co-op, for instance, had a series of commercials which began with a guess-the-noise moment. One opened with a succession of bangs and thumps and in-and-out sawing noises, followed by a voice explaining: 'This is the sound of a Co-op butcher giving a customer exactly what she wants . . .' I liked the potted history drama-documentaries on Saturday mornings, in which great feats of scene-setting were performed by the sound effects department announcing the onset of the French Revolution with gunshots, cries of 'Sacre bleu!' and a burst of the Marseillaise on the accordion.

But the constant backdrop to my reading, writing essays on Yeats's *The Tower* and grilling pork chops, was Irish music. Throughout my childhood in London my father had played it between recitals by Bridie Gallagher and John McCormack; but then it had been hardly more than a diddly-diddly-dee sound, a type of comforting sonic wallpaper. Now I started listening to it seriously, taking in its tonal shifts and random improvisations, the gorgeous layering of guitar on mandolin, on flute on fiddle . . . I went to concerts and met a band just starting out called Stockton's Wing. 'You must go to London,' I assured them. One of their recordings, an eight-minute, double-stranded courtly rhapsody called 'The Belltable', became a lifelong favourite, one of the tunes you know you'd pick if you ever went on *Desert Island Discs*.

At weekends I endlessly patrolled the gentle swell of the Killiney Hills that overlook the crouching bear of Howth Head, where Leopold and Molly Bloom went a-courting and she kissed him with her mouth full of seedcake. I took a Belgian fellow-student called Brigitte on a romantic picnic to Phoenix Park beneath the fantastic obelisk that was Dublin's tallest landmark. But although I was discovering the city, I wasn't managing to connect with the Irish I'd set out to find, to link myself to them in a new blood relationship. None of my fellow-students was English, or Irish; they were mostly Americans, Germans and Japanese. Most Irish graduates had generally had enough of Yeats, Joyce, et alia, force-fed to them at school and university to consider studying them at greater length. British graduates would, naturally, look for a graduate course at a British university, where they could get a grant. I was therefore the only representative of either nation. Being a kind of English-Irishman, I spanned the cultures (or so I liked to think) but I wasn't meeting any Irishmen of my age with whom to share my thoughts.

So, I immersed myself in the MA course. Taking its starting point as 1800, with the publication of Maria Edgeworth's small but rich and ironical novel of Big House feudalism, *Castle Rackrent*, the course twined discrete strands of Irish culture into a single braid. It was the brainchild of Roger McHugh, a white-haired and pugnacious academic of uncertain temper, who gave us a gruffly perfunctory opening lecture and left us to it. His teaching team was an intriguingly varied crowd, representing several strains of nationality.

The Yeats classes were taken by Augustine ('Gus') Martin, a portly cove with the palest blue eyes I'd ever seen and an ebullient manner; a backslapping bonhomie you'd otherwise find only at rugby internationals. He had a fruity, acktorish delivery but was an uncertain reader of poetry. Though he'd been teaching Yeats for years, he discouraged any fancy theorising about the mythic underpinnings of famous lyrics. As far as he was concerned, the 'glimmering girl' who turns up in the 'Song of Wandering Aengus' was a tantalising babe from Yeats's erotomaniacal imagination, rather than any manifestation of the unreachable soul, as expressed in *A Vision*. 'Very interesting, now,' he'd say if you brought up the mythic dimension. 'Good man. A very interesting contribution,' and move on to something more down-to-earth. You got the impression that Dr Martin would have liked to give this essentially ethereal figure a bit of a seeing-to if only she'd stuck around a bit longer.

By contrast there was Seamus Deane, a gaunt, chain-smoking, harassed-looking Derryman who took classes in Joyce's prose. He'd been at school with Seamus Heaney and was doomed to live forever in Heaney's shadow, under the sobriquet of 'Seamus Not-Quite-So-Famous', that is until he almost won the Booker Prize in 1996 with his family memoir, *Reading in the Dark*, but won the *Irish Times* award for it instead.

Deane was a curly-haired Republican with a very uncurly disposition. He breathed academic combativeness and political passion. He tried to conceal his boredom at having to teach a crowd of clueless Americans, Germans, Belgians and me, and covered it up with a gritty aloofness that put everyone on their guard. One morning he gave the most extraordinary lecture. He was introducing Joyce's *Ulysses*. The talk began with the intellectual fallout of the French Revolution, and presented a brisk *tour d'horizon* of Western thought in the early nineteenth century, and its expression in Tom Paine, Coleridge, Wordsworth, Shelley, Byron; the efflorescence of the novel in England, France, Germany, Russia. He explored a dozen disparate tendencies of formal experiment and stylistic expression through Dickens, Eliot, Trollope, Thackeray, Flaubert, Stendhal, Tolstoy, Turgenev, Dosteovsky. Whole swathes of European literature were briefly caught up, inspected for their part in this onrushing spiral of cultural history, and just as briskly dismissed. Suddenly we were at the turn of the century: Zola's grubby-petticoat realism versus Henry James's cathedrals of psychological enquiry; the influence of Ibsen's Nora and the European short story on George Moore's *The Untilled Field* and *Esther Waters*; and the spiral was suddenly tightening down to England and Ireland, to focus on the contrasting outputs of London and Dublin as the new century arrived and with it the breaking of forms that was known as Modernism, and this great, whirling, pan-European dialectic of thought and literature was pulling in, like a zoom-lens camera, towards a single city, Dublin, and a single day – 16 June 1904, Blooms-day – the day on which almost the whole action of *Ulysses* is set.

Deane subsided. I sat there stunned and delighted. I've known people since then who can give the impression in conversation that they are talking about a dozen different subjects apparently at the same time. But at twenty-two, I'd never known a performance to beat it. So here he is, I thought – the most brilliant scholar I've ever met.

The others couldn't but seem a little dowdy after Deane's omniv-orous dazzle. Maurice Harmon, who took classes in modern Irish poetry, was a nervous-seeming chap, like a grammar-school classics master, sure of what he knew already but never likely to start foaming at the mouth with enthusiasm for anything else. He had written a small, cautious appreciation of John Montague. He would produce a small, judicious account of Brian Moore.

Christopher Murray, the drama tutor, was a mild, rather than a dramatic man, punctilious about details. He could become exasperated about, say, the inept dispersal of footnotes. He led us relentlessly through some unforgivably bad late works by Sean O'Casey, when the self-mythologising dramatist had lost his demotic rage and become drenched in sentimentality; Dr Murray only seemed mildly put out to hear O'Casey abused by the likes of myself.

More problematic was J. C. C. Mays, a pale, highly-strung English-man who introduced the class to Beckett's prose, and was himself full of Beckettian mannerisms. He flinched at harsh lights, and could not enter a classroom without asking that the strip lighting be switched off. He wore polychromatic spectacles that darkened or lightened as the weather outside the windows changed through the afternoon. It meant you could be looking directly into his alarmed blue eyes at the start of a conversation, and be gazing, by the end, at two circles of darkness, as if their owner had sloped off and gone into hiding. He was fastidious to the point of pain. His practically whinnied with distaste when one of the Germans opined that the point of *Waiting for Godot* was surely that the characters were socio-economic failures.

There was an uncoordinated young English bluestocking called Susan who took us for Irish prose. She lived in the east wing of an Ascendancy house in the Blackrock suburbs. We were once invited to 'take soup' with her and duly traipsed out to the run-down Protestant mansion that was her dreamy dwelling-place.

And there was Alan Bliss, a wolfish, no-nonsense former Oxford don who taught us dialect and was a repository of unusual information. While studying the Irish famine, for instance, he'd been intrigued by the idea of a population surviving on potatoes and buttermilk and nothing else, year round. So he asked a dietician to investigate the potato's balance of vitamins, enzymes and therapeutic properties and see how they matched the needs of the human body. Back came the reply: they match absolutely. The humble spud contained everything the body needs in order to survive. The problem, said the dietician, is the numbing boredom of having it every day, a regimen that your system might finally react against psychologically, by slowing down, enervated by the constant procession of boiled and mashed tubers. It gave you a startling new perspective on the psycho-physiology of 1840s peasantry.

And that was the line-up. Among the teaching staff, as exemplars of Irish academe, we had one Dublin bar-room chorus leader, one steely Northern poet, one civil-servantish academic, one school-masterly thespian and three English people in varying degrees of odd-ness, two of them parodically British and the third wrapped up in some Big House dream. I wasn't sure that, in my attempts to integrate the two halves of my identity, this was the best place to start. For the moment, though, I tried to enjoy Dublin as a destination rather than some kind of psychic territory.

One of the odder entertainments available to us was to join an extra-curricular literary group that was trying to tease all the myriad levels of meaning out of *Finnegans Wake*. It was run by a man named Roland McHugh, an odd but charismatic academic who had proved too weird for the universities to handle. He ran an exegetical salon just off Stephen's Green and seemed to be otherwise self-employed. He had read nothing but Joyce's *Wake* for the last eleven years, he said, and could envisage reading nothing else for the rest of his life. He was obsessed with the 'sigla', a kind of encryption code in Joyce's worknotes that suggested various running themes that hadn't been glimpsed by critics before. And he attended brainstorming sessions of the International Joyce Brotherhood, where they'd take one sentence at a time and unweave all its semantic strands until it yielded up every possible layer of meaning.

McHugh would allow us, his audience, a glimpse of these proceedings by taking a small phrase or word, and asking us to guess what other phrases or words were buried or echoed or alluded to in it. The *Wake* word 'cropse' was thus dissected to reveal a portmanteau of 'copse', meaning a little wood, 'corpse' and 'crops' — a tiny cycle of death and renewal in a single monosyllable. We were invited to join in, but only on the understanding that Professor McHugh already knew everything that was worth knowing about Joyce's tantalising dreamscape. One evening he confessed that the most recent convention of Joycean super-brains had stumbled over the made-up word 'insimples', which turns up in a paragraph of what appears to be musical notations. The assembled academics had puffed their pipes and devilled away, looking for meanings that had something to do with instruments and performance.

'The word "simples", as in herbs and simples, is in there, of course, with its sense of healing and the healing power of music,' said McHugh. 'And "symbols" is implicit too, with the pun on "cymbals", but I'm sure there's something missing. There must be some reason Joyce began the word with "in". It cannot be merely arbitrary. He is far too . . .'

'Stop me if I'm being too obvious here,' said a woman in the audience. 'But isn't it "*ensembles*"?'

'What?' asked McHugh, peeved at the interruption. 'What did you say?'

'It's "*ensembles*", surely,' the woman persisted. 'Although it sounds better if you say "enn-sembals". Surely that's only two vowels and one consonant away from "insimples". Or not? Just a thought.'

The professor's face was a picture. He stared at the floor, like a man teasing something out of his molar with an exploring tongue. He mouthed the French word *ensembles,* then the English transliteration. At length he raised his head and looked at the audience.

'Ensembles,' he whispered, 'that's *it*.' The audience gave the exegete an ironic round of applause, but the professor stopped them. 'This is not a *game*,' he said. 'This is an invaluable contribution to Joyce studies. I'm most grateful to you, madam. Now if we could look at the phrase "tauftauf thuartpeatrick" . . .'

We went home feeling as if we'd been initiated into the mysteries of creation.

To me, Dublin was a place where grandeur and decay did not go just hand in hand but virtually danced in the streets. Along O'Connell Bridge, hennaed-haired tinkers sat with their children, proffering cardboard trays for people to put money on, as if they might be contaminated by hand-to-hand contact. A mile away, the calm white dome of the Four Courts loomed like a great graceful umbrella, promising justice for all. And between the two locations you could find yourself walking through half a dozen levels of socio-economic achievement. On the Quays, beside the Liffey, there were shops that seemed to have been unoccupied for years with Scotch tape stuck over the broken glass in their windows. But beside the gorgeous lattice of the Halfpenny Bridge, there was a treasure trove of secondhand bookshops, probably the same ones at which Leopold Bloom buys the work of Jan de Kok for his wife in 1904. At Bewley's Café in Grafton Street, waiters ferried plates of braised beef with gravy and vegetables, a dish familiar to my mother's generation; but on Dame Street there were fancy new American diners, all chrome and flash lighting effects. The city, in its elderly finery, seemed to be aching to join in with the modern world, but seemed unsure how to do it. If seventies Dublin were a fictional character, I thought, it would surely be Miss Havisham in *Great Expectations*.

I tried to introduce the Yanks on the course to Dublin life. I took them to The Stag and the Abbey Tavern and McDaid's, where Paddy Kavanagh and Brendan Behan and Flann O'Brien used to drink their lives away; to the Long Hall and the Bailey, where the front door of Number 7, Eccles Street (the real-life front door of the fictional home of Bloom and Molly) had been rescued from demolition and cemented into the wall; to the famous trio of Baggot Street boozers – Toner's, Nesbit's and O'Donoghues – where you might catch some fiddle music on a Friday night, surrounded by flop-haired Dubliners. The guys on the course, Bill and Patrick, Gerry, Fred and Wolfgang, liked it all well enough, but the American girls just looked around with haughty, daughters-of-the-Mayflower distaste. They were not used to pub culture and this was not how ladies were treated in Thunder Bay or the Hamptons. There you didn't get thumped in the ribs every few minutes, or were asked to sit at a bar that was sticky with spilt beer and have smoke blown in your eyes. The Americans were unused to Dublin's closing-time rodomontade. When the pubs emptied in the afternoon for the mandatory holy hour (from 2.30 to 3.30 p.m.), the man in Toner's would hasten our departure by yelling in our ears, 'Now lads, c'mon. Now Lads, please, *now PLEASE!*' on a rising note of hysteria until the Yanks visibly flinched.

Windy spring turned to bosky summer. The trees along the Grand Canal, where Patrick Kavanagh celebrated his post-op return from the dead, came into flaming bosomy leaf. Dublin women in sensible shoes and pencil skirts lay in attitudes of abandon on Stephen's Green, soaking up the midday sunshine. And on one such day my sister arrived in town. Now twenty-three, newly fledged from a post-graduate course in tourist management, apple-cheeked and *soignée*, she flew in to the Irish Tourist Board looking for work. On her way to the interview, the Dublin taxi-driver surveyed her critically in the rear view mirror: 'You're not goin' looking for a job in them clothes areya?' he asked with brutal directness, dropping her off by a pub to change in the ladies.

She didn't get the job, but she did become friends with her inter-viewer and, through him, met a network of other Bord Failte employees. My favourite was David Hanly, a ginger-bearded glittery-eyed cove who wore a flat cap and drank at Smith's Bar beside Baggot Street Bridge. Hanly and I drank gallons of Guinness together and argued about literature. He had no time for any novelist, Irish or English, except for John Banville, whom he considered a genius; all the others were as fake as plastic shillelaghs. I would go on into the night about Aidan Higgins or John Broderick, only to be met by Hanly's invariable response: 'But the man *just can not write!*'. He was enraging and funny and dreamed of escaping the Tourist Board and decamping with his wife to a paradisal land called Tinahely in County Wicklow, there to write a novel. Which indeed he did a year later, before becoming a famous broadcaster.

Finding young Dubliners to bond with was beginning to be a problem. I was anxious that they didn't think I was English, or an outsider like Wolfgang from Hamburg or Fred from Pittsburg. I had become Irish; I had a library of Irish writers on my shelves and the literary history of the last 200 years under my belt. I knew all the songs, I knew where Leitrim and Cavan were, and what river ran through Cork. I had cousins, actual *family*, who lived in Rialto and Rathfarnham. I could say 'it's raining' and 'God be with you' in Gaelic and I could muster an immaculately authentic Galway accent. I felt fatally drawn to Irish girls, to Irish music and Irish landscapes. I'd taken to eating potato cakes at tea-time in a downstairs café near the Shelbourne Hotel. I rhapsodised about the quality of the *colcannon* (Irish bubble 'n' squeak, only with cream and onions, utterly delicious). I ignored the creeping spread of globalisation (like the arrival of McDonald's in Grafton Street) and concentrated instead on the special-issue poetry chapbooks in the Eblana bookshop, the ancient humidor smell of the tobacco shop across the road from Trinity College and the elegance of Brown Thomas's – the Liberty's of Dublin – and other such manifestations of genuine, authentic, old Irishness. I tapped my foot to the flute-and-fiddle buskers in Nassau Street. I nodded in respect to the great stone head of the über-Fenian O'Donovan Rossa in Stephen's Green. I made the pilgrimage to Davy Byrne's 'moral pub', where Leopold Bloom had a cheese sandwich and a glass of Burgundy on Bloomsday. I was as Irish as Irish could be. But maddeningly, the expected transformation didn't work.

Longing for authentic Irish company, I used to call at the house where three Galway sisters I knew lived together. One made documentaries for RTE, one gave piano lessons and the third worked in a bank. But Chekhovian parallels weren't appropriate – none of the sisters was married, they didn't pine for a far-off Moscow since they already lived in the heart of a capital city, and they all worked too hard to feel stifled by aristocratic ennui. I would take them for drinks, chat in their kitchen, tell them grotesque stories about the Americans on the course, listen to the news from home and shamble off into the night. They were all good-looking career women who could hold their drinks with any man. I basked in their company and, in time, found myself mesmerised by the middle sister, the piano teacher. She had vast cat's eyes, which widened like searchlights as she described some scary incident in the badlands around her home. Her mouth would set in a sarcastic smile that went up at one corner. She was skinny but her bosom sprang away from her ribcage like a maddened schnauzer on a tight leash. She had a way of adjusting the sleeves of her black sweater – pinching the underside of the material to pull them back from her wrists – that affected me as if it were the preliminary move in some indescribable act of darkness. I adored her. I came to see all three girls, and if the piano player was absent, would spend the time happily with the other two. But if – let us call her Imelda – was there, I would follow her around the house like a spaniel, unable to let her out of my sight, desperate to woo her, as might any other Dublin beau trying his luck. In a massive push to impress her, I took her to a Dr Feelgood concert; but the walls of speakers obscured our view of the band, and my attempts to shift our seats resulted in our being flung by bouncers into the side aisles like rubbish bags.

She ignored me. That is, she ignored me as a potential lover. She was friendly, as one is to people dimly connected with one's home town – or as you might be nice to the brother of the paperboy from your parents' village, were he to turn up in Dublin looking for a bit of a crack in a bar. She treated me like a brother. Worse, she sometimes treated me like a *girlfriend*. One late evening, drinking in her kitchen, I was trying (perhaps a fraction too hard) to impress her with my grasp of Irish prosody, when she hoicked up her black top: 'Have you seen me new brassiere, John?' she asked. 'Isn't it *lovely*?'

It was red and very full. I don't remember much else.

'Go on with what you were saying, anyway,' she'd said, but I'd lost interest in the subject. I knew that, whatever I was doing, it was not stoking the fires of passion in this Dublin female.

Imelda and her sisters apart, it was hard to make friends among young Dubliners. They were an exclusive lot. The undergraduates of UCD wouldn't talk to elderly twenty-two-year-old foreigners on the masters course; they stuck to their own, creating little villages of gossip and romance in a simulacrum of home. The young Dubliners I saw in pubs tended to be invariably absorbed in the most urgent conversations; they'd sit across table for hours telling each other things as if their lives depended on it. The Dubliners I met at parties mostly lived at home in the posher suburbs of Mount Merrion and Stillorgan, Dalkey and Killiney, with a lovely view over Dublin bay, the home of lawyers, surgeons and senior managers who drove Mercedes and Volvos and drank vodka-martinis and attended the theatre. They would have slotted easily into the stockbroker belt of Kent and Surrey, and so would their children. But they weren't really my sort of people, and I wasn't really theirs. I could get on fine with a twentysomething Blackrock lawyer, talking about music or current affairs or the iniquities of the nation's 50 per cent tax burden; but should some other suburban achiever enter the conversation, I was instantly marginalised. Suddenly it was them against the English intruder. You could practically hear them asking each other, sotto voce, 'Who's yer man?'

Emboldened by my success singing for the company in Galway, I'd occasionally play the guitar at Mount Merrion parties. It wasn't a success. I tried a heartfelt version of 'The Old Bog Road' – a classic folk song that would have gone down a storm in Mills's Bar, Killaloe. I wasn't two lines into it before the girl on the chair beside me snorted derisively: 'Oh Christ, not *that* old thing. My *mother* used to sing that. Don't you know anything else?'

'Okay, then,' I said, slightly miffed. 'This is a new song by Loudon Wainwright III.' And I sang 'Rufus is a Tit Man', a brilliant if slightly risqué number about the American songwriter's baby son:

Rufus is a tit man, sucking on his mother's glands,
Sucking on the nipple that's sweeter than the ripple wine.
Oh it's sweeter than the wine.
You can tell by the way the boy burps, it's gotta taste fine . . .

By the end of the first verse, it was clear that this was no better. 'Well that's charming, I must say,' observed the lady in the chair. There was, evidently, no pleasing some people.

The year drifted by, offering small upsets and rewards. Halfway through a lesson on *The Candle of Vision*, a numinous piece of mystical wool-gathering by Yeats's friend George Russell (whose nom de plume was 'AE'), the lady from Thunder Bay, Canada, asked: 'Wait a minute. Are we supposed to take any of this stuff about the Great Memory *seriously*?'

'Well not exactly,' said Susan, the teacher, mildly. 'But mysticism played an important part in the nineties Zeitgeist.'

'Yeah, but it's all so *turgid*. And it doesn't make any sense. Is this book supposed to be a work of Great Literature?'

'Well, no,' conceded Susan, 'admittedly its appeal hasn't lasted.'

'So why are we studying him? As some kind of *phenomenon*?' The class broke up by mutual agreement shortly afterwards. The late George Russell found himself on the Eternal Slush Pile, as far as the course was concerned.

More sinister was the Beckett Experience. James Mays, the neuras-thenic Englishman with the ever-deepening shades, told us we would now embark on the Beckett trilogy. Portentously, he wished us luck. We were to read *Molloy* and re-convene in a week, having simply made sense of its narrative structure. The following Tuesday, we discussed it and were told to read the middle book, *Malone Dies*. 'And are all of you feeling *okay*?' he asked, 'everybody happy in themselves?'

Sure, we replied, why the mystery? The next Tuesday came. We discussed our responses and were sent to read the final book, *The Unnameable*, like troops being waved off on a difficult mission.

A week later, in mid-discussion, Mays unfolded a piece of yellowed newsprint. The headline read: 'Irish Writer Cracks Up English Student.' A couple of years before, it turned out, a woman on the course had reacted to the *Trilogy* as to a creeping virus of insanity. Naturally withdrawn and shy, she had become noticeably quieter after reading *Molloy*. During the class discussion of *Malone Dies*, she had begun talking to herself, in a stream of consciousness rant that was increasingly hard to ignore. Halfway through reading *The Unnameable*, so the story went, she had a nervous breakdown. And guess what? An ambulance arrived to take her away to the asylum that figures in Beckett's *Murphy* under the name of the 'Magdalen Mental Mercyseat'. 'That's literature for you,' was a popular local opinion. 'All that book-learning, it'll do for you in the end.'

It was a good story, despite its implausibilities, and left us feeling like ragged survivors of some psychological assault course. But I confess I wondered if there was a faint whiff of triumphalism in the newspaper headline – as if the victim's Englishness were an issue, as if an Irish audience could be proud to think a new way had been found of screwing up the old enemy.

I got to know the Beckett Experience closely, as I fell under the thrall of his prose. In the summer months, I rented another student bedsit in the leafy environs of Mount Pleasant. It was the kind of place where, having no fridge, you'd leave a carton of vanilla yoghurt sitting on the windowsill for two days and discover, on returning home one night, that it had exploded all over your bed.

In these new surroundings, I set to read every word Beckett had ever written. Nothing in twenty years of reading had prepared me for the voice of the *Trilogy*, of *Texts for Nothing*, of *Mercier and Camier* and *The Lost Ones*, of the *Dialogues with Georges Duthuit*, the art criticism, the dementedly precise production notes for *Endgame* and *Godot*, the final fragmental experiments and impossible landscapes, the self-cancelling prose of *Imagination Dead Imagine* and *Lessness*. I was amazed by the way the voice went round and round my head, naggingly, excitably, birth-and-death-confusingly, endlessly drawing near to the discovery of what cannot be said and how the artist might yet say it. I'd go to bed with Beckett's voice, wake up with it, move around the bedsit with it winding through my matutinal thoughts, coax an omelette into shape on the stark iron cooker with one hand, while writing notes on little pink file cards with the other.

I began to recite certain sentences over and over, like a talisman. One line from *Krapp's Last Tape* reverberated in my brain: 'Crawled out a few times before the summer got cold. Sat shivering in the park, drowned in dreams and burning to be gone.' I was, I suspect, going a little mad. Should I make an appointment at the Magdalen Mental Mercyseat?

One morning I was trying to write at my desk, when I heard a burst of massed clapping from somewhere outside. I went on writing. The applause came again, some minutes later, with appreciative cries of: 'Oh . . . !' And again, a minute later. Evidently, some sporting event was taking place somewhere near my front door. But there was no park nearby that I knew of. And what sport, I wondered, drew such applause, such genteel clapping, several minutes apart? It couldn't be tennis (the intervals would be shorter). Or football or hurling (nobody claps at a goal in either). Golf maybe? As I tried to concentrate, interrupted by further muted bursts of applause, it dawned on me that the impossible was happening: a game of cricket was in session not a hundred yards away from me.

Cricket in Ireland? Impossible. The great sporting symbol of British colonialism had never taken any popular root in Ireland. How could it be happening on a Wednesday morning in the heart of Dublin? The only explanation lay in the text before me. Beckett was a keen cricketer when young; he was the only Nobel prize winner ever to have appeared in *Wisden*. Somehow, my brain had conjured up an arena in which he could return, steel-framed spectacles flashing in the sun, to make a hundred before lunch as I, his most recent acolyte, beavered away making sense of his new book, *For To End Yet Again*.

I went out into the street to take a look. At the end of the cul-de-sac, a small wire-mesh opening revealed a whole undiscovered neighbouring cricket pitch, across which a tall, hairy-moustached man was running up to bowl with long-limbed grace. I could see a small crowd sitting in the sunshine, listlessly greeting any half-hearted strike by the batting side.

I took a bus into town. There I witnessed, through a television-rentals window, the same match being relayed on a dozen screens. It was,

'Thommo and Lillie,' said the owner. 'Nice havin' the Aussies in town.'

A wave of nostalgia hit me. The touring Australian team were in Dublin. The world-defying combination of Jeff Thompson and Dennis Lillee had been outside my front door, and I'd never noticed. Nor had anyone I knew in Dublin had the faintest clue it was going on, or thought to tell me. A long-standing fan of test matches, I instantly yearned to be back in London, at the Oval, listening to the ball-by-ball commentary on Radio Three, with the joshing interpolations of Henry Blofeld and Brian Johnson ('Ah, look – here comes a pipe – and there's Fred Trueman on the end of it') while surveying the action through binoculars, as I'd done on countless summer days before.

And it struck me – what on earth was I doing in Dublin? I liked it fine, from the posh fanlights of Fitzwilliam Square to the brick tenements of Rathmines. I liked the wan autumnal twilight, the gulls on the Liffey, the National Library in Nassau Street and the snugs of Mulligans Bar; but I did not feel the deep throb of home I'd expected. For me, fatally, there was something too settled and too inert about the place. I had conceived a passion for my Irish family past, only to discover that I couldn't settle in its capital city. Through three suburban districts, thirty pubs, forty Saturday nights, endless wanderings, hill-climbs around Killiney and Howth, bus rides, bicycle rides, cinema trips with Patrick from Chicago, fruitless romantic assaults on the Galway sisters, frowsty Sunday mornings and that unique brand of urban misery that is compounded of turfsmoke, aerials, rain and brick-work, I had chased my Celtic soul down Dublin's long streets. I had longed to find my Irish self over there. Instead I'd just become more English – fastidiously unable to accept a life whose priorities were different. I'd assumed it would somehow all slot into place. I was quite certain I'd fall in love with an Irish girl, introduce her to the cousins in Graig Abbey and the friends in London, before settling down (à la David Hanly) to write a book in my own private Tinahely. There I would hold great dinner parties with Irish bread, English puddings and French burgundy. I'd have become an Anglo-Dubliner, at home exactly midway between London and Galway.

But I'd been wrong. The experimental Irishman I'd tried to become had never really cut the mustard. And the Ireland I'd looked to as home had disoblingingly refused to be any such thing. It hadn't been the heart of *my* Hibernia. It wouldn't have been my father's either. I suspect he would have been as out of place here as I was.

The exams passed in a blur. When they were over, Patrick and I got royally drunk and smoked cigars to celebrate our liberation. He was going back to Chicago, to wait at tables at night and write masterpieces during the day.

I said goodbye to the Irish sisters. They said: 'Cheers now, and if you're ever back here, look us up.' I said goodbye to my last landlord, who complained about the exploded-yoghurt stains on the carpet and withheld my deposit. I said farewell to the nice old man in the tobacconists round the corner. 'Come soon back!' he said cheerily, as I left to pack. Yeah, right, I thought. I was going back to where I started. I was apparently doomed to be an Englishman after all.

XIII

PARTING OF THE WAYS

'I'm going back for good this time,' said my father.

It was 1983. He had lived in London for thirty-three years. '*We're* going back,' he corrected himself.

'Yes, but not to *live*, Dad,' I said. 'It's not possible, is it?'

He did that thing you read about in G. A. Henty novels but rarely see off the page. He *set* his jaw.

'This is different. We're going back to live in Ireland. The thing is, are you coming too?'

He had had enough. My father and his adoptive country had never forged much of a relationship. He might have adopted England, but it had never really taken to him. He had become part of its medical strength, part of the NHS, part of the British electorate, part of the *Daily Telegraph* readership, part of the BBC viewing figures, part of the parish of Battersea, an aficionado of Burton's the tailors, Tesco supermarket and Arding & Hobbs department store; he'd become an avid consumer of English products: Guards cigarettes, Gordon's Gin and Schweppes tonic, Bird's Eye jelly (strawberry flavour), Jacob's Cream Crackers, English beef on Sundays. But he had never bought himself into the English soul.

My father rarely showed any signs of actually disliking England but he mocked English culture and English accents whenever he could, like a rebellious teenager who can't quite understand whether his impulses are hostile or satirical. As my accent got more pronounced in my early twenties, he would repeat things I'd said; the word '*aaactually*' drove him into paroxysms of contempt, twirling an invisible curly moustache like a squadron leader. He looked upon my English friends with suspicion, as if convinced they would somehow betray me, run away and leave me for dead at any moment. Once at a party, I watched, cringing with embarrassment, as a pissed Etonian named Bertie called my father 'my *deah*' with a Wodehousian yap, and told him stories about the legendary stupidity of the Irish. Dad regarded him with interest. 'He must be an awful nice feller, that Bertie,' he remarked to me later, 'if he can get as drunk as that without turnin' violent.'

With English girls he was fantastically gallant. He liked making them laugh. He was a compulsive squeezer of flesh and encircler of waists, a bringer of special-issue, limited-edition drinks of weapons-grade alcoholic content, as though offering them a Valentine's gift tied with a bow. His conversational mode with them was always conspiratorial, no matter what the subject matter. He liked the way English women pretended all the time, the way they let on to be tremendously impressed by *this* or so terribly concerned about *that*; so thrilled by some piece of information, so frightfully cast down by, say, the news of the build-up of nuclear warheads beyond the Ural mountains. He would look into their eyes as they affected their most *faux*-worried frown about matters of health; he knew when they were 'playing up' to him as my mother called it. Once, my girlfriend Elizabeth, came to him about her aunt.

'She's been diagnosed as having a prolapsed womb, Dr Walsh,' she said, breathlessly. 'Is that dangerous?'

My father considered.

'She's not in any *mortal* danger, Elizabeth,' he replied gravely, 'unless of course she prolapses in the middle of the road . . .'

There was one subject, however, that was serious in a way that could not be undercut by charm, and that was Northern Ireland. Since the Troubles had re-started in 1969, things had become increasingly sticky and unpleasant for all Irish people living in England. With each new atrocity of shootings, kneecapping and revenge demolition, with the entry of the words 'Provos' and 'sectarian' and 'Bogside' and 'three-minute warning' and 'Shankhill' into common currency, the abrupt arrival of bombings on English land and the territory we ourselves walked – Oxford Street, the City, even Lavender Hill police station (where a famous IRA bombing trial was carried out, overseen by Special Branch helicopters, across the road from where I used to borrow library books), with every new reminder of Ireland's ancient wounds at English hands, and her long, unforgiving culture of reprisal, the English-Irish came in for troubles of their own.

No matter how faithfully they might report the IRA's campaign, the newspapers seemed determined to consider domesticated exiles from Cork or Waterford to be just as implicated in the violence as if they'd come straight from Sinn Fein HQ. A century after *Punch* cartoonists routinely pictured the Irish as thick, ape-jawed, stove-hatted and blunderbuss-carrying seditionaries, the papers ran cartoons featuring my parents' countrymen (and, as far as I was concerned, my own) as maddened, blood-lusting, implacable bombers, all staring eyes and (for some reason) sharp teeth. Jak in the London *Evening Standard* was a special offender. But then the *Standard* seemed to nurse a special animus against the London Irish. Several of its regular columnists in the seventies, such as Angela Ince and Lord Arran, regularly wondered aloud about the dark side of the Irish character that could find expression in acts of senseless public mayhem.

The issue of repatriation, too, reared its head at this time: following his 'rivers of blood' speech about the influx of black Britons, Enoch Powell came to suggest that other 'immigrants' besmirching British soil, the ones with green passports, might be helped on their way home by government intervention at some future date. I remember my father gripping the *Standard*, the evening paper that he'd read so faithfully over the years, and taking in the news that his English neighbours would be happy to see him get the hell back where he came from.

'Immigrants,' he said, as if the word had been 'criminals'. '*Immigrants*. The bloody nerve of it. After everything Ireland's done for England. Didn't the Irish fight for them in two world wars?' (Technically this wasn't strictly accurate, since the Irish Republic declared itself neutral in the Second World War, but large numbers of Irish joined up, wore British uniform and died as a result.) 'And didn't the Irish build half the buildings in London, and half the ships that sailed out of Liverpool? . . . and where in God's name would English hospitals be without Irish nurses, and who built bridges all over the British Empire, if it wasn't feckin' Irish engineers . . . ?'

He paused, red-faced. A super-orbital vein stood out an inch on his hot forehead. I had rarely seen him so angry. And as I looked at him, I was aware of him looking at me, regarding him. What was he seeing? An Englishman regarding an Irish immigrant? His own son, with the studiedly English voice and manner was suddenly one of the throng of British people who had decided they didn't want to have their uncouth Celtic neighbour around any longer. My father was suddenly transformed in front of me, from an exile (about which you could sing any number of sentimental oh-for-my-little-homestead-in-Leitrim melodies) into an immigrant (about which you couldn't sing anything, except perhaps a glum chorus of 'Deportees'). He hated it. He was the local Battersea GP, for Christ's sake. He was a man of stature and learning, held in respect by his patients, by the community of the sick, not some dubious alien who had arrived in the cargo area of a long-haul truck. Immigrant indeed.

It wasn't even that his sympathies went in the direction the *Evening Standard* assumed they would. Or did they? My father, born in 1916, grew up a natural Republican. His family had had encounters with the Black and Tan enforcers during the Troubles of 1922 ('the absolute scum and vermin of the lowest English prisons, that's who they sent over to keep the peace'). His people had learned the arts of silence and saying nothing, of keeping alert for traitors and informers and people who wanted to know your business, of combining a seeming passivity with sudden bursts of passionate, implacable, do-or-die patriotism. They had learned to define themselves by opposition, and by a kind of Homeric sullenness in the face of tyranny. And they had passed it straight into my father's genes. He had no sympathy for the IRA. He was as appalled as our London neighbours when the news arrived, week after week in the seventies, of letter bombs and pub explosions and detonated flesh. But he had a strong attachment to the *old* IRA, the freedom fighters in the hills, the IRA of *Shake Hands With the Devil* and Sean O'Faolain's stories, and 'Come Out You Black and Tans', the IRA of Moran in John McGahern's *Amongst Women*. I doubt if my father had ever knowingly met a genuine IRA man in his pre-London life; but he had a patriot's admiration for the type.

And now? He steered clear of voicing any opinion, most of the time. Whatever he thought, he said nothing. If the conversation at home turned to Ulster or the IRA, he would look grim yet knowing, an expression that became standard on London-Irish faces in those years. Talking about personalities offered a way round uttering statements of approval or dismay: it was easier to mock the Reverend Ian Paisley than to talk about Freda, the daughter of my mother's Sligo friend Margaret, who had got picked up by the Garda as a member of a Provisional cell in Dublin, because one might then have to voice some opinion about the daughter's sympathies or commitment, or about the value of arresting her.

In my father's dining room and my mother's kitchen, the London Irish subtly evaded the subject of Irish terrorism; it went beyond diplomacy; it was a thing of murmurs and tiny wisps of agreement, like an old-boy network. It was discreet, fastidious, muted. It was unbelievably *British* – or at any rate, a complicated complicity of both British and Irish reserve.

Only once did the murmuring get any louder. It was when Mountbatten died. I remember going into the living room to get a book, and finding my father, his friend Eddie from Wicklow, and the local curate sitting in a suddenly tight silence. My father grunted. 'You have a point, there,' he was saying, whatever the point had been.

'They simply had it comin',' Eddie from Wicklow said, evidently for the second time. 'You cannot say they weren't warned.'

Another silence fell.

'Well, they'll learn their lesson eventually, I'd say,' said the priest.

I stopped in the doorway as it dawned on me what they were discussing. 'Are you talking about Mountbatten?' I asked.

'Go on, John, hop it,' said my father. 'This doesn't concern you.'

'You were talking about the English Royal Family being taught a lesson, were you?' I asked in amazement. 'You don't mean you think they deserved it, do you?'

'This has nothing–'

'That they were asking for it?' I interrupted my father. 'Is that what you're saying? You think Lord Mountbatten deserved to be blown up because he's an English Royal?'

'John –'

'How can you say that? How can you say anyone deserves to die because the IRA decide they're a good representative of the enemy?'

'What the IRA said about the bombing,' said the curate, 'was that they wanted to tear the sentimental heart out of England. And by God that's what they did.' He nodded. He stopped just short of saying, 'and fair play to them.'

What could I say? None of these men thought it was right to kill. But they were faced with an absolute division of loyalties to which I had no access. The rest of the conversation is a confused recollection of raised voices, somebody saying there was a war on but I didn't realise it, and my father frowning at me because I wasn't showing respect to a man of the cloth.

It was not a pleasant encounter. Their conversation was only possible because they were all in private agreement; they didn't want to be part of a debate. They weren't sure they liked what had been done. They were really sorry about the two children. But they couldn't condemn the grandeur of the gesture.

My father was a deep-dyed sentimental nationalist. He thought the British should get the hell out of the North, but he meant it historically – not just the British in 1975, but those who were planted there in the early seventeenth century. To my father, they were still invaders; like the English milords given estates in Munster and Leinster under Cromwell. He disapproved of them all, for two reasons: one, they salted the population with English voices and manners, a constant source of irritation to one as wary of condescension as he; and two, they were mostly Protestants.

I was often surprised how much Catholicism meant to my father. Unlike my mother, Dad took a pragmatic view of religion. 'Listen to me, John,' he once advised. 'Keep the faith – or you'll never have a day's luck.' In vain I would argue that faith is supposed to be a matter of belief and devotion, not of superstition and utility. To him it got you somewhere. 'I've never have got through my final medicine exams without the miraculous medal hidden under the paper,' he once confided. But beyond trusting to luck, religion was, for him, a rallying-call. Catholicism was what got you to Heaven and educated your children, but it was also a tribal identification. He could never, I suspect, have trusted a Protestant. It wasn't sectarian hatred in his case, simply the indoctrination of the Catholic classroom, with its insistence on calling anyone who wasn't a co-religionist of the nuns and priests a 'non-Catholic', as if the word were cognate with 'non-event' or 'non-person'. When he finished singing 'Boolavogue' or making a speech at my sister's wedding, or seeing late departing guests off into the night, he would call out that same injunction he once urged on me: 'Keep the faith'. It meant a good deal more than urging people to remain Catholic. It was tied up in his mind with a potent hymn, whose chorus went: 'Faith of our fathers, Holy Faith/ We will be true to thee 'till death' – about the importance of remaining true to the ancestors, to the old ways and the hidden histories and secret freemasonries of Irish society. Keeping the faith, in a way that English people, even your own beloved (though now sadly English) son, could never understand.

I had always found religion terribly divisive and said so. In my early twenties, I had an awful set speech about how, from the Crusades to the Falls Road, the religious impulse, which was supposedly a striving for love or transcendence or the worship of an ideal, mostly expressed itself as a nasty desire to annihilate anyone whose forms of belief were different from your own. It was a jejune but heart-felt speech because I saw the possibilities of it happening in my own family. I lost my awe about God and Hell and Satan and Con-fession when I was fifteen, but I couldn't stop going to Mass until I went to university, so great would the pain and shock have been to my parents.

When at last I told them I was no longer available to attend Mass, walk up the aisle, pray for the souls in Purgatory or take part in family devotions, their twin reactions were extraordinary. My mother, whom I would have expected to prostrate herself on the floor in a hyperventil-ating heap, was weirdly cool about it. 'So *that's* what these grand friends of yours have been up to,' she said shortly. If she could blame my loss of faith on my impressionable nature and the serpent-like arguments of some awful Protestants at Oxford, it was okay; that was the way the world worked. I would get over it. She would see to it. She'd call in priestly reinforcements. I'd eventually be brought back to the Papist harness with a twitch upon the thread. That's what Catholicism was like. It would be a bit of a chore, an unnecessary bother, but it would be done. She would see to it.

My father's reaction was quite different. I found him in the kitchen late one night, reading the paper and listening to the stocks and shares report on the ancient wireless. (He had taken, late in life, to monitoring share movements, as if he had a portfolio of blue chips and equities the size of Adnan Kashoggi's; in fact he had about hundred shares in Rio Tinto Zinc, but that was all). We talked about this and that, then he said:

'Your mother tells me you're not going to Mass any more.'

'Yes.'

'Ever again.'

'Well yeah. I just . . . kind of lost it. Whatever it was.'

'You just lost it. Like losing a – a – shoe?'

'I just stopped believing in it all, one day, ages ago, if you must know. It's not a big deal. It just means we believe in different things now, you and me.'

'Oh? And what is it you believe in now?'

'Well, nothing really,' I said, sounding pathetic. 'I mean, nothing *organised*.'

Dad was silent. He had turned so that he was facing the far wall, with its jaunty wallpaper pattern of carrots, turnips and other root vegetables. He put his hand up on the high mantle shelf as if blindly searching for matches to light his late-night Guards filter tips. Only he didn't find any matches. His hand stayed where it was. He seemed to be resting his whole portly frame against the far wall, the carrots with their limpid crowns of green.

'I'd be sorry if you were never to go back to your religion, John,' he said in a strange voice.

'But why, Dad? I mean, we're all grown-ups here, right? Surely I can believe what I like now, can't I?'

'It's just–' he said, and his head bowed slightly, 'it's just I'd be afraid there would come a time I'd never see you again.'

I began to say, 'Oh for God's sake, don't let these differences of belief come between us, we'll always be friends . . .' when I realised he was talking about death, and judgement, and Hell and Heaven; and I further realised that my father was crying. I'd only seen him cry once before, when he was opening the back door in a hurry and the metal circlet of a key-ring had punctured his thumb and got stuck under the flesh like a tiny steel trap, and he'd been in agony until we got it out again. He was leaning into the wall with the root vegetables and his big frame shook, just very slightly, as if a small train were going by overhead. I remember standing there and biting my lip, unsure as to what I could possibly say to comfort him, and thinking: well once again, fuck religion, this time for making my father cry.

He and I had been having a curious relationship, especially about Irishness, over the last couple of years. We had both endlessly criss-crossed the Irish Sea, passing each other like *currachs* in the night. He had been back and forth in search of a home in the West, where he could retire with my mother and be happy again, and all his family and old friends would come and find them and celebrate the community that should always have been theirs, and his life would be, as it were, *lived again*, re-made with everybody he wanted there, intact and alive, just as he had left the place thirty-three years earlier. It wouldn't be retirement as such, it would be a fresh start in the oldest place he knew, a country refreshed and moneyed, subsidised, newly confident. If only my mother could be persuaded that the life she had made in England was a temporary, contingent thing, made up of patients and tradesmen and the friendship of other exiles, and the ceaseless procession of priests who never stayed very long without drifting back to Ireland in relief. If only he could persuade this regrettably Anglophile woman that her roots were the most important part of her stubborn Celtic make-up, then all would be well.

I, meanwhile, had been unable to leave the place alone. A form of schizophrenia had turned me into a cultural chameleon. In London and Oxford, I was completely at home. I spoke in a pure, received-pronunciation, window-rattlingly posh voice. From three sentences of spoken English I could identify the likely home, background and current socio-economic circumstances of any other Englishman or woman I met. I was an enthusiastic consumer of English newspapers, English popular music, English cars and English beer. I found English women the most appealing, most capricious, most intelligent and most attractive in the world. I dressed in English sports jackets and corduroys, effortlessly achieving a moth-eaten 'young fogey' image some years before it was supposedly established by A. N. Wilson, Gavin Stamp and their friends. I was English in spades.

But in Ireland, I was myself in a completely different way, or so I thought. A whiff of turf on the breeze at Athenry Station hit me like an injection of morphine, its sweaty-incense smell working you into a dreamy rapture. The sunken houses of little Irish towns, their silent shops and windswept main streets, made me ache with pathos. The cows and sheep doing nothing on the hillsides, the precarious immortality of the dry-stone walls got to me as if I existed only to see them, to paint them or write about them. A little late in the day, I was having a Wordsworthian *Prelude*-like vision of Ireland, full of rearing mountains and hissing-steel careerings across frozen ponds.

While I was admiring the landscape, my father was worrying about land, the actual soil and stones of his bit of Ireland. When he left Galway in his twenties, he had relinquished a large inheritance of land.

Henry, his father, had died in 1938, leaving several hundred acres to his sons. The eldest boy, John, had just been ordained a priest, with the attendant vows of poverty, chastity and obedience, so Henry divided the land equally among the others – Walter, Paddy and my father, Martin. When Martin became a doctor, there was nowhere for him to practise in the depopulated west of Ireland. All the parishes that could sustain a panel of patients were fully subscribed. So he decided to head for England in search of work, like a thousand other Irish doctors in the late 1940s. What should become of his inheritance? He asked Walter: would he look after it for him? I'll do better than that, said Walter. I'll take it off your hands entirely, for the price of a car plus your college fees.

A car? It's hard to imagine, today, giving up your claim on two hundred acres for such a paltry exchange, but my father agreed. Land was cheap, money was scarce, cars were a luxury, and it must have seemed an attractive trade-off for a go-getting young medic heading off to seek his fortune in the English capital: leaving the bleak landscape of home for a future cruising down English roads, scattering London pedestrians, miles from the management of grazing cattle and crop rotations.

Over thirty years later, his perspective had changed. Galway land seemed to my father as magical, as important, as in-the-blood, as Scarlett O'Hara's Tara. Dad wrote to Walter and his wife, Agnes. Would they consider, he asked, letting him have, say, ten acres of the family fields? Dad was now sixty-seven, retired, pining for home. All he wanted was a few meadows to walk across, to raise a few hens, maybe a pig or two, some soil to clutch in his hand and plant an allotment in. Perhaps they would let him know?

It was an exciting prospect. He waited for an answer. He could, maybe, build a house on the land, not too monstrously modern, not one of those rancho-deluxe bungalows – the curse of the rural Irish landscape in the last few years – something a little grander, neo-classical perhaps, with pillars and a gateway. He sat in his downstairs surgery, night after night, drawing plans and pictures of his new Irish retreat. He would need an outhouse where he could paint, a second one where he could entertain private patients, a barn where, in due course, there would be parties, fairy lights, a minstrel's gallery . . .

A letter came. It was curt and to the point. 'Thank you for your enquiry,' it read. 'If you look in the "Property For Sale" section of the *Connaught Tribune*, you will find any number of acreages for sale, at very reasonable prices.'

That was all. He was downcast, then furious, then resigned. He tore up the plans he'd made, the little diagrams of outhouses and allotments and garden fountains, he consigned the booklets about drainage and silage and goat husbandry to the surgery wastepaper bin, and sulked in a haze of cigarette smoke.

But I couldn't, just could not, empathise. I had tried to think of myself inheriting all the Ballybacka land. What on earth would I do with it? Myself as an Irish landowner of all these acres, this rainy hinterland, these fields of corn and barley, of cows and sheep and tractors and harvesting machinery and milking machines: the image stuck in my head for a few days. I just had no passion for ownership. I was too young, too urbanised, too Londonish. I had as much interest in owning land as I had in driving a tractor down Battersea Rise in the rush hour. It was nonsensical.

But to my father, land was now everything. He had to go back. I had watched him for years flirting with returning to his roots: his solo trips to Ireland, his impulsive purchases in Tuam and Galway and Killaloe, his endless letters to old friends in the West proclaiming his grand intentions, his bid to settle in a corner of his old homestead.

And then came the red letter day. He had bought a house in Oranmore, a small, charming town on Galway Bay, a well-upholstered dormitory town to the increasingly trendy quasi-metropolis of Galway, and announced he was leaving London at last.

'You're really going?' I asked.

'And about time,' he replied. 'But I'm worried about you.'

'Me?'

'It's all very well going back at last,' he said. 'But I hate leavin' you out on a limb like this.'

'Out on a limb?' I was amazed he should think such a thing. 'But this is London. It's my home. My friends are all here. Everything I know about is here. My work is here. How can I possibly be out on a limb?'

He looked at me sadly. 'You'll come over to see the old man from time to time, will you? And your mother?'

It seemed to me the sort of thing you'd say to a son going into exile in Canada or New Zealand.

'Sure,' I said. 'Sure. Trust me.'

So they packed up Battersea Rise, my mother going along with it in a sort of daze. There was such an accumulation of English stuff from her thirty years in London, so many things to be picked up, rediscovered, wrapped up and packed, that I suspect she simply shut out of her head the fact that she was 'going home'. But there was little home left in her own backyard of Sligo. Her youngest sister, Winnie, had died. The older ones were still alive but embedded in Boston, Massachusetts. The farmstead had been sold. There were no old folks to go back to, except my father's family; and after the debacle over land, and the small ads in the *Connaught Tribune*, she had no great desire to see them again.

My father, though, had reached a cunning compromise. By moving to Oranmore, they would be circumventing Athenry (eight miles further from Galway) and all it meant as the birthplace of the Walshes. They would be near a city, if my mother pined for big-city life, for shopping sprees and avant-garde hairstyles (she didn't, as it turned out; she pined only for her London friends). They would be near Madelyn, who by now had moved to Ireland to work in tourism, had spent weekends in Athenry, met and married the town vet, Frank Brody.

And in this happy setting – foreshadowed in a song sung in the old days by the company around my father's dining-table: 'If you ever go across the sea to Ireland/ Then maybe at the closing of your day/ You can sit and watch the moon rise over Claddagh/ Or watch the sun go down on Galway Bay' – beside an old castle, excitingly near the new golf club, surrounded by neighbours and a colony of nuns, they would start a new life together.

He was sixty-seven. She was seventy-three. They might, he told her, have ten good years left in them before anything 'happened'.

The only thing to be resolved was me. Could they leave me 'out on a limb' in London, while three-quarters of my family relocated in their ancestral land? Apparently yes, but it didn't seem to bother anyone. For why could I not go with them, if I wanted? Had I not become the most passionate advocate of Irish ways? Hadn't I proudly held an Irish passport since I was sixteen? Had I not become just as Irish as the Irish, or at least discovered my secret identity, the authentic jumping of my Celtic blood, over the last few years? And now that my parents were turning the family wagon train and heading for home – shouldn't I go with them?

No, I just couldn't do it. I'd lived in Dublin and watched it trying to turn itself into London, and I'd wanted to get out. I could, of course, try to live in the west, to be near my parents and the cousins in whose company I basked so happily, and so immerse myself in the place that it would become like normal life to me. But, I realised, I didn't want that either. I didn't want the smell of turf on the air to become so ordinary a phenomenon that I'd never notice it. I didn't want the view from the windows of Graig Abbey, or at least my own scaled-down version of it, to become a tired image of mere fields. The prospect of becoming a writer in Ireland and paying no tax on my creative earnings was attractive, but the lure of Fleet Street and literary London, in which I was then just making my tiny debut, was much stronger.

Becoming a journalist was itself a symbol of the parting of our ways. It was not an occupation of which either of my parents approved. It wasn't a profession. It meant writing down your impressions of the world and making them public, something my mother's smart English friends would never have dreamt of doing, something quite anathema to my father's secretive soul. He composed letters to the newspapers about trade unions, taxation and the incidence of *brucellosis* in humans, but never sent them. When he saw the book reviews I was writing for the papers, he would whinny with alarm: 'You must be mad to publish stuff like that,' he'd complain. 'Sayin' the feller "cannot write", sayin' he has "the intellectual grasp of a paintbrush". Jesus, John. He'll take you to court, and you'd better not look to me to bail you out . . .' But I was set on my course and stuck to it.

I can see in hindsight that my work was carrying me in a different direction from the one in which my parents were going. Journalism was an engagement with the wider world, a radiating out into all sorts of new areas. It meant deadlines and thinking about new things, instantly reactive and immediate. It was the precise opposite of going back to one's roots and drawing the curtains on the past. It was putting out new branches and leaves.

And so the day itself came, and the huge lorries. Battersea Rise, home of a thousand hoolies, was packed up into tea chests and crates and cardboard boxes: all the rosewood furniture bought over the years from Edwardes' Furnishing across the road, the brown-and-blue soup tureens, the Paul Henry landscapes, the Waterford crystal goblets, my mother's ancient *batterie de cuisine* and flouncey taffeta Irish Club ballgowns, the bed in which Madelyn and I were conceived, the three-piece suite on which a succession of priests had settled softly down to instruct us all in how better to live our lives; the little tables on which Dad and I had played endless games of chess on Tuesday nights; the piano on which I had mangled both Schubert sonatas and arpeggiated English pub tunes ('Oy, Padarewski! Will you for the love of God play us something we can *sing*?' my father would shout through the study door); the Ladro ornaments and glassy figurines which sat for years on the dining room mantelpiece, overseeing our revels and hiding their faces from the alarming parish priest; the 'Welcome' mat on which the English patients wiped their feet for fear of being bitched at by the Irish doctor's wife; the fancy coal scuttle disguised as an occasional table (I wrote about it once in a school essay, 'Describe your favourite room'. My mother was horrified: 'What did you want to go telling everyone we've got a *scuttle*?' she cried); the fifties cocktail cabinet with the pull-down-flip-up front, at which Dad stood manu-facturing industrial-strength cocktails and handing them, with his this-is-a-special-one-just-for-you manner, to the quaking recipient . . .

It all went. And then they went. I had to go to work the day they took off back to Galway and couldn't wave them goodbye. The sky didn't fill with portents. The veil of the temple wasn't rent. They didn't even have a goodbye party. They just went back to Ireland one day, as easily as they might have left on any day in the last thirty-three years.

They went back to end their days in an Irish idyll, composed of rural harmony, neighbourliness, ancient values, hunt gossip, village marts, nuns, Gay Byrne on *The Late Late Show*, soda bread for breakfast, barm-brack for tea and floury potatoes for supper. They expected a flood of relatives to call, a network of new chums in Oranmore, a series of glad-handing encounters with long-lost friends in the streets of Galway. But of course Ireland had moved on.

In the eighties, the Republic was changing completely. Galway had become trendy. Oranmore had gone further; it was gentrified. Its inhabitants were now smart young business people, Galway University lecturers, people who understood computers. Where Dublin in the seventies had tried to be a simulacrum of London, Galway in the eighties looked towards Europe for its inspiration. Dutch and German tourists wandered through the streets. British rock stars resting between tours chilled out in Renvyle House, on the farthest edge of Connemara.

Sinead O'Connor and U2 had replaced the sentimental old stuff about shawls and bog roads, while traditional Irish music – the most brutally purist, Chieftains-style instrumental Irish music – was all the rage on the Continent and, by a kind of mirroring phenomenon, all the rage in Galway as well. In London, a wonderful London-Irish band called The Pogues interspersed breakneck-speed instrumentals and songs about piracy and the Maze prison with ragged versions of the come-all-ye's I had heard in my youth. I once interviewed the band's leader, Shane MacGowan, a snaggle-toothed drunkard and phenomenal song-writer, and ill-advisedly suggested that there was once a time when us London-Irish teenagers had thought the Clancy Brothers singing 'The Wild Rover' and 'The Holy Ground' were appallingly uncool. MacGowan leapt from his seat in a fury. No they weren't, he snarled. They were *always* deserving of respect, and that's why The Pogues played their stuff.

My parents came to a changing Ireland, where matters of land and neighbourliness and old decency were being left behind by a new brash confidence. My mother blinked in disbelief at discussions of oral sex on *The Late Late Show*. My father sought out his old friends, and was surprised to find how offhand they were about his return from exile. When I came over from London three months later to see how they were getting on, they threw a small party and got their new neighbours round to inspect the London offspring. It was not a success. Everyone sat on chairs with spritzers and glasses of mineral water in their hands (they had to get up for work in the morning) and made polite conversation. There was a librarian, a bearded fundraiser for a cancer charity, a female magistrate and their respective spouses. Nobody sang (though my father demanded I had a go). We talked about current affairs, about cooking and the idiocies of nouvelle cuis-ine. Instead of my being treated like a curiosity from across the great divide, instead of being asked to report on 'anything new or strange' from beyond, they all agreed that Mrs Thatcher had done a fine job sticking up for British interests in Brussels. It was worse than being in London. Mother knocked up some plates of chicken and potato salad, but the guests declined; they'd already had their supermarket rogan josh meal-for-two, wolfed down in half an hour while watching the early evening news.

My parents had retired to an old world that desperately wanted to be a new world, an Ireland that was embracing modernity like a teenager in her first immersible blue denims. The relatives didn't come a-calling. My father no longer talked about having a few acres of land to stride across; it wasn't the way of things any more. The way of things now was a lawnmower salesman cold-calling my mother, demonstrating how the thing worked in her pitiful little patch of grass and then charging her £40 for mowing her lawn.

And then my father fell ill. Not long after he moved to Oranmore, he complained of feeling awful, drained of energy, bothered with cramps, eaten away inside. He knew the score. He knew, from horribly familiar text-books, there was something badly wrong with him. A year after the big move, he went for tests at Galway hospital.

It was leukaemia. A form of cancer usually visited on children had taken him over at the age of sixty-nine. He went into Merlin Park hospital outside Galway, to have the initial treatment. We all went along, Mother, Madelyn and I, and watched as he perked up from gloom to delight when he discovered the young female doctor was the daughter of a former chum of his from medical-school days.

He was given a cocktail of drugs rather than chemotherapy. He rallied, sank, rallied again. There was much talk of 'platelets' and 'white corpuscles' and we monitored the progress of both over the succeeding weeks.

He and my mother travelled to Dublin, where there was a special clinic that could bombard his wrecked bloodstream with wondrous anti-toxins. Mother stayed by him from morning until night and slept with him until dawn, finding him food, drinks and encouragement.

He became withdrawn and uncommunicative. When I tried to talk to him, he would short-circuit my sympathetic chat with demands that I go out and find a book called *Principles of Histology*, in which he could read a step-by-step preview of his impending extinction. A Galway cancer specialist met him to discuss the prognosis. 'You're a doctor, Martin,' he said. 'You know how these things go. Check your will, say goodbye to a few friends and accept it. That's it, I'm afraid.' I could never forgive the cold-hearted scumbag for saying such a thing to my poor father.

He was given a lot of dreams of 'remission' by the hospital but he knew it was all over – the long life he'd spent, endlessly moving between his beloved Ireland and his co-opted (rather than adopted) England, the doctoring and fathering, the singing and loving, all the bulky romance of which he was capable. He knew he was 'for the high jump', a euphemism I'd heard him employ a dozen times about a patient in dangerous health.

Christmas was difficult, with this guillotine over our heads. For a present, I bought him a hat in Galway, a charming Irish trilby with a peacock's feather stuck in at a rakish angle. It didn't fit. I knew my father's hat size. How could it have changed? Should I conclude that his head had shrunk? We drove into Galway, he and I, and there I went through one of the sorriest scenes of my life.

It was a clothes shop, just north of Eyre Square. 'I bought this hat for my father,' I told the sales girl, 'but it's a seven and three quarters and doesn't quite fit. Have you a seven and a half in the same style?'

She checked. No they hadn't, she said but he was welcome to try on a few others.

'How about it Dad?' I asked. 'You've got the run of the shop. Trilbies, homburgs, fedoras. Maybe a Stetson . . . ?'

I settled a black homburg on his head, amusingly.

'How's that look?'

'I look a complete fool. Why do you want to make me look like a complete—'

The sales girl reappeared.

'Now,' she said brightly. 'What about the trilby? It's about the right size.'

Dad once again regarded his reflection in the glass.

'What's the use?' he whispered. 'When will I ever wear it?'

'But Dad,' I said. 'We're nearly there. How about this lovely wide-brimmed thing with the feather?'

He tried it on. It looked ridiculous. 'No,' he said with finality. His utterances were getting shorter and quieter.

The salesgirl brought a few more. 'Would you like to try this tweed one?' she asked. 'They're a very popular line.' She put it on his head, without asking. He looked old and shrunken. He looked like he didn't care any more.

'I don't think that's really him,' I said and regretted it instantly.

'Would he like to try a cap on?' she asked.

Between us we had consigned my father to the third person, as if he were a cripple. He stood between us, lost in bitter sorrow, his handsome face suddenly stilled like a child's, devoid of animation, while the sales assistant put a foolish-looking Norman Wisdom cloth cap on his head . . . then another . . . and another.

'What size is it again?' she asked, clearly keen to get this tiresome customer fitted and gone from her busy life.

My father looked at himself in the long mirror. 'I'm a right-looking eejit,' he said mournfully. His face suddenly wore the mask of death, the hopelessness of carrying on any more.

'Or this maybe?' said the salesgirl, putting another awful cap, this time in leprechaun green, on his head.

I lost my temper. He was standing there so still, his eyes nowhere, his head as foolishly innocent as a baby fontanelle, having these undignified trappings plonked on him as if he were a donkey on a beach being kitted out in a straw boater.

'Or the brown one . . . ?' asked the girl.

'*Leave him alone!*' I shouted at her. 'Can't you see he's not well?' The girl shrank back. She had only been trying to please.

We left the shop in a hurry. We went home in silence, no longer caring about which form of headgear would suit a man in the final throes of leukaemia.

I was in London when he died a few weeks later. They'd let him go home. He thought he was in remission, but they were only being kind. He was for the high jump after all. The last time we spoke was on the telephone. I said how wonderful it was that he had a few months to tend his allotment with Mother before the next round of treatments, the next cocktail of drugs, three months hence. 'Will you for Christ's sake phone your mother more often?' was the last thing he said to me. 'Don't you know she needs to hear from you when you're stuck over there?'

So I was 'stuck over there' was I, still in need of rescuing? He must be feeling better, I reasoned, if the old Ireland versus England battle was still working in his veins. Four days later, I was in a taxi taking me from a book launch in Bloomsbury to the Duke's Head pub in Putney to see some friends, when his image came into my head and I knew something was wrong. In the pub, I talked desultorily to the literary agent pal and the fashion-magazine pal, then remembered the moment in the taxi. I rang Madelyn's home from the public bar, shovelling in twenty-pence pieces, each of which bought barely a few seconds of conversation between a fusillade of bleeps:

'Madelyn's out at the hospital,' said the young baby-sitter. 'She'll be back later. By the way, your *fatherighted*, John.'

Beepbeepbeepbeepbeep . . .

I couldn't hear properly.

'What? Did you say my father's *all right*?'

'No, your father *died*,' said the tiny voice. 'About an hour ago.'

After all our to-ings-and-fro-ings across the Irish Sea, it seemed oddly appropriate that the plain and awful fact of his death should come to me on a battered public payphone in an English boozer by the Thames, by way of a stranger beside the Irish Atlantic, and that I should hear it through a din of bleeps, the bass thump of a jukebox, the dull thud of darts landing on the double-top and the voice of English yeoman irritation calling out: 'Come on you lot. Haven't you got homes to go to?'

XIV

THE FIELDS OF
ATHENRY

I got to know Galway a lot better in the years after my father died. Its dry-stone walls and flat meadows gradually became a less romanticised landscape to my London eyes. The city itself continued to go through various changes of identity during the eighties. Because of a libertarian ruling by the city fathers, the backstreets that led down to the harbour had been reclaimed and reinvigorated by the entrepreneurial youth of the West, and a necklace of restaurants and trendy clothes and crafts shops had twined its glittery and polished loops around them.

The *jeunesse dorée* hung out in the Quays Bar, where, as you walked in, a pall of chatter and cigarette smoke and filtered sunlight settled on you, and it took a moment to adjust your eyes and see that the clientele was predominantly teenaged students, not cloth-capped old farmers. Beside the Quays, the River Corrib, dotted like a cottonfield with drifting swans, sparkled in the light as it ran out to join the Atlantic. Here was the Curragh, whose main feature, a century ago, was that its womenfolk used to wear red petticoats; and here was the Spanish Arch, where the merchants from Cadiz used to drop anchor and come ashore for days. Some of them stuck around, entranced by the Celtic light, the music, the potato-and-buttermilk suppers and the local beauties, which is why some western-Irish people have the very un-Celtic combination of blue eyes and black hair.

Five miles away, beside Galway Bay, lay Oranmore where for twelve years my mother was ensconced as the Widow. I would visit her twice a year, meet her neighbours and the support-system of friends and helpers who'd run errands for her, and the nuns from the local convent who'd arrive on her doorstep with home-made puddings. She would bring visitors into a long, warm, swirly-carpeted room like a well-upholstered train carriage, with a TV and armchairs at one end and a bookcase and breakfast table at the other. She'd arrange cushions underneath and behind them, adjusting and pummelling and flouncing the bosomy silk and brocade until the guests felt themselves thoroughly adjusted and pummelled too. She would fuss about, making tea and arranging cakes on a stand and, should they stay beyond six o'clock, direct them to the kitchen cupboard where the sherry and gin bottles lay. And if they were non-drinkers, it was a subtle way of getting them to leave.

For twelve years she sat in the carriage-shaped room receiving visitors. After the first couple of years by herself, she stopped going out to other people's houses. They would have to come to her if they wanted some company; she was past the effort of going places. She just wanted the raw chat, the tea and sherry, as it were, straight from the neck.

In her house, I would sometimes unlock the door of the big living room where all the London furniture had been consigned, and look in. It was all there, relocated from Battersea Rise in just one room: the rosewood table with its handsome fleur-de-lys chairs, the french-polished sideboard crammed with Waterford crystal, the raffish fifties cocktail cabinet where my father mixed gin-and-its and presented them to visitors as if they'd won them in an expensive raffle; the glass case where her collection of fragile teapots and cut-glass cruets on glass shelves seemed to hang suspended in air; the rocking chair upholstered in violent purple; the umpteen 'occasional tables' from Edwardes' Furnishing. It was like furniture in a museum, illustrative of some long-lost era. My mother rarely went into the room herself, except to hoover the carpet. It couldn't have been more obvious that she wanted to let the past bury itself, unless she'd wrapped a series of dust-sheets over each squashy armchair and spindly gate-leg table. Sometimes she let guests look around the house, but they were never invited to sit on the London upholstery. It would, I suppose, have seemed an offence against the past, against the texture of a period she had cheerfully consigned to oblivion: her doctor's-wife years.

The one photograph that had pride of place on her mantelpiece, surrounded by family snaps but always eclipsing them, was taken on a trip to Rome in the mid-1980s. It showed my mother in the midst of a gaggle of London-Irish ladies meeting the Pope. The women seemed to be wearing identical fawn-coloured mackintoshes and were stretching out to the Polish prelate, like star-struck teeny-bop fans meeting a boy band. You can practically hear the cries of '*John Paul! John Paul!*' The great man is smiling and relaxed in the picture, as he tries to calm the howling throng. But if you take a closer look at this forest of outstretched arms and pleading hands, you notice that the Pope's hand is touching just one set of fingers – and if you track along the wrist and back up the arm to the shoulder and beyond, you find my mother's delighted face at the end. It was a nice God-creating-Adam moment of communion between the Supreme Pontiff and the Widow of Oranmore, who was his biggest fan. 'I got him, you see,' she'd say later, smiling. 'I was a bit quicker off the mark.'

Mother had lots of callers. Whenever I went to see her, she would complain of boredom and loneliness, of the lack of company and the absence of conversation in her days, of the terrible list of things that needed to be done, the keeling-over bird table, the gas-canister refills, the bolted hedgerows, how none of her family ever came to see her – and then the doorbell would ring, and she'd greet her friend Siobhan, or Maureen from up the street or Patricia from the estate with her pretty daughter, or Pat Raftery, her first real friend in Oranmore, whose husband went to the same school as my father. Or it would be a giggling brace of nuns, or Joe the gardener, or Noel to mend the heater. They were her back-up, her stock company, her court. They chatted to her for hours, like old pals.

I listened in one day as Gerry, the man from the rental shop, came to mend the television and told her about a new apparition that had been seen in Ireland (something you'd rarely hear from a TV mechanic in London). It was the days of the Rocking Virgin of Ballinspittal, when gullibility was in the air. The local priest, he said, was convinced the apparition was the Devil disguised as the Blessed Virgin, mouthing heresies to outrage the ears of the faithful. 'So didn't he get one of the boys to fill a mug with holy water from the church and when the apparition next appeared and spoke to the children in their ecstasy, didn't he throw the mug of water at the space in the air where the Virgin was supposed to be standing, and the Devil let out a yell you could have heard two counties away . . .' Mother would keep a baleful eye on me for the slightest hint that I found these revelations amusing. 'Go on, Gerry, what happened next?' she'd ask. 'Isn't it a desperate world we're living in?'

She was a re-born Irishwoman, the Widow of Oranmore, and she drew friends around her as she'd drawn the faithful in London, and before that in the Home Counties among the silver soup tureens. Although she'd always resisted my father's dream of returning from exile, she'd had no trouble at all settling in to this pleasant town and assimilating with the new generation of Irish neighbours.

My father didn't last long enough to assimilate. He was genuinely upset by the non-reaction of Irish friends to his triumphant return. They just said: 'Howya Martin?' and promised to come and see him one of the days. But he'd wanted more than that; he wanted the life he'd left behind thirty-three years earlier. In London, he had always felt an exile; while my mother throve in her new role as the doctor's wife. Then he'd come back and felt out of place still, while she had adapted once more. She was never 'out of place'. She was always 'in place'. What was I to make of this?

Soon after Dad died, my mother travelled to the shrine of Medjugorje in former Yugoslavia, where the Blessed Virgin had once appeared to some village children warning of terrible but unspecified things (the shrine is located, eerily, on the exact site of a Croatian massacre several decades ago). After that one-off, intrepid burst of wandering, she hardly went anywhere. I tried to lure her back to London, to see her Battersea friends like Jo Fitzpatrick, or to stay with me and my new family, but she declined. '*I am not able*', she'd groan, a literal untruth and an all-purpose excuse. Even a trip to Dublin would, she said, put a desperate strain on her heart. Instead she stayed in the carriage-like room, welcoming people who had stories to tell, offering severely Catholic advice about sexual relationships to unheeding young neighbours, and becoming obsessed with quiz shows: 'Isn't she *marvellous*?' Mother would sigh about the young Irish TV hostess who had the difficult task of asking a Wicklow matron which river ran through Cairo.

I would occasionally send her articles I'd written, although the ups and downs of the British literary marketplace didn't hold much excitement for her. She was scornful of my passion for Samuel Beckett. Though the fellow was allegedly an Irishman, he was obviously just a Frenchified atheist, and a Protestant one to boot. 'I saw a thing on television about him the other day,' she once told me on the phone. '*Awful* stuff. Terrible slow. He was just standing there at a window, staring out at nothing. And I felt he was – *looking* for something he'd never had. Something he sorta needed to *believe* in. . . .'

Only Mother could have advanced such a thesis: Sam Beckett, the would-be Catholic.

She'd show my articles to her friends, who'd marvel at them and say: 'God, I'd love to read that one day.' They all approved of a magazine interview I'd conducted with a more acceptable Beckett, Sister Wendy, the art critic. But this was mostly, I suspect, because in the accompanying portrait photo of the toothy nun, my face could be seen in dim profile. 'Look at the way she's smilin' at him, Anne,' her friends said. 'She musta had a crush on young John . . .'

I lived for her in photographs and phone calls. And when I came to see her in the flesh, and met her friends, I was conscious of playing a role. I was the son who'd gone to England one day, turned into an Englishman and was now back with his chalk-striped suit, designer ties and Oxford voice.

I hammed up Englishness for her. I said: 'my dear Mamma . . .' and 'surely the point is . . .' and 'perhaps we could contrive to meet . . .' Why? Because she loved it. Because I'd turned, before her very eyes, into one of the gentlemen who had sat beside her in the Kent and Surrey mansions in the 1940s or invited her out motoring in the countryside in their plus-fours and MGs and intellectual spectacles. It was a pretence, a series of courtly playlets. But our genuine fondness for each other survived it.

Once, I'd driven across Ireland in a rented Fiat, en route to interview Seamus Heaney in Derry on the first night of his first play, *The Cure At Troy*, and I made a detour to Oranmore. Over late night coffee, Jameson's and biscuits, which kept her up beyond midnight for perhaps the last time in her life, I read her Heaney's sonnet sequence, 'Clearances', written for his own mother who died in 1984. They were simple, intensely moving epiphanies of everyday love and its unexpected power of transcendence:

> *When all the others were away at Mass*
> *I was all hers as we peeled potatoes.*
> *They broke the silence, let fall one by one*

Like solder weeping off the soldering iron:
Cold comforts set between us, things to share
Gleaming in a bucket of clean water.
And again let fall. Little pleasant splashes
From each other's work would bring us to our senses.
So while the parish priest at her bedside
Went hammer and tongs at the prayers for the dying
And some were responding and some were crying
I remembered her head bent towards my head.
Her breath in mine, our fluent, dipping knives –
Never closer the whole rest of our lives.

She loved it all. Even the moment when the mother dies in the seventh sonnet and, 'The space we stood around had been emptied/ Into us to keep', which my mother said she didn't understand but I was to understand all too clearly, three years later.

Eight miles beyond Oranmore was Athenry, my father's home town, and now also the birthplace of my nephews and niece. It was starting to mean more and more to me. Madelyn and her husband Frank moved house in the town and fetched up in a solid, grey, classically Irish-bourgeois mansion with a grand sweeping staircase and a high-ceilinged and half-timbered kitchen. The neighbours trooped in here every day, savouring coffee and gossip all morning. Reminders of the house's history could still be seen – in the dissecting room where Frank sliced open family pets and poorly lambs for inspection, you could see, stuck into the ceiling, the hooks from which flitches of bacon and maturing beef used to hang, tantalisingly, in the run-up to the labourers' harvest supper in decades gone by.

Frank and I always regarded each other with caution. We liked one another well enough, but were wary of our extreme differences of circumstances and temperament. He was intensely physical, down-to-earth and unpretentious, a man of strong appetites and direct action. He spent his time outdoors, in muddy fields and corrugated sheds, plunging his arm inside cows and mares, delivering lambs, testing cattle, riding to hounds. He treated animals with neither sentimentality nor brutality. They were patients; a job needed to be done to stop them sickening or dying; he would do it, take his money and leave.

But I noticed how often he would tell his children you should never tether a horse like that, never underestimate the feelings of a dog, never use a whip, always remember to feed the proliferation of kittens, guinea fowl, roosters and assorted fauna that milled about in the back yard.

He was a tender-hearted chap, but shy of expressing tenderness. It took a few years of buying each other drinks, singing duets and riding horses together before we started to bond. Suddenly he would introduce me to farmers in local pubs as: 'Do you know John, my brother-in-law?' rather than saying: 'This is Madelyn's brother . . .' and letting it hang in the air.

A couple of years more, and we would fall into a manly embrace on meeting and departing. The first time I kissed him on the cheek (it had become the smart fashion in London), he stiffened, as if I'd gone a bit far. But he learned to live with it. We fell out now and again. Once, when I'd been talking perhaps over-much about the London book-launch circuit, he said: 'I don't know John. It's an odd sort of life you have over there. There's not much call for reading books over here. Or for reading newspapers much.'

Stung by this dismissal of my whole career *raison d'être*, I snapped:

'Yeah, well there's not much call for vets in south London, come to that. A very *marginal* activity.'

It was rude of me. In Athenry, when my father was growing up, and still now, the vet was crucial, central in the Irish town community, at the top of the social hierarchy along with the doctor, the parish priest and magistrate. There was no call for disrespect.

Frank treated signs of London sophistication with brusqueness. If I raised an 'oh, how-can-they?' eyebrow at the odder cocktails requested when it was my round (Guinness and blackcurrant; brandy and creme de menthe), he'd say, crossly: 'John, just get the drinks in and don't be passing remarks.' One evening just after Christmas 1990, we were getting ready for the Hunt Ball in Galway. I'd bought a new dinner suit in Covent Garden, with moiréd lapels and satin seams. Awash with underarm deodorant, I put on the suit and arrived in the kitchen. Frank was still in his work clothes, polishing his evening shoes. I placed my hands on my tight-fitting hipster waistband, extended one leg in a kind of ballet-star pose and said:

'What d'you think of the strides, Frank? Aren't they gorgeous?'

He all but exploded. 'Jesus!' he shouted. 'No man calls his trousers *gorgeous*. And no woman neither.' A slight *froideur* existed between us for an hour or two.

Once, having eaten their provisions for a solid week, I decided to cook Madelyn and Frank a 'special supper', the kind of thing (I explained) that we London sophisticates routinely enjoyed every evening. It would be an Alistair Little recipe: 'Wrapped Breast of Chicken with Wild Mushrooms', a dream of warring flavours presented in a beautiful pink and green parcel with a cascade of tender *funghi* on top. It couldn't be simpler: put the chicken breasts onto slices of prosciutto ham on top of scalded, then 'refreshed', Savoy cabbage leaves, sticking knobs of butter between each layer, wrap the lot in aluminium foil and cook on a roasting dish in the oven with a generous selection of ceps and morels and little chopped shallots stewing aromatically alongside the foil packages in white wine and herbs. Yum yum!

I set off to Quinnsworth's supermarket with a list in my hand. But there wasn't any Savoy cabbage ('there's some perfectly nice ordinary cabbage over there,' the girl said); there weren't any shallots ('but the onions over there are pretty small,' the girl reasoned); there weren't any ceps or morels ('but the button mushrooms will do fine, I'd say,' the girl confided). There wasn't any prosciutto, nor pancetta, nor any other Italian substitute ('but sure, what's wrong with good Irish ham?' the girl asked, a little peeved by now. 'Isn't it all from the pig, one way or the other?'). There were, however, some chicken breasts and I bore them away in triumph, along with some wine and my many recipe substitutions.

Back home, I plunged the cabbage leaves into boiling water, then cold water, and watched as they lay in a wilted mass on the side of the sink. This never happened with stiff, crinkly Savoy cabbage from Sainsbury's back in south London. I laid the chicken on the ham slices on the cabbage leaves, rolled them all together and asked Madelyn for the aluminium foil. 'We used it all up at Christmas,' she said. 'But perhaps you could wrap it with some string.'

Oh *please*, I thought, this is so *typical* of Ireland – so keen on making-do, so hopelessly given up to mediocrity, so *not terribly good* at things. I rolled the wrapped chicken breasts in their soggy pale green shrouds, laid them face down on the roasting dish, surrounded them with sliced mushrooms and wine, and closed the oven door. It'll be fine, I told myself, you cannot screw up the essential *integrity* of an Alistair Little recipe.

Half an hour later, the smell of roasted greens was all over the house like a gigantic fart. The children protested. Annabel, holding her elegant nose, threatened to move next door until the terrible pong subsided.

'Uncle John,' said Giles scornfully. 'Don't you know how to make bacon and cabbage?' By the time the scorched cabbage leaves were dished up, their edges twisted with incineration, I felt about six inches high.

'So this is the sort of thing you get for forty quid a head in Soho, is it John?' asked Frank. 'Very nice . . .'

As time went on, my children came to check out the Galway relations. I was worried. Would it be like my own early experience of Ireland? Would they see poverty, rain, bleak religiosity, blank fields, nondescript towns? Would they scurry back to London, relieved to be out of that close, thick-textured, armpitty fug of the Irish family kitchen?

I needn't have worried. The minute Sophie, my eldest daughter, met her cousins, Annabel and Giles, she was sold. At the age of seven, she had her first inkling of Irish community life. Walking down the main street of Athenry with Annabel, then eleven, Giles, then nine, and an assortment of tiny associates, without any fussy grown-ups monitoring their progress (a thing she'd never be allowed to do in the mean streets of London), she found herself in Brady's the butcher shop, opposite Athenry church. Five hundred miles from London and after two plane rides and a taxi from Galway airport (perhaps the longest journey she'd taken anywhere) they seemed to know who she was. The butcher, John-Joe Brady, greeted the children: 'Hi Annabel. Hello Giles. And who's this little girl? Don't tell me, let me guess. You're John's daughter, is that right? I heard he was in town.' 'Gosh,' Sophie said to me later, 'They *know* me here. There isn't a single shop in London where anyone knows who I am. But they know here.'

My son Max first encountered Athenry in the snow. My consort Carolyn and I had flown to Shannon, hired a car, piled her sister Jackie and the three children into the back seat and headed into the mystic West. Around Ballinasloe, the snow had started coming down, leaping out of the sky at the windscreen with a mad Valkyrie violence. Outside Ardrahan, we stopped to consult the map for the turning to Athenry. The snow stopped leaping. It fell instead in a graceful, angelic descent through the lamplight outside a pub.

'We're nearly there,' I reassured the dozing family in the back. Max was wide awake. His huge brown eyes watched the big falling flakes, thick as turkey sandwiches, as he wondered how a cumbersome sleigh could safely pass across this cascading sky. It was Christmas Eve. 'I just can't *wait*,' he said, with four-year-old passion, 'to get to Ireland.'

Once there, he was introduced to a boxful of kittens, a houseful of shadows and huge, strange rooms, an enormous smelly Newfoundland called Wendy, and a bedroom where he bunked down with Giles and his brother Justin, Max's senior by a year or so. As the years rolled by, he and Justin became a horrible twosome, both of them fascinated by the grosser elements of veterinary work. When a cow was brought into Frank's surgical outhouse one morning for a Caesarean operation, no amount of parental shooing-away could stop them feasting their eyes on the blood, the yanked-out womb, the slimy caul around the huge, new-born calf.

Max and Justin fetched out tiny milking stools and sat on them, eating crisps and watching the amazing sights of blood-drenched birth like a messy cabaret. Then they had an idea. Aged seven and eight, they rigged up a sign saying 'hole in cow – 50p', tacked it to the tree outside by the main road into Athenry, brought out more stools and sat waiting for an audience to arrive.

Back in London, my children wrote cards to their Irish cousins, and demanded to be taken back there. One day, I was driving Sophie and her friend Bethan to a party. 'Dad,' said my daughter. 'Can you put on "A Fairytale of New York"?' She had heard me playing The Pogues' anthemic classic of two Irish exiles failing to get on in Manhattan and she liked the rude middle verse ('You scumbag, you maggot, you cheap lousy faggot/ Happy Christmas me arse, I pray God it's our last') and the girls duly guffawed at the rhythmic abuse in the middle eight. At the end I was startled to hear my daughter tell her friend, 'the man singing that is called Shane MacGowan. I like him because he's Irish. Like me.'

Somewhere, Sophie had picked up the notion that being Irish made her more exciting, more interesting, more something-or-other than being a boring old English, Anglo-Saxon person, minding her Ps and Qs and being *sensible*. My vestigially Celtic heart leapt in its bosom.

★

The people of Athenry started to be friends rather than holiday acquaintances. When I was in town, I would make a beeline for Hanberry's Hotel, the small, cosy bar where I used to meet Uncle Walter and his drinking buddies, Willie Higgins and Father Joe Fitzsimons. Miss Hanberry, the Sitwellian proprietress, had departed this life, and the bar had been taken over by Lily and Martin O'Beirne. Martin was a sleepy-eyed, growly-voiced Midlands gentleman who would usher even the most pissed and determined late-stayers out of his sight with the utmost courtesy; Lily was, and is, a formidable figure, capaciously bosomed, gossipy and fond, taking no nonsense from anybody, but possessed of a soft heart. 'You're welcome back, John,' she'd always say, as I wandered in at 10.30 p.m. 'How's your poor mother?' And we'd talk symptoms, move onto how the children were doing, then onto what I was up to in London, then back to Athenry news, at which she'd toss her head, as if to say 'news? Around here?'

But there always was news. I didn't know any small towns in England so I had nothing to compare it with; but in Athenry, with Lily, there was always news. Nothing that might get into an Important National English Newspaper, but information, speculation, trial and conviction. You could hear it all in Hanberry's Hotel, as we all sat around the low tables in the public bar: Tom and Anita, Taig and Patricia, Mary Sherlock, Athenry's rather thrilling female judge, her first husband, Noel – who sang 'The Streets of New York' in a powerfully projecting voice, and who died when his car backed off the quay into the Corrib one awful spring day – and then Mary and Conor, her second husband, a legal hawk who made us all welcome in his turn.

And there were always parties, raucous and seductive and irresistible, full of triple-whiskies and barrels of Guinness, the kitchen filled with plate-loads of chicken and coleslaw, buzzing with sexual intrigue and alive with singing. I'd find myself in conversations about horse breeding or Atlantic fishing – subjects of which I had no experience of any kind. When still under forty, I'd find myself standing with elderly farmers, our glasses of Jameson's clutched to our chests as we agreed that yes indeed, the old days were the best. I'd be invited upstairs for a private little chat with someone's cousin, a Jane or a Bridie, who was only in town for a couple of days and didn't really know anyone at the party. I would play the guitar and sing. It became a natural thing to do after midnight. We would play songs by The

Pogues, or 'The Fields of Athenry' by Paddy Reilly, or new airs by the *nouvelle vague* of Irish women singers like Dolores Keane and Mary Black, and we'd intersperse them with old songs and invigorate both.

I enjoyed evenings with one of Frank's in-laws called Charles Clancy, who ran a supermarket in Kilrush, Co. Clare. He sang in a floor-shaking bass tremolo. He could take a song like 'The Man Who Broke the Bank at Monte Carlo' – an ancient comic number and my mother's father's favourite song – and perform it as if it had been written the day before. He played the piano with nervous energy. We had some wonderful duets. Frank Brody habitually ended the evening singing a medley of 'Take These Chains From My Heart' and 'I Can't Stop Loving You'. He would conduct the crowd as it danced around him or stood on chairs to join in the final shouted chorus, with Charlie pounding the high treble keys and me scrubbing the chord of A7 that would lead us all into the climax, a wide-brimmed hat tipped over my eyes, and a fag burning between the strings at the top of the guitar neck. I doubt if I was ever happier at any gathering in my life.

At Christmas 1998, Mother looked alarmingly thin and frail and I knew she wouldn't last much longer. I had just returned from America to hear, on St Valentine's Day, that she had been diagnosed with cancer and had gone into hospital. I didn't know she had only a month to live and I spent that month there. Galway was now my own back yard. It was like returning to where I was born, where Madelyn was raising kids and where Dad lay buried near his brothers and his own parents.

After Ash Wednesday, things at the hospital moved on a little. They'd fitted a morphine syringe on a spring release into Mother's arm, a device that gradually, and more or less constantly, injected her with blissful waves of unknowing. She was in good spirits. She greeted most of her visitors with a pleasure bordering on ecstasy, but ignored less-favoured callers by pretending to be comatose. She seemed to be emotionally rinsed out: her awareness of whom she liked and whom she disliked was suddenly sharpened by the approach of the Great Clarifier. She clutched Sister O'Keefe's hand more convulsively than before. When her neighbour Sarah (who had once charged her errand-money for getting some shopping from the local SuperValu shop) came a-calling, Mother froze her off, and lay, silent and glassy-eyed, until her ex-friend departed.

She wasn't disposed to talk much to anyone, although I would press on her any items of local gossip I could dredge up: how this one's husband had an accident while cleaning a big industrial oven at the infirmary, how my cousin's fiancé had misbehaved at a London party. Mother's mouth would smile indulgently, like a queen having to put up with some unusually boring courtiers.

To visitors she would say a prayer that had become like a mantra to her. A connoisseur of the invocation, the ejaculation, the novena and the petition, she had prayers for every eventuality: from a trans-atlantic flight to a lost shoe. This prayer was targeted at the infirm, to be said while going upstairs at night time. It began:

Take my hand, O blessed Mother,
Hold me tightly lest I fall.
I am nervous when I'm walking,
And on you I humbly call.

She recited it over and over, enunciating the final '*Ay*-men' with a passionate flourish. '*Lovely*, Anne,' the visiting ladies would say at the end, 'I never heard the like of that before.'

Raising her on a mountain of pillows to make her comfortable became a major event, somewhere between an embrace and a rescue. It was a physical business, like slinging livestock between two ships. Madelyn (or one of the nurses) and I would lean across Mother's front overlappingly, each clamping a steadying hand under the far armpit, then, with a one-anna-two-anna-*three*, heave the patient skyward as if throwing her towards the ceiling with loud *huzzahs*. Mother would settle back on the yielding feathers with a sigh as soft as the newly replenished pillows.

'That's *won*derful,' she would breathe sensuously, as if it were the greatest treat in the world.

She existed, still, on a diet of 7-Up and vanilla-flavoured gunge, with occasional wary excursions into breakfast tea, which she would take though a cup with a sipping lid. Then she would sit up to be winded, and I would press my hand against her spine, circling it with firm pressure, as I'd learned to do with my children, and as I expect

248

she used to do to me. 'God bless you,' she murmured once. 'You have wonderful hands.'

Strange invasions troubled the ward. A travelling woman with bloated legs was laid up in the women's medical ward, and her children hovered around her bed, darting looks here and there as if about to be apprehended by the Guards. Then her partner arrived. You could hear his deafening progress from a hundred yards away. He moved slowly up the corridor on a stick, pulling himself upwards and forwards in surging movements, like John Hurt in *The Elephant Man*. He was enormous – six foot four or five – and dressed in threadbare tweeds and ditch-digger's trousers. A smell of stale whiskey wafted along with him and settled like germ warfare on the trolleys and sterilising equipment.

'Where is she?' he bellowed, halfway along the vinyl flooring. 'Where's Sadie?'

A young nurse appeared and strove to quieten him, but he waved her aside and lurched among the beds, like an ancient Chanticleer in this surgical hen-run, until he found the woman in the corner. 'So *this* is where they gotcha, wha'?' he asked accusingly. 'Coom back with me now.' And he started to pull her from the bed, until restrained by nurses and orderlies.

One day I arrived to find a young man wandering about the wards with his hands encased in pink balloons. He was in his early twenties, had a lock of hair over one eye like a football celebrity, and glided up and down in a black dressing-gown. His arms were held up before him like surgeons' arms after the scrubbing-up ritual, and two great latex globes wobbled on the ends. When he drew closer you could see that his hands were horribly burnt, the fingers purple and distended, like hands of exotic bananas. They were held up for inspection, glowing and heat-sealed inside their rubber shrouds. God knows what had happened to him, but he seemed keen to show off how bad his injuries were.

Among Mother's companions, Rosamund had got worse, more blackened around the limbs and desperate about the eyes, more disposed to fall asleep on the edge of her bed, head laid on the wooden tray that was supposed to hold fruit and flowers. Mary the Snow-Haired now cried out at night, like a child, but was more serene during the day, as the threat of ever more radical surgery seemed to recede, and more of her flourishing family came to see her. Mary the

Yank confided snippets of family history interspersed with bursts of fantasy. 'You know that Clive Anderson, the fellow on the TV?' she asked me one day. 'I knew his mother. She used to run a market stall in Donegal. I remember the time he won a prize for singing at the fair. He sang "The Rose of Mooncoyne". He could only have been seven or eight.'

She glowed with the memory. Yes, I agreed, Clive has certainly done very well for himself, considering . . .

Madelyn and I had become regulars in the ward. We waved at the stricken ladies; they waved back and introduced us to their families. Some mornings, after hours with Mother, Madelyn would take a break and talk to other patients, sending her mamma into a childishly envious fury. I came to marvel at my sister's instinctive capacity for helping people out – massaging someone's sore foot while talking to them, picking up a spoon mid-conversation, and feeding them the remains of their abandoned lunch without seeming to make them eat; the way she'd apply lip balm to my mother's dry mouth, her finger tenderly circling in the honey-scented pot, as unconcerned as a child with finger paints.

Madelyn brought one of her children's Sony Walkmans from home and helped the stricken Rosamund twiddle the dial until she found a Roscommon station; thereafter the old lady listened to it all day, grinning as though being told stories by an old friend. My sister did it all without a thought, like breathing, because it needed to be done.

I knew I wasn't like that. It would take me days of lists, aide-mémoires, shopping expeditions, personal organisers and inner dis-cussions of my motivation, before I could bring someone what they most needed. All I could bring my mother, at this late stage, was myself. I had come to her deathbed. I had become upset, rallied, blown my nose, said a gruff goodbye, returned to London, been summoned back, panicked, returned and told her I'd stay with her until she was better. But when she said, 'You must be worrying about your family,' I said: 'Yes, the poor children, what will they think of their father spending so much time in a hospital?'

'Minding his mother,' put in my mother.

'Yes of course but I've never been separated from them for so long . . . and from work too, though of course that's less –'

'John,' said my mother, fixing me with a gimlet stare. 'You *cannot* go back to London now. Think what'd happen if you'd just got back and Mad'leen had to ring and say: "Mummy is dead"?'

It was beyond me. 'What would happen?' I asked, heartlessly.

'Sure, you'd go out of your mind.'

She always knew, better than anyone else, what would happen to people. But she was declining. She now slept most of the day. She ate absolutely nothing. Her breathing was getting more and more shallow. Sometimes it stopped completely. Every second of silence, as you listened, expanded into a panic-stricken element outside the normal drift of time. Was that the Last Breath? Or is it this one, coming now? But no, her breathing returned with a sudden fussy intake, a sorry-I'm-late inspiration to compensate for the breaths not taken.

We took to sleeping by her bed at night, like faithful dogs. Madelyn would sit beside her in the best ward armchair, while I stretched out on an agonisingly uncomfortable chair, the kind reserved for unwelcome visitors, my feet propped up on another. This way, we could be sure of being around for the genuine Last Breath finale.

In the morning, when the nurses arrived to wake her, change her position, sheets, nappy and drips, I lowered my legs from the chair. They felt as though they'd never reach the ground. The weak March sunlight fingered the window, unenthusiastically. I was so stiff, I could barely stand. 'Oooh we're very *cross* today,' said Pat, the orderly.

The waking corridor looked at its bleakest. To think of spending even a brief stay here, to think of working here, to think of – no, try not to think of it – of *dying* here. It seemed too dismal a thing to even contemplate.

The days crept by. I went for walks into Galway, recuperative strolls that described the same trajectory every day. I resolved to write a hospital column for the newspaper, or keep a diary, or start a crime novel (*The Third Amaryllis*) or send letters to my children, and walked into town to find some stationery. I wandered the streets of Athenry in the mornings, reacquainted myself with the shops and bars and houses I'd come to know over the years. Somers the grocers, Morrissey's the paper shop, Reilly's the baker where they made a spectacular pear gateau of unearthly lightness.

I talked to my nephews and niece. Annabel was now fourteen and alarmingly grown-up. She regarded me with a Garbo-like *hauteur*, as if wondering what I was doing still hanging around her house. Giles was twelve and a film buff. He wanted to be a director but was settling, *pro tempore*, for being merely a screenwriter. He talked in cool but heartless movie clichés. 'Let's go', he'd say if I was dawdling in the hallway: 'Let's blow this popsicle stand.' He could recite pages of dialogue from *films noirs*, thrillers and gangster movies, though he was, technically, too young to have seen a frame of any of them. The biblical riff that Samuel L. Jackson used before blowing people away in *Pulp Fiction* ('And I will strike down upon thee with great vengeance . . .') was a particular favourite. I became used to having my reveries about mortality and the precariousness of life suddenly interrupted when the barrel of an enormous gun was suddenly clamped against my temple and my nephew's otherwise quite pleasant face appeared, contorted with the Vengeance of the Lord.

One evening at the hospital, a carnival atmosphere supervened in the ward. Two of the nuns were by mother's side, talking to a visitor about Medjugore. Cousin Mary, Aunt Peggy's daughter with the sparkling eyes was there, and Frank's glamorous sister Carmel, in her immaculate Chanel jacket and her spun-gold hair. Father O'Dwyer had looked in on one of his don't-blink-or-I'll-be-gone visits. Father O'Connor had arrived, pulling out his rosary beads. I tried to escape, but there was no chance. We intoned the Rosary, my mother joining in the 'Holy Mary, Mother of God' choruses with a fervour I hadn't seen in her for a while.

She was always keen on the idea of divine grace, that curious substance so lovingly invoked by priests – the Catholic *karma*. When I was young, I thought of grace as a magic treacle, somehow both liquid and solid, a spiritual oil that stole around and into you like the sea around a sandcastle only more slowly, that gradually insinuated itself inside all your angles and crevices and nooks, something you couldn't escape, but wouldn't *want* to escape – divine oil, unimaginable treacle, entering your system like virtuous heroin. It had always put a spring in my mother's step. Now it seemed to have returned. All her sorrow and disappointment that God had failed to deliver her from cancer had, apparently, evaporated. As in George Herbert's poem 'The Collar', she had ranted and railed at the Almighty, she had 'rav'd and grew more fierce and wild'. But she had come through: 'At every word methought I heard one calling, Child,/ And I replied, My Lord'. It was something to celebrate.

'John,' she said. 'Sing me a song.'

'I can't, Mum,' I said. 'Not in a ward full of sick people. It'll only make them worse. And not in front of Father O'Connor and the nuns. It wouldn't be right.'

'Sing "All my bags are packed . . ."'

'But Mum . . .'

'Musha, wouldn't you sing it for me?' And she turned upon me the sweetest smile I had ever seen, a look of the tenderest love at the moment of departure from what it loves most. The visitors melted into the background. I looked at her face and saw it shining, as if all the love of decades had suddenly been rolled together and let glow in a single burst. I couldn't look away. A whole lifetime of knowing someone is not preparation enough for leaving them, however you may have rationalised it, however little more there is to be said.

'Go on,' she said. I brought my face close and, amazingly without embarrassment, sang:

All my bags are packed, I'm ready to go,
I'm standing here outside your door,
I hate to wake you up to say goodbye.
But the dawn is breaking, it's early morn,
The taxi's waiting, he's blowing his horn,
Already I'm so lonesome I could cry . . .

So kiss me and smile for me.
Tell me that you'll wait for me.
Hold me like you'll never let me go . . .

It was a favourite song of hers – John Denver's 'Leaving on a Jet Plane'. Whenever I used to sing it to her in the seventies, she would look into my eyes, disconcertingly, as if it was sung by a lover. It didn't take a genius to see it as her sign-off. The others joined in the chorus, but Mother didn't mind. From beyond her screens you could hear the three men sitting at Mary the Snow-Haired one's bed joining in as well:

Oi'm leavin' on a jet plane,
Don't know when Oi'll be back agin
Oh babe I hate to go . . .

Their intention may have been sarcastic, but it didn't matter. Everyone laughed and clapped at the end, and the nuns went to talk to Mary's melodious guests. Father O'Connor said: 'Well Anne, I never saw you look so good in a long time,' and she beamed up at her favourite pastor. The morphine was coursing through her veins at a steady clip, making her perpetually high, but there was euphoria in the air. Mother got the company to sing, 'It's a Long Way to Tipperary', waving her hand like a baton. If she'd been in a pub, she'd have been thrown out for rowdy behaviour.

Afterwards, when Siobhan from Oranmore arrived, and cousin Marjorie and the nuns and in-laws stood talking together, Mother beckoned Madelyn and me to her side.

'John, you stand *there*,' she said, sitting up and pulling my arm. 'And Madelyn you go *there* on the left. Now hold my hand. Not there, put your hand round my wrist, so I've got you properly. And Madelyn, you do the same. Good girl.'

Mother looked at Father O'Connor's noble, weatherbeaten head. She looked at my sister and me. With a small dramatic flourish, she lay back on the mountain of pillows. 'Now!' she said.

But she didn't die then, as she wanted to. There were two final stages, one undignified and upsetting, one peaceful and terminal. In the former, they tried to reduce Mother's intake of morphine because it was making her sleep virtually all day. This was not a success. She became doubled over with pain. Her arms ached. Her legs and feet, both horribly swollen, hurt like hell. Everything became minimal – the sounds she made, the amounts she fed on, the words she spoke, the pressure of her hand on mine. I watched her taking a sip of tea. It was the smallest sip in the world. Her breathing got worse, rough, irregular and punctuated by an occasional cry, a kind of 'Ha!', upon which she would pitch forward in the bed. Madelyn and I held her up together. She hacked and strained, and we soothed and reassured her, but we all knew it was hopeless. She had started saying 'I want to die!' with snarling clarity.

The morphine was increased again. She lapsed in and out of consciousness. She had periods of delirium, full of prayers blended together:

Mary help me,

Mary help,

Mary mother of God,

Pray for us sinners,
Pray for us sinners,
Now and at the hour of our death,
Mary help me,
Mary mother of God,
O Blessed Mother, hold me tightly lest I fall.

Once or twice she emerged out of the sleep and delirium, to startle the group around her. I was talking across the bed to Sister O'Keefe about some encounter in the hospital café. My mother lay back on the pillow with closed eyes.

'So anyway,' I was saying. 'The girl behind the counter said to this guy, "Wouldja ever feck off?" and he was so startled, he–'

My mother sat bolt upright in the bed, jolted awake by the obscenity. She looked furious, then fake-furious because Sister O'Keefe was smiling. She glared at me, raised a fist in the air and narrowed her eyes. 'I'll give you such a *clout,*'she said, and relapsed back into her dreamy hinterland. It was the last thing she ever said to me.

She slipped into a coma and lasted three days, her body hunched over in a foetal posture, as snug as a bushbaby. She looked *aghast*. She lay utterly stricken as if mown down by a truck. Realising that she was not going to rally or improve now, they moved her into a side room. They shifted the impedimenta from her bedside. I made an inventory of the last things she owned, or held, or saw in her life: her blue gingham slippers; the thick walking-stick on which she leaned for the last of her eighty-seven years; her (rather cool, I thought) Gucci handbag; three sets of rosary beads and a crucifix from Sister Teresa (the nun who had Padre Pio's only glove); a two-litre bottle of Clipper spring water flavoured with pink grapefruit; umpteen almost-finished bottles of 7-Up; three phials of eyedrops (whose names – Philocarpine, Tears and Betoptic – sounded like the Eumenides, or that troika of spirits from the Burning Fiery Furnace); one plastic Virgin Mary statuette filled with holy water from Medjugorje, one bottle of Lourdes water; one canister of Sprilon foot spray ointment (how I'd come to loathe the words 'ointment' and 'fluid'); one jar of Vaseline, one honey-and-glycerol lip-balm; one cloudy bottle of Mycostatin with its own pipette; two spare tins of Ensure Plus (vanilla flavour); a fluffy cuddly dog with sad eyes and a pink ribbon; the death's head nebuliser hanging on its slender elastic thread; one half-eaten box of Roses chocolates, one of Posies tissues; one last amaryllis – the fifth, that she would not now see bloom; two spout-lipped cups from which she took her last sips; one pack of Rich Tea biscuits (half-eaten) . . . the Mass cards and the Get Well Soons, the Thinking of Yous and Phone Me When You're Betters had all been cleared away. Had we all hardened up? Were we saying 'that's quite enough of *that . . .*'?

Visitors were discouraged. Go on back to your homes we said, like policemen at the scene of a crash, there's nothing to see here. In the private room, we sat around her quiet-breathing frame. Frank came with the children, Annabel and Giles and Justin and Simon, all of whom kissed their grandmother as she lay stricken. I was puzzled. I wouldn't have brought my own, London children to see a disintegrated old lady, for fear that they might be upset. But these wholly Irish children seemed unbothered by the evidence of decay. It was just their granny asleep and looking a bit past it. We talked desultorily, and chatted to Siobhan from Oranmore who called to see if anyone needed help, and to Mother's devoted Sligo nephew, PJ, who was overseeing some building work in Galway. When they'd gone, someone switched on the television. *Coronation Street* came on and we gazed dumbly at the crowd in the Rover's Return. Frank suggested we say the Rosary. I refused. 'Well, it'd be a lot more respectful of your Mother than us sitting here watching the box,' he said scornfully. He was right. We raced through the Rosary in a fast, embarrassed mumble, needing her conscious presence to imbue it with any meaning. Without her, we felt like a pagan crew.

The next day, as I was writing a piece for the newspaper back in London, Madelyn rang from the hospital. 'Are you *ever* coming in today?' she asked with an edge in her voice.

In the private room, a small table had been moved in for the Last Sacraments, covered with a white cloth and bearing a statue of the Virgin, a rosary and two candlesticks. I rang Father O'Connor. He was out. I tried a relative of his in Galway, who thought he might be at the golf club. Finally I tracked him down and said he was needed. 'I'll come later on,' he said. 'Maybe I could look in this evening.'

'How about *now*?' I asked.

'No, no, this evening will be all right, I'm sure.'

'Only if you want to be praying over a dead body,' I said, shortly.

He came within the hour. He stood at the foot of her bed and said the Prayers for the Dying. They were beautiful, full of the welcome and greeting she might expect at the gates of Heaven. They would all come out for her, all the virgins and martyrs, saints and guardians, apostles and evangelists, the whole community of the upper sky would come down the lane to the Pearly Gates. 'Anne,' they'd all say. 'Is it you at last?'

The prayers were over. Madelyn blew out the candles. PJ went off to his construction site. Beside the bed, Sister Teresa was showing Madelyn a length of pale blue silk ribbon she had bought to make a Legion of Mary sash for my mother to wear. There was nothing for me to do except read a book.

Then I noticed my mother had opened one eye. It was the first sign of conscious movement in forty-eight hours. She was looking, it seemed, *through* me, at something beyond. Her face was still buried in the pillows like the Tollund Man in the turf of pre-history, but her eye was as bright as a seagull's.

'Mad . . .' I said. My sister was still talking ribbons. 'Mad,' I hissed, 'her eyes are open.'

'*What?*' Madelyn came round the other side of the bed from me. 'Mummy? Are you awake?'

I took her wrist, to check her pulse. Madelyn squeezed her hand. We were now on either side of her, as she had stage-managed us days before. We were even, by coincidence, holding her hands as directed, with fingers halfway up her wrist.

Mother's breath gathered itself up into a single heave, taking her shoulders with it. Her torso seemed to rise up into a vast shrug, as if all the cares of the living world were not worth worrying about after all. Then she let out a giant breath and died.

What I remember was this: that she had woken to die; she had looked into me, and through me, and had passed on all she was, all she had been, all her Sligo-colleen smartness, her maternal Irish *there*ness with my sister and me, her dreams of English acceptance, her doctor's-wife equilibrium, her tough Catholic zealotry, her flirtatiousness, her bosomy, perfumed, enveloping love — all of this had been transmitted into me to keep and to draw on for the years I had to live.

Pat the orderly, as brisk as a bee in a moment of crisis, took charge, while Madelyn and I wandered about saying our farewells. We went into the little four-women ward, to take our leave of Rosamund and Snow-Haired Mary. They murmured the standard Irish condolence:

'I'm sorry for your trouble', and we agreed that she was out of pain and didn't she have a great oul' innings?

'Good luck now,' we said, stopping just short of adding, 'keep in touch', as if we were tourists coming to the end of a holiday.

We said goodbye to the nurses. Eilis, who had brought the meals trolley round, asked if she could pop in to the room and say goodbye to my mother. It was an odd request – they had hardly been close, and why would anyone outside the family want to say goodbye to a corpse? But I said, 'sure.' Other nurses joined in. A little procession of people came in through the door to where my mother was lying. Then Pat shooed them all out, so that they could wash my mother and lay her out, something she had often done for others. (Some patients, she once told me, like to be able to identify whoever will be performing this last and most profoundly intimate rite on their bodies.)

I went back when it was all over. She was tucked inside the sheets so tightly, only her head showed. Half a dozen snowdrops lay on the coverlet. Her hair had been severely brushed back, and I couldn't recognise her. The skin on her face seemed to have been pulled back at the sides, making her look like a dead Japanese soldier. Her marmalade hair revealed a whole inch of snow-white roots. She would have hated to be seen like that. It showed how long she'd been in hospital, how long since she'd looked in a mirror. Mother had wanted to be an auburn beauty all her life. Here she was, given away by her roots at the end.

Madelyn's children arrived. They came to say goodbye to their grandma, typically unbothered by the image of death. Giles kissed her on the forehead, but without, thank God, reciting his 'Ah-will-smite-thee-down' speech. Simon, aged two, was lifted up to do the same. If I had been two again, I would have screamed and wriggled and made a scene. He just got on with it, to murmurs of 'Good man, Simon'. The orderlies had taken all my mother's bits and pieces, the eye drops and vanilla canisters and what-have-you, and had bundled them – casually employing the most elementary symbolism of all – into orange plastic refuse sacks. They stood by the door: five sacks. I looked at mother's Japanese-soldier face, at the newly emptied room, the dull view from the window, the pointless sink.

'C'mon Giles,' I said. 'Let's blow this popsicle stand.'

XV

GOING THE LONG
MEANDER

I stood in the hospital corridor, three floors up, waiting for the signal to depart for good. Suddenly I was an orphan, albeit at forty-five, and eternity had stopped being an impossibly far-off cloud. Through the window of St Anne's ward I looked at the streetlights coming on, though it was barely 4.30, scarcely tea-time. Unlike my mother, the day was dying young, switching on the lights of the cathedral, the university, the students' digs, the little houses I couldn't see along the backroads to Eyre Square, as if the whole city were suddenly afraid of the dark.

They call Galway 'the City of Tribes'. The men of Connaught built a fort on Galway Bay in 1124. In 1232, Richard de Burgh – scion of a Norman family from whom my aunt Dolly claimed descent – colonised the area with fourteen tribes. Cromwell's men called them 'the Tribes of Galway' because they stuck together so clannishly, but the phrase became a badge of honour, a mark of distinction. You can hear it still in the voice of Irish radio talk shows: 'Come in, Aisling, from the City of the Tribes . . .' It was in Galway also that the famine ships gathered in 1847, to take refugees away from death to the New World.

Tourists romanticise Galway, with understandable logic, as the vertiginous edge of Europe. The Cliffs of Moher, where I dragged any number of English friends in my younger days can seem, in their chasmal beauty, the Final Shore, the last beach of the civilised European continent, before everything turns into wild ocean and windy disarray and the long transforming journey into the melting-pot of America.

I wondered where I fitted into this metaphorical picture. Perhaps I'd spent too long in a hospital, but I was bothered by the idea of the Irish soul.

How do you measure where you really belong? Genetically, I was as Irish as Bertie Ahern, and rather more Irish than De Valera. Accent- and behaviour-wise, I was as English as Stilton. My supposed Irishness had veered and tacked this way and that for years. When it suited me, I had identified various promptings in my heart as being utterly non-Anglo-Saxon. Any time that English phlegm, English dullness, English awkwardness about passion or social restraint, any time the company of English public schoolboys seemed too much to bear, I retreated into the happy dream that I was fundamentally Celtic. Like anyone with two nationalities, I could take comfort in this otherness. I didn't want to be *just* British. I wanted a counter-life, a dark underbelly, a passionate European descant, a Hibernian, grit-in-the-oyster wildness. But was it all just a chronic act of wish-fulfilment?

In his book *The Irish*, Sean O'Faolain writes about the dualism of the early Hibernians (just after the first conversions of St Patrick) and how they tried to have it both ways. 'There may be an overlay of stern Christian morality,' he wrote. 'At the bottom there is a joyous pagan amorality. They believe in Hell. They also believe in the Happy Isles. They believe in the Christian doctrine of punishment, and compensation in the afterlife. They believe, simultaneously, in the continuance of life's normal mortal joys and sorrows for all beyond the setting sun, and, behind, the dripping udders of the clouds.' He portrays the early Irish as having two 'lobes' of the mind. With one, they live a life of impetuous independence, full of passion and conflict, war and adventure, full of awe and marvels. The other lobe is all craven acceptance, passive obedience, a willing giving-in to a higher authority, and, says O'Faolain, it 'must unseat their lusty human joy, their gay reliance, leaving them hung in mid-air between their various heavens and earths'.

There was that image again, from Synge by way of Milton, of the falling angels, stuck in mid-air for a lifetime of in-betweenness, never quite becoming one thing or another. Of the straying and exiled Irish who could never quite settle in their adoptive England, yet never quite come home; the puzzled Irish who came to London as though to a neighbour in the street, expecting help, sympathy and a welcome, and found a culture so radically different from theirs, that it was always a foreign country. The ex-Catholics like me, who never became bad enough to warrant Hell, but could never shake off the trace-elements of Papist guilt in their bloodstream. The Cromwellian Irish, herded by the Protector beyond the Pale, as Milton's Son of God herds Lucifer's defeated angels before him in his blazing car, flocking them to the far crystal wall of Heaven and the door through which they will be flung to Pandemonium; the famine Irish, herded by poverty and need to the edge of their land – not the wall of Heaven but the Galway coast and the ships bound for death or America, falling off the edge of Europe.

Years before Milton wrote about them, the angels were objects of appalled sympathy. In Canto Three of Dante's *Inferno*, the narrator encounters the same unfortunate throng, hearing 'strange tongues, horrible outcries, words of pain, tones of anger, voices deep and hoarse, and sounds of hands among them . . . a tumult which turns itself unceasing in the air, forever dyed as sand when it eddies a whirlwind'. Who, asks the narrator, are these unfortunates? They are, he's told, 'that caitiff choir of the angels who were not rebellious, nor were faithful to God; but were for themselves'. For themselves alone: *sinn fein*. Dante describes how 'Heaven chased them forth to keep its beauty from impair; and the deep Hell receives them not, for the wicked would have some glory over them.'

And here we were, on the edge of Galway, another caitiff choir after a death. And the tribes, all fourteen of them – though I didn't keep count of who was represented – rallied round, from the first moment of Mother's departure into the final Catholic night.

Irish funeral arrangements are amazingly brisk. There's no question of hanging about for a week, as in England, waiting for a gap in the burial schedules. There's a strict sequence of events – Death, Announcement, Removal, Church, Wake, Mass, Burial. It's conducted over two days but starts within twenty-four hours of the heart ceasing to beat.

Louise, my doctor cousin appeared, had a word with the nurses, then she, Madelyn and I hastily scribbled a death notice to go in the *Irish Times*. We composed it in the corridor, and wrote it out on the windowsill among the overflowing ashtrays. It was as formulaic as a haiku. The thing was to get everyone's name in, and the parts of the world where the family had fetched up:

> The death has occurred of Mrs Anne Walsh of Oranmore, Co. Galway, widow of Dr Martin Walsh of Athenry and formerly London. Greatly mourned and missed by her children Madelyn (Athenry), and John (London), her sisters Catherine and Bridie (Boston), her nephews John and PJ (Sligo), and Jackie (Boston), her nieces Bridie, Anne-Marie and Marion (Boston), her brother-in-law Paddy and sisters-in-law, Dolly (Graig Abbey), Peggy (Monivea) and Sister Rosalie (Preston, Lancs), her grandchildren Annabel, Giles, Justin and Simon, Sophie, Max and Clementine (London), other relatives, friends and neighbours. Removal from the Memorial Chapel Athenry, Saturday 6 p.m. Funeral at Oranmore Church, Sunday 11 a.m.

'It's customary,' said Louise, 'to end with some line about resting in peace, or being in God's hands, that sort of thing. But only if you fancy it.'

'What d'you think, John?' said Madelyn. 'Some little sign-off?'

'How about: "Left on a jet-plane"?' I suggested.

Madelyn wrote: 'Take my hand, O blessed mother' which was, at the same time, sentimental, horribly religious and absolutely perfect.

We returned to Athenry. Nobody wept. Instead the car was full of chat about the most recent hospital visitors and the news they'd brought, little satirical swipes at anyone who'd been fulsome or pretentious. It was the beginning of the Irish response to death, which is to greet it with open arms, buy it a drink, display it, prod it and poke it and chat about its uniquely levelling properties. The Irish do not romanticise the Reaper. They don't utter cries of horror at its approach, nor sentimentalise it with too much religion. Instead, the atmosphere of the song 'Finnegan's Wake' takes over, with its central conceit that, at any moment, a mis-hurled bottle of whiskey might revive the stricken figure in the bed. Death is an event to be celebrated almost as much as marriage – perhaps more so. Marriage offers a lot of pious hopes of happiness for the union of two people, while Death concentrates the minds of all present on the single individual and – all pious hopes left behind – considers what he or she made of the hand that was dealt them seventy or eighty years earlier. It's a form of enquiry about what exactly you *do* with a life; every new death prompts the question of how it could have gone at any time in the previous three-quarters of a century. What's important at a wake is discussing how they lived in this life, not what they may be going on to in the next. Priests take a backseat. They know it's a secular sign-off. The prayers and the holy stuff will come later.

There was already a throng in my sister's kitchen when we got home. Word had spread, from the nurses at the hospital, from someone who knew her at the *Connaught Tribune*, from the Garda who had to be informed of such things, the estate-agent fraternity of Oranmore and Galway ('Beech Grove is up for sale; pass it on'), from God knows which second cousin of the catering staff in the hospital café – a whole network of gossip had put her demise on the local social airwaves.

People squeezed our hands and explored our faces for signs of fatigue or emotional strain. After an hour of such attentions, you tend to dramatise your responses, choosing the happiest form of words your mind has hit upon:

'Yes, she went very peacefully. Yeah, a good send-off, like putting a ship out to sea.'

Madelyn and I sometimes passed each other as we circulated the kitchen. We had been through so much together – talking, keeping watch, keeping each other sane, dining together every evening for weeks in all Galway's restaurants. We both knew the other remembered the 'Tipperary' evening when Mother wanted to die but couldn't. It made the final scene more bearable.

The crowd chatted and laughed. They sat around the breakfast table, drinking gin and hot brandy or lolling against the work surfaces, flooring pints. What were they talking about? Not Mother – the time for that was later at the wake, after the coffin had been delivered to the church. Rather than commiserating, everyone behaved as if they'd just met in a pub. They talked and flirted and ignored any signs of distress from Madelyn and her immediate family, not out of heart-lessness but out of tact. They were like a mobilised party, like Nathan Detroit's floating craps game in *Guys and Dolls*, available at short notice to rustle up an atmosphere of bustle and chat; an Irish white noise to defeat the silence of death. Everyone acted at being normal, as if to say, 'Life goes on. The crowd in the kitchen are always going to be there, always talking, always on the point of singing.'

At around 11 p.m., Frank summoned me. 'We have to go for a little walk,' he said.

'You can't be thinking of going up to Hanberry's on a night like this,' I said, crossly. Really, Frank's passion for draught Guinness . . .

'We're going to talk to the undertaker,' he said. 'We have to choose a coffin.'

Five minutes later we were there. The Athenry undertaker had three coffins on display, long and capacious, like wardrobes laid out on the rough mat floor, but polished to a rare housemaid's sheen.

I couldn't think where to begin. Did you enquire about durability? All-weather, hard-wearing imperviousness? Special features? I'd no idea. I seized a passing thought and said,

'How much is this one?'

Damn. It sounded as if I was looking for a bargain,

'I mean, which is the most expensive one?'

'This one here, Mr *Welsh*,' he said, indicating an enormous mahogany sarcophagus, the kind of thing seen on the banks of the Nile in the time of Pharaoh. 'Eight hundred pounds.'

'Okay. And the one next to it?'

'Ah, that'll be eight hundred pounds as well. But the other one is six hundred and you wouldn't be wanting that.'

No indeed, I said. 'And these brass handles – are they extra?'

'They are indeed. But they're not really brass. They're just made of tin. Take care now – on no account pick up the coffin by the handles, for fear they might snap off.' Scenes of disaster at the graveyard filled my head. I'd have thought that if you're willing to pay a thousand pounds for your mother's coffin, the least you could expect would be some decent handles on it. But here they took a pragmatic view. No point in wasting good brass or silver or gold (even the crucifix that was finally clamped to the top of the coffin was a horrible tin novelty, like something out of a cracker) if it was only going to be buried out of sight and ruined by the elements.

I shivered. It was freezing in there. It seemed excessively cold even for March. I looked around the undertaker's shed, suddenly understanding why they might keep the temperature down. Were there a dozen unseen corpses lurking in the shadows, waiting for someone to buy them a place to sleep?

'Who'll dig the grave?' Frank was asking.

'I would've asked Jamesy and Noel, but they're away,' said the undertaker. 'And PJ and Michael won't do it any longer.' He turned to me, with a harassed look. 'That's what this country is comin' to. All the local lads you could once rely on, they won't do that sorta work any more. They all want to be biochemists.' He snorted with derision at this unseen side-effect of the Celtic Tiger economy.

'Maybe,' Frank mused, 'Martin over at Hanberry's would know of a couple of lads.'

'The very thing. Unless . . .' He looked at me, then at Frank. Then they both looked at me.

'What?' I said. '*I* don't know anyone I could ask to dig a grave.'

It was only much later that I realised what they had meant. They were asking: 'Why don't *you* do it?' It's a family tradition that is creeping back into Irish rural society, as the grave-digging trade dies out. To dig out a hole in the ground for your family is a decent thing, a mark of respect for one's own. But it didn't occur to me for a second that that was what they had in mind. There could be nothing so wholly antithetical to my life as a Londoner as the idea of standing in an ever-deepening hole, stripped to the waist and sweating like a racehorse, surrounded by sheer walls of mud through which worms and old bones poked, until I had become part of the earth.

When I finally realised, of course, I bitterly regretted not doing it.

The next day, Friday, was weirdly still, like a Sunday when I was young, or those Good Fridays when neither of my parents surfaced from their bedroom all day except for tiny collations of cold meat and eggs, and Madelyn and I played together in the house unsupervised, as if we'd been deserted.

Nobody seemed to be around. Nothing was urgent. For once no one was making any meals in Madelyn's kitchen. Justin, aged seven, normally the noisiest child in the Western hemisphere, glided about like a small Trappist monk. Most peculiarly, the telephone didn't ring. The telephone is *always* ringing at my sister's house – patients calling the vet, local committee members calling Madelyn, teenage friends of Annabel ringing to destroy someone's reputation. Today, you'd think we were all forgotten. But we weren't. The town was just leaving us in peace.

I suddenly remembered the *Independent*, that newspaper I used to work for a hundred years ago. I'd tape-recorded an interview in Washington with Elmore Leonard, and promised the magazine I'd send off a 2,000-word piece in the midst of my vale of tears. So soon after my mother's death, I had another deadline looming, 2 p.m. that day. Obviously, I should ring them up and cancel it. Instead, I'd just sit here in the kitchen, or go for a moody walk, or play some mournful music, or read some comforting pages of Dickens. Which book? *Bleak House? Hard Times?*

On the other hand, no. Instead, I rang Frank's sister-in-law Kathleen, who lived across the road. Their house possessed not only a computer but an atmosphere of unearthly calm. I could work there. Kathleen said, 'Yes of course you can write an article here,' never once remarking on what a heartless swine I must be, that I could think of doing such a thing with my mother hardly cold in the mortuary. Instead, Kathleen ferried coffee and biscuits up and downstairs, her hand squeezed my shoulder and I was grateful to have such an understanding friend in town.

Back in Madelyn's kitchen, we wondered where to have the wake. Mad was all for booking a reception room in an Oranmore hotel. I wanted to hold it at Mother's house, where there hadn't been a party since my father died. We decided to have the wake in the old lady's last home.

Mid-afternoon, I overheard Madelyn talking to a friend in the kitchen.

'Have you been down?'

'Yes.'

'To see her? You saw her?'

'Yes.'

'How does she look?'

'Oh terrible.'

'That bad, huh? And her hair?'

'Awful white. Desperate.'

'Hmmm.' I could hear my sister considering. 'Maybe I'll go down myself in a while and put a bit of lipstick on her.'

''Twould be nice.'

I couldn't bear to think what was going on. I faxed the article off to the newspaper. I rang some friends in London and told them of the death. They were sympathetic but guarded, as if I had made a social gaffe in telling them directly about Mother. I realised that, in England, I'd only ever heard about people's bereavements from a third party, as though it wasn't really done for you yourself to spread the news about your dead parent. Then I put on my best *Reservoir Dogs* suit and Timney Fowler tie, and we headed off.

If the death notice says 'Removal 6 p.m.', people arrive to pay their respects anything up to two hours before. So we got there at 3.30. The chapel resembled a grim Eastern European dancehall, with chairs around the walls and a small electric fire to keep out the chill. In the middle of the carpet, on two trestles, my mother's coffin lay open.

Around her nestled a great quantity of white crêpe, folded and pleated into a long ruff that ran the whole perimeter of the casket. She was wearing her sensible blue tweed suit, a rosary twined around her fingers, a blue Legion of Mary ribbon coming to a V-shape around her neck. She looked in good shape for someone who had checked out twenty-four hours earlier. Her hands had lost their nasty black–brown bruising. The ancient Nippon militiaman had gone from her face, and she seemed quite her old self. Her cheeks were a subtle, peachy glow and a spectacular Joan Crawford crimson gloss outlined her thin lips. And her hair . . .

Her hair was astonishing. Where, at the hospital, there had only been giveaway, snow–white roots, there now sprang away from her head a rich chestnut brown with orange highlights.

'*Annabel*,' I hissed.

She adopted her most mutinous expression. 'What?'

'Is this your doing?'

'*No*. I was just helping Mum.'

'What is it? Some kind of disco highlights aerosol spray?'

'No, it's just a bit of colouring pen.'

The children clustered around the coffin. They wanted to see how cold their grandmother was. Justin stuck out his finger and twiddled her cheek. The baby, Simon, did the same on the other cheek. They lifted the fingers of her hand. They patted her forehead. It was, apparently, the custom of the tribe to pat dead people on the hand, and adjust the set of their chin, to smooth the line of their grave-clothes and kiss their frozen forehead and tell them off for going away and leaving you.

An old song came back to me, a sentimental thing by Count John McCormack called 'Pretty Molly Brannigan'. It ends with the words:

I'm as cool and collected as any salamander, ma'am.
Won't you come to my wake when I go the long meander, ma'am?
I'll think meself as valiant as the famous Alexander, ma'am,
When I hear you cryin' o'er me, 'Yerra, why did you die?'

The family began to arrive around 4 p.m. Aunt Peggy from Monivea, with her daughter Mary, she of the glittering eyes and angelic face, her brother Michael and their spouses. Marjorie's two sons, Christopher and Tristan dwarfed their gorgeous mother and Louise's son and daughter towered over theirs, as if some mighty Walsh gene had skipped a generation and was bursting into efflorescence in the newest one. Maurice's daughter, Lizzie, turned out to be the dead spit of cousin Michelle. John Louis arrived, red-faced, white-haired and genially wicked, his wife Stephanie, of the New Zealand oceanographer family, contrastingly elegant and restrained. Cecily, the nurse, with whom my mother had always felt a professional empathy, was weeping. Caroline had left her mother, Aunt Dolly, in someone else's care for an hour back at the family homestead.

And then they all came, in a seemingly endless procession, the twin populations of Athenry – where my father was born, and my brother-in-law, and where both my parents and many of my ancestors would soon be buried all together – and Oranmore, where my mother had lived in widowed contentment for twelve years. They came along the line, as along a wedding line, shook hands and said: 'I'm sorry for your trouble', until the words passed beyond one's hearing, into a comforting music. It was the community gathering itself about its own folk.

Madelyn stood beside me and supplied a running commentary on the arriving multitude:

'This is Jim and Violet, you know, Eileen Sweeney's sister, she lives in Oranmore, and Charlie King, you know Charlie who went to Canada, that's Martin Burke from the gift shop down the town, and Michael Melia, a great character, he runs the *other* gift shop. This guy's Eamonn Neary, who's on the Heritage Committee with me, so's this chap, Dermot Monaghan, Daddy was very friendly with *his* dad, you know Aideen and Etienne, the big fellow with the beard is

Padraig Judge, oh sorry you've met him a million times, and Antoinette his wife who's Mrs Duddy's daughter, she used to sell you chips at her front door after the pubs closed, and here's Mrs D herself, you've sung enough times with Pascal O'Dowd, do you know his wife Geraldine? This is Peggy and Conn Walsh from across the road, Peggy who started the women's group, and Maura and Stevie Duane, Mary and Conor you know, this is Mary Foran, a friend of mine, and Dolly's nephew Paul and his wife, Bridie, and Michael Fox, he's a neighbour of Peggy's in Monivea, this here's Enda Finnerty, whose mum was in the bed next to Mummy in Rita's Ward last June, these two are Francis and Peter Connolly, brothers-in-law of cousin Cecily, and Peter Feeney, from the community council, and Teresa Ruane from the Athenry festival, here's John Feeney and Teresa, neighbours from Ballybacka and friends of ours, Finbar and Stephanie O'Regan from next door but you've known them for years, and Paddy Coen from Carnaun, he was a friend of Daddy's, here's Frank's uncle, Eamonn Madden, and Fonsie his other one, and Eilish his wife, Pearce Coffey from Ballybacka, Tom's brother and Giles's teacher. And here's Christie Morrissey, and Michael Morrissey, Christie's a nephew of Paddy's, Michael's his brother, he has a newsagent shop in town where I get the paper every day, his daughter's a friend of Annabel's. And Michael Kelly, from Castle Lambert, the farmer, and Gerry and Kate MacMahon, you know them well, that's Martin O'Grady from the Heritage Committee, and Seamus Cullinane, headmaster of the Tech, and Anne, who knew Mummy through the prayer group in Oranmore, and Carmel Farragher and her daughter Martina, and here come Walter and Pat Raftery, Mum's friends from Oranmore, Walter was at Daddy's school, he grew up near Ballybacka, but you knew that. Here's Norman Patterson, the Oranmore vet, a friend of ours for years, and Maureen and Sean Lawless, and Tricia and Taig Costello, you've met them in Hanberry's, and Paddy and Olive Coffey from Dobbin and Coffey's, the bar where everyone holds their parties, and Ruth her sister who lived in Lavender Sweep in Battersea and were patients of Daddy's, and Martin and Lily from Hanberry's, and Anita and Tom Coffey, late of Ballybacka, and Rita Walsh from Lydican, Daddy's cousin and her son Pat, and Michael Ford from Carnaun, neighbours of Daddy's, and look who's here but Willie Fahy, another neighbour . . .'

They kept on coming, a river of sympathy, dividing at the coffin, milling around it to right and left, coming to clasp hands with the family and with me, who was family but also a stranger. They seemed not to care that I was from 'beyond', and hadn't met some of them ever before. They just looked into my eyes with the utmost sympathy and offered a kind of absolution for my not having been home enough. Suddenly I, rather than my parents, was the exile returned to the family plot and gruffly welcomed back.

It seemed to go on for years. I said, 'Yes, Mad, I know them' to one name in three, and began to realise I knew Athenry very well. I could almost have been a part of it. Over the years I'd become saturated in its lore, its seasons and gossip, the days and nights spent in the company of the town. It was the community I'd missed when I was growing up, when nobody in Battersea knew their neighbours and the wandering Irish exiles of south London congregated in my mother's kitchen to form a chatty village enclave of their own.

We walked to the graveyard. My father was buried there, his headstone surmounted by a white Madonna in a crown. Over a decade had gone by but the grave plot, with its floor of white chips, might have been laid yesterday. At the base of the stone, we'd had the words of his favourite song, sung by Aunt Dolly in her tremulous English soprano: 'Better loved ye canna be/ Will ye no' come back again?' engraved on the white marble.

I wondered who the elderly, white-haired and intense-looking couple beside the grave could be. I'd seen them in church, while worrying about my funeral mass speech, and couldn't quite place them. 'John,' said Madelyn, 'You haven't said hello to Mary and Joseph.'

The penny dropped. It was Mary Lynch, my father's nicest, most congenial and successful partner in the Battersea GP practice, Mary from Donegal, whose name was on the headed writing-paper of all the letters I got from my father when I was running up bills in Oxford and playing at being landed gentry in Killaloe. Mary and her husband Joseph, who taught English at the local school in Clapham and had laughed at my jejune notions about Dickens, in some of the hundred-and-one evenings they'd spent at the house.

'Mary?'

'John . . .' She looked shocked at what the years had done to me, my white hair, the bags of tiredness under my eyes. She did not say 'I'm sorry for your trouble.' We knew each other too well for that, although it was twenty years since we'd last met. We stood smiling, uncomfortably aware of the passage of years, and the few that were left to either of us.

'Hi, Joseph.'

'Well John, you old con-man . . .' Joseph was never a chap to let sentiment get in the way.

At the grave, Father O'Connor said prayers, the chilly March wind scouring his face, the snowdrops and primroses leaning their innocent heads away from the northern blast. The coffin sat on its wooden moorings until, at a signal from the priest, the pall-bearers, myself included, stepped forward, fed the ropes under the coffin and gathered them up, as if clamping a saddle under a mare. Six of us took the strain as Michael Moran, my aunt Peggy's son, and Cecily's husband, PJ, pulled the wooden struts aside and the coffin dangled in sudden space. It seemed to be lurching at a crazy angle, Mother going head-first into the oblivion of earth, nose-diving into eternity – but it righted itself and we lowered it down.

Father O'Connor said more prayers about commending the body to the earth while the spirit flew off above it. People around the grave's gaping mouth crossed themselves. Those of us with floral wreathes prepared to throw them in. We said a decade of the Rosary in a freezing mumble.

Then Frank, heedless of his good suit, seized the shovel that lay sunk in a pile of earth, shovelled up a pile of soil and handed it to the priest to throw onto the coffin. He didn't just offer it to him, he *brandished* it, two-handed, as though presenting him with a gun to fire. There they stood, the vet and the priest, the practical man and the transcendental, seeming to wrestle above the lip of the grave on the edge of the Atlantic. While, all around, the tribe of friends and relations and neighbours hung their heads and prayed for the repose of all dead souls. It could have happened at any time in the last 300 years. It was a snapshot from the past.

The Graig Abbey cousins never let me down. Marjorie and Cecily, and my mother's favourite nephew, the endlessly omni-capable Maurice, and John Louis, my disreputable soul-mate, and Caroline and Louise, the harp-playing dreamboats I'd gazed at longingly in my teens, all of us now grown fatter and more lined, incontrovertibly middle-aged and freighted with enormous children, they all crowded round Madelyn and me, bringing the blanket warmth of a family to this bleak landscape. Here was the tribe, unsinkably at home. Uncle Paddy stood beside his sister Peggy, looking at the family grave and wondering when they would follow their siblings. There was Madelyn, surrounded by her Irish brood, and Frank, whom I had failed in my London-cushioned way when I had not leapt at the chance he offered me of digging the grave myself. And at the centre of it all lay Dad's redheaded Sligo bride, whom he'd met in Rome and married in Kensington. The queen of all she surveyed in Battersea had come home to the ancient Galway turf with which she'd had this on-off relationship all her life, a falling angel never comfortable at home, never quite herself in London, crashed to earth at last.

They were together in this small patch of land. All my father had wanted, at the end of his busy time in London, patrolling the bustling acres of Clapham and Wandsworth Common, was a small patch of Galway land in which to hang out with my mother. Well, he had it at last. His earth, his Irish home, his undeniable birthright in the fields of Athenry. I suddenly felt proud to be a Walsh, to be part of this Celtic gang.

The flowers were thrown. The earth closed in. It was over.

We trudged past my father's grave, down the lane to the wrought iron gates and the cars that would take us to Hanberry's Hotel, to while away the afternoon with Guinness and whiskey and memories.

I fell into step beside Joseph from Port Laois.

'This may be the wrong moment to bring it up, John,' he said. 'But there's an absolute dead cert running at Leopardstown this afternoon. Nine to one. It can't miss. You could stick a tenner on it if you're quick.'

He surveyed my face and the Londonish tears on my cheek.

'Oh well,' said Joseph. 'Just a thought.'

XVI

BEYOND

A century had passed since the Irish writer, John Millington Synge, had landed on the Aran Islands for the first time. He'd come to Inishmore, the largest of the three, on 10 May 1898, left its comparatively bustling social life for the peace of Inishmaan, the middle island, after a few days, and stuck around there. He had returned every summer for the next four years, speaking Irish to the islanders, gathering folk tales as raw material for his plays, and marvelling how stories he'd encountered in European mediaeval folklore, in Florence, in Wurtzburg, and as far afield as Persia and Egypt, should turn up on the lips of 'illiterate native[s] on a wet rock in the Atlantic'. He had photographed the island girls with his cumbersome modern camera down by the harbour, and entertained the locals by playing curious physical tricks: he could lift a poker with his bare toes and riddle the grate, this serious and haunted aesthete; he could bend over backwards and pick up a set of keys with his teeth. I'd always liked the sound of John Synge. As a small act of homage, Madelyn and I set off that summer for Inishmaan.

It was the culmination of a long sentimental journey I'd made after my mother died. I'd gone back to Killaloe for the first time in twenty-five years. Matty was long dead. His 'Select Bar' was renamed Dalcassians, after Brian Boru's soldiers at the Battle of Clontarf. The town was even better looking than I remembered, but more chocolate-boxy, more tidied-up and prettified. Expensive cabin cruisers of European provenance lined the Shannon shore. Whelan's Stores was still there at the bottom of the hill, but there was now a cashpoint in the wall. The Crowes' house had become a dress shop. There was no sign of the butcher's where we used to be given slugs of poteen. Beside Sean Collins the chemist, a new Celtic Cat Gift Shop was selling artfully wrought metal *objets*, mirrors and leprechauns: the town had become a Heritage Centre and was now on the tourist itinerary of every visitor to Ireland from anywhere in the European Union.

Mills's Bar was still there, amazingly unchanged. The bar itself which had once been a simple counter with bottles on a shelf behind, was now stocked with *à la mode* liqueurs and malt whiskeys. Posters and photographs of sporting triumphs lined the walls. The barman was still Tony Mills, but a different Tony, quieter than when he'd dished up twenty-drink rounds on relays of trays and had shouted for silence at 1 a.m. when the Garda sergeant's Cortina had been seen coming over the bridge. After five minutes of meaningful gazes, I said:

'You're the Tony Mills who's always run this bar aren't you?'

'I am,' he said. 'There's been no one else.'

'Well I'm sure you wouldn't remember but I came here a lot, one summer, a whole quarter of a century ago – me and my sister and about twenty friends of ours from England. We used to play guitars and sing. We were very friendly with the locals. We all lived in a big house in . . .'

He tilted his head. He scrutinised the white hair, the crow's feet, the scribbled signature of age across my face.

'Dance, Dance,' he said. 'Was that the song?'

We talked about who was still in the town and what the English ones were doing now, those of us with whom we'd kept in touch. Then he disappeared upstairs and didn't come back. Bridie, his wife, our welcoming barmaid from twenty-five years ago, said he might be feeling a little moody about the past.

I climbed the hill in Killaloe to the surgeon-general's house that had been the site of our revels. The present owner Mrs Wood showed me around and I registered, in a series of shocks, how little had changed inside. The old Aga, the bath in the middle of the carpet, the wrought-iron stanchion protruding from the staircase, the wooden shutters, the downstairs lavatory with the disastrously long run-up. And there was the ancient mirror, mottled and silvered, in which our nineteen-year-old selves had preened and inspected the storm damage of the night before. I looked in the bedrooms and couldn't relate them to the sock-reeking crash-pads they'd been in 1973, where you could never be sure who'd be sleeping in which room from one evening to the next.

Mrs Wood and I looked through the top floor window that overlooked the town and I saw, beyond Ballina, a new estate of houses stretched across the fields, dull and uniform, a kind of dormitory village for Killaloe, now that it was so Continentally popular.

In the garden, she showed me the blooms she'd planted where once there were only empty cans of Harp and dead whiskey soldiers. The yard where Paddy Crowe and I had once constructed a rudimentary barbecue for the English visitors now seemed impossible small. I crossed the lawn, past the thin, twisty trunk of the magic tree, and approached the far wall like one approaching a shrine. The Shannon river rose beyond it, sparkling heartlessly away, though someone had removed the wooden ramp that used to poke out into the current for the amusement of water-skiers. A chilly wind blew off the water and round my ears.

I said goodbye to Mrs Wood beside the front door with the wrought-iron birds tweeting away on their metal branch. They looked, I said, just fine.

'Thank you,' she said. 'You wouldn't believe the trouble I had scraping all the paint off. Took me years . . .'

I drove all over the west, to Clare and the Cliffs of Moher, where I'd brought English mates and girlfriends, and to the pub in the fishing village of Doolin, where we'd watched Aran fishermen steam and subside into sleep by the bar in their dripping yellow sou'westers.

I'd hardly ever been to Ireland in midsummer. The landscape was painted with many colours: purple-pink fuschia hedges, an ivory froth of meadowsweet, yellow ragwort, the back-to-school flowers of montbrethia, the brown jewellery of dog asphodel, the white bog cotton.

I drove around Sligo, my mother's county, looking for clues as to what she may have felt in her young days. Crossing the Black River, I saw a big farmhouse painted pale lemon with a white picket fence and a paddock for two horses. It was the essence of rustic bourgeois settledness in the middle of nowhere. It was too awful to contemplate how a modern family could think of living there.

A mist was creeping over the brown moors and the turf quarries – the sods of peat laid out in a pattern, like tyre tracks – as I reached Lough Talt on the Mayo border. The mist moved like a thing possessed, sweeping across pines and fir forests, and the steep and awesome incline of the Ox Mountains. Black-faced sheep with little rectangular pupils and blue bottoms stumbled across the raggedy turf and regarded me disdainfully behind wire fences. No other car moved for miles in any direction. The ladylike fuschia hedges blew about in the turbulent wind. Boats bobbed uncomfortably among the reeds at the edge of the lake. 'White waves riding home on a wintry lough' – was that Heaney? I stopped the car for a stroll by the water's edge, as I'd once done, for no particular reason, by Carratubber Lake near Graig Abbey.

It wasn't a good idea. Within a hundred yards, I was lashed and stung by the rain. The lake water, whipped by the rain, seemed out to get me. I felt like the hawthorn, forever harried by the elements. Get me, I thought, the hell out of here. Suddenly I knew how my mother might have felt about the prospect of staying in Ireland, back in the thirties, and why, as an old acquaintance of hers had told me, 'she'd have licked the road to get away'.

To the passing motorist, it was a gorgeous landscape, authentically wild beyond any oil painting. But to anybody actually living there, it was a nightmare, an uncompromising elemental assault. Nature raw, hard, freezing and bullying.

Tubbercurry, my mother's home town, had made great modern strides. The flower shop was called 'Guns 'n' Roses', the beauty salon offered leg waxings and sunbeds; at Coen's Electrical Store you could buy a 'steam facial and nasal inhaler'. The old ways were respected by Traditional Music Week, by twenty-five year-old *Irish Timeses* and *Sligo Champions* in a shop window, an old glass-covered well outside McGuinness's bar, and a notice advertising the sale of 'Lowland and Mountain Sheep' at Cloonacool in a week's time.

In Charlestown, where her cousins lived, I looked in the phone book and found over seventy Durkins, the family from which she sprang. Unlike my mother and her sisters, the modern family had chosen to stick around in large numbers. The town had been modernised, zoned, and landscaped since she knew it before the war, its modern architecture full of East European efficiency: the Marist Convent resembled a house of correction.

In the local church, St James's, where she certainly would have gone to Mass, I found the images Mother carried with her all her life: a stained-glass window full of saints and virgins with staring eyes, the Little Infant Jesus of Prague, a statue of Christ showing off his Sacred Heart, the little girl's Catholic heroine, St Teresa the 'Little Flower'; an icon of Our Lady of Perpetual Succour – my mother's favourite holy picture, in which the Madonna is looking calmly at you, while the child in her arms is being shown by angels the cross and the spears on which he will later be hung, and impaled; one sandal is falling off his left foot in horror, as his tiny black hands clutch his mother's thumb.

This place was where it all came from, the image-bank of Catholic mythology that she'd passed on to Madelyn and me. She'd managed to get away from here, fired by amateur dramatics and an ambition to be grander than her rural Sligo peers. But these images came along with her, along with her arsenal of prayers and indulgences. And they went with her into exile, like baggage.

I tried to imagine what her life might have been if she'd never set foot in this church – what kind of person she might have become, how she might have brought us up to be different people. But I couldn't. This was the Ireland that created her, with its staring-eyed divines, its flayed Sacred Hearts, rainy hills and wind-lashed hawthorn bushes; its air of barely survivable mediocrity, its basement-level self-esteem.

It wasn't the Ireland I wanted. Coming here I thought I might tap into some spiritual essence, something that would show me where I fitted in. But if I'd had any impulse to return, this place told me loud and clear that I just couldn't hack it. I couldn't be John Wayne in *The Quiet Man*, returning to his roots and attuning himself to Innisfree, to live forever with Maureen O'Hara in a bosky Celtic Arcadia. This sentimental journey had only confirmed my unreconstructed Englishness.

Confronted with the elemental heart of Ireland, my instinct was to turn and run.

Back in Galway on a gorgeous sunny day, the sky striated with long, herringboned clouds, Uncle Paddy – gentleman farmer, master of Graig Abbey – died, three months after my mother. There was bunting in town for the Athenry Agricultural Show, a fluttering of flags, even outside the church. Cars lined up along the lane by his house, as neighbours came from miles around to pay their respects. Paddy was laid out on the bed in the drawing room where'd he recently taken to sleeping, as if anticipating his own end. He'd been saying: 'I'm finding the time awful long . . .' to his daughters weeks before.

He lay in a pale green check shirt and mustard waistcoat, as the mourners clutched his hand, stroked his cheek, said a few respectful valedictory words to him. There was an aggressive tilt to his chin as he lay dead in the bed. He seemed to have improved, to have become younger. Just a few months after his eightieth birthday, he looked barely sixty.

Outside Graig, people milled around in the Sunday afternoon sunshine with pints in their hands. The hallway with the lion painting was a crush of mourners saying: 'I haven't seen you for *ages*.' and 'Where did *you* come from?' as if at a party in Fulham. There was a thriving spirits bar in the grand piano room with the pictures of the yearning monk and the nun at the window. Only close friends were allowed down the stone-flagged hallway into the kitchen where Dolly, the widow, was being attended.

John Louis, my old hero, my duet partner and most profoundly dissolute influence, was on the wagon. We hugged each other. I told him about a book I'd been reading by a journalist called Liam Fay, who had dressed as a priest for a day and gone round Dublin buying a gross of condoms, drinking vodka from the bottle's neck, emerging dishevelled from a ladies lavatory; he had tried to find the church where Gay Byrne of *The Late Late Show* worshipped, so he would ask the resident priest to let him say Mass – just for the moment at Communion, when he could look at the great TV star, extract some unleavened bread from the chalice and say, 'And now, here is your host, Gay Byrne . . .'

I persuaded John Louis to have a small whiskey with me, in Paddy's honour, which he did. By cruel irony on his way home to Charleville, his car was crashed into by a hired Volvo full of vacationing Scandinavians, driving on the wrong side of the road. Nobody was hurt. But for everyone back at the funeral it was the worst reminder that you might be next. In Ireland, it sometimes seemed inevitable that you might die at any moment; in England, the prospect had always seemed remote.

★

Then Aunt Dolly died and Graig Abbey was crammed once again. The remainder of Dolly's family, the Browns (descended from the Burkes of Clanrickard and before them from De Burgos who came over with the Norman conquest), arrived to pay their respects.

She lay in her small white single bed, before the fire in the living room where I had slept before Marjorie's wedding. She looked angelic, a sleeping thirties doll. Lipstick emphasised her perfect cupid-bow mouth and red nail polish, her graceful hands. Something of the English flapper had returned. Her white hair lay dramatically across the pillow. Above her head waved a spray of tiny white flowers called Baby's Breath. Someone had threaded a rosary through her cold fingers. Dolly saying the Rosary? As far as I knew, she was never a natural worshipper. She believed much more in style. Religious observance wasn't her thing, though she did have an often-expressed concern for what the point of existence might be.

'If Dolly woke up now,' a fellow mourner whispered in my ear, 'she'd look at the rosary in her hands and say: "Who gave me this? Take it away. Get me a hot brandy. Give me a fag . . ."'

In the crowded hallway there was much talk of Dolly's Englishness. How she was the daughter of a sergeant in the Royal Irish Constabulary before the 1916 uprising – an Irishman working, technically, for the British crown. How his family had emigrated to be educated in the UK, and how Dolly had pined for Bangor, North Wales, where she went to school, and for Ashford in Kent, where she spent happy teenage years. Like my mother, she had fallen for an image of classy English life, within striking distance of society balls and royal garden parties; but she had never been able to settle back here. Sitting in Graig, looking at the unfathomable fields, she had been a kind of exile from her own Irishness, pining for a life she could never replicate in Ireland, even while happily assimilated into Irish family ways.

I fell into conversation with Sister Brid, from the Presentation Convent in Athenry. We talked about Dolly's in-between status – how neither she nor Anne could quite stay, or grow, or become 'really themselves' in England; but neither could they go back to what they'd known and rejected in Ireland. I told the nun about my own wonderings about where my home was.

'It's very simple,' she said. 'Wherever your parents may be buried, your true home is with the next generation. So with you it's London, where your children are growing up. But the human heart allows itself to have *sacred spaces*, where you feel most alive, even if they're not your home.'

That sounded about right. But I still hadn't found the home I sought, somewhere between London and Galway, sharing the essences of Englishness and Irishness, somewhere beyond both.

By the end of the summer, my sister and I found ourselves on Inish-maan, where Synge had once lain and sunbathed on the huge slate rocks. Our landlady was called Angela. She folded her arms across her bosom like a Northern seaside landlady. Her voice was startlingly English. Yes, she said, they were planning to turn McDonough's house, where Synge stayed every summer, into a memorial museum, with a room where visitors could have some peace and quiet. Yes, she'd seen the *Leenane Trilogy* by Martin McDonagh, his amusing cod-Synge playlets about life in the Arans, that were now entrancing the Americans on Broadway — and frankly she was disgusted. A travesty of island ways and people, she said — just as the crowd on the first night of *The Playboy of the Western World* had regarded Synge's portrayal of murder, connivance and hero worship in County Mayo with shocked provincial disdain.

The man in the local shop had a smooth English delivery too. It was only when I read Tim Robinson's introduction to the Penguin edition of Synge's *The Aran Islands* that I discovered why he spoke like that.

When the O'Briens and the O'Flaherty's were fighting over the islands in the 1560s, the former appealed to the English to decide who owned the place. The Arans were confiscated by Queen Elizabeth I and given to an Englishman to run, on condition that he build a garrison there. An English fort stood untroubled on Inishmore for nearly a century. After the Irish rebellion in 1652, the islands were recaptured by an expedition of renegade Catholics from Connemara. 1300 soldiers and a battering captured the fort and extended it, making it a prison camp. 'There was a military presence on Aran thereafter until early in the next century, writes Robinson, 'with the result that today Aran's bloodgroup pattern is similar to that of northern England, where Gaelic and Saxon stock have intermingled'.

Aha! I fell on the information with delight. So the Aran Islands were not, after all, the Irish back-of-beyond, a savage non-civilisation even wilder than Connemara. Instead they were a windswept, stony, English-Irish platform on the sea that used to take Irish exiles, like my mother's sisters, to Boston and a new, un-Irish life. Whatever the evidence to the contrary, the old women in their crocheted shawls passing through the streets, unchanged from the day Robert Flaherty filmed them for *Man of Aran* in 1934, this was a place with vestiges of English blood. The Aran rocks became a glowing metaphor in the midst of my sorrows. They bound up the cruel past with the welcoming present.

Madelyn and I went to the island's only pub in the evening. We talked to the landlord, whose voice was precisely that of a London-Irish barman. He was called Sean Brian Thomas. Was Thomas his surname? No, he said, islanders know each other by their given name, then their grandfather's, then their own father's. It was a tradition. Me too, I said, having been christened John Henry Martin at the Battersea font.

Next morning, Madelyn and I set out across the island. We found 'Synge's Cottage' and poked about the rooms: here was his bedroom, here was the window through which he looked every mooring, with its direct sight line down to the jetty where the ferry and the mailboat pulled in. We walked up to 'Synge's Chair' – an arrangement of heavy white stones which, one hundred years earlier, the playwright had fashioned into a throne from which he could regard the Atlantic waves and the threshold of Ireland. It was the highest coign of vantage around. We looked at the sibling islands on either side, lying so low, crouched discreetly out at sea, beyond exile and dreaming, a flat and basic territory of stones on which your imagination could go to work.

Neither of my parents had ever been here. I thought of them looking out to sea – my mother, young and toothily glamorous, lost in an acting dream, staring at the Atlantic from a Sligo town, longing to escape from the bleak wind around Lough Talt and the deadening farmland of Tubbercurry; my father, in his cool, medical-student corduroys and his George Raft haircut, his arm encircling a young Bridget or Philomena, gazing at the orange sun disappearing beyond the grey plates of the Arans, wondering how he could ever leave Galway but knowing he'd have to.

I looked to the right, where the Cliffs of Moher bulked in the sunlight, showing a more friendly, piebald aspect than ever before. I looked left and saw the edge of Connemara, the great lunar landscape of Galway rock, from where the airplane would soon land to take us back to civilisation. The Cliffs and the stone desert, my favourite sights in Ireland, seemed suddenly drawn together, forming a mystic triangle, somewhere beyond England and Ireland. Here, where Synge's Aran fisherman believed that angels were always falling through the air and wreaking havoc in the world, here was the place where they might fall to earth at last.

'Madelyn,' I said. 'How'd you like to build a house here?'